Mapping the Evolution of Platform Society

Mapping the Evolution of Platform Society: Multidisciplinary Insights from Social and Political Sciences

EDITED BY

VALENTINA GOGLIO

University of Turin, Italy

AND

CECILIA BIANCALANA

University of Turin, Italy

United Kingdom – North America – Japan – India – Malaysia – China

Emerald Publishing Limited
Emerald Publishing, Floor 5, Northspring, 21-23 Wellington Street, Leeds LS1 4DL

First edition 2025

Editorial matter and selection © 2025 Valentina Goglio and Cecilia Biancalana.
Individual chapters © 2025 The authors.
Published under exclusive licence by Emerald Publishing Limited.

Reprints and permissions service
Contact: www.copyright.com

No part of this book may be reproduced, stored in a retrieval system, transmitted in any form or by any means electronic, mechanical, photocopying, recording or otherwise without either the prior written permission of the publisher or a licence permitting restricted copying issued in the UK by The Copyright Licensing Agency and in the USA by The Copyright Clearance Center. Any opinions expressed in the chapters are those of the authors. Whilst Emerald makes every effort to ensure the quality and accuracy of its content, Emerald makes no representation implied or otherwise, as to the chapters' suitability and application and disclaims any warranties, express or implied, to their use.

British Library Cataloguing in Publication Data
A catalogue record for this book is available from the British Library

ISBN: 978-1-83608-029-9 (Print)
ISBN: 978-1-83608-028-2 (Online)
ISBN: 978-1-83608-030-5 (Epub)

INVESTOR IN PEOPLE

Contents

About the Editors — *vii*

About the Contributors — *ix*

Acknowledgements — *xiii*

Introduction: Mapping the Evolution of the Platform Society — *1*
Cecilia Biancalana and Valentina Goglio

Section 1: Education

Chapter 1 Collective Intelligence Online Experiments: A Learning Method and Its Pedagogical Applications Through Online Collaborative Work Platforms — *13*
Pablo Bautista-Alcaine, Tatiana Íñiguez-Berrozpe and Javier Fernández-Albás

Chapter 2 A Better Skilled Workforce for the Digital Transformation: What Role for Platform Education? — *27*
Valentina Goglio

Section 2: Discrimination

Chapter 3 The Use of Digital Devices and Digital Platforms in Social Work: Challenges and Risks — *49*
Giovanni Cellini and Carlotta Mozzone

Chapter 4 'Made in Italy': Online Hate Speech Targeting
Gender-Normative Defiance at the Sanremo Music Festival *65*
Camilla Borgna and Antonio Martella

Section 3: Media

Chapter 5 Can I Have Some News? Local Journalism Gaps and the
Role of Platforms *89*
Pedro Jerónimo and Luísa Torre

Chapter 6 TikTokisation of the News: News Media Content
Production Strategies in Portugal *107*
Antonio Martella and Pedro Jerónimo

Section 4: Institutions

Chapter 7 Digital and Financial Literacy and the Development of
e-Government Platforms *133*
Anna Lo Prete

Chapter 8 Ruling the Digital Environment at Last? *149*
Enea Fiore, Daniela R. Piccio and Antonella Seddone

Section 5: Environment

Chapter 9 Environmental Challenges in the Platform Society:
Insights From Mobilisations Against Data Centres *171*
Cecilia Biancalana

About the Editors

Valentina Goglio is an Associate Professor of Economic Sociology at the Department of Cultures, Politics and Society of the University of Turin (IT). Her research interests are at the intersection between education and the labour market, with a particular focus on the implications of the digital transformation for education and work. She recently published *The Diffusion and Social Implications of MOOCs. A Comparative Study of the USA and Europe*, Routledge 2022, and *Job Insecurity and Life Courses*, Bristol University Press, 2024.

Cecilia Biancalana is an Assistant Professor in the Department of Culture, Politics and Society at the University of Turin. Her research focuses on political ecology, party change, populism and the relationship between the internet and politics.

About the Contributors

Pablo Bautista-Alcaine, PhD in Education, is a Researcher and full-time Professor at the Faculty of Education in Zaragoza. His research specialises in collective intelligence and issues related to digital health and its risks, all linked to primary and secondary education students.

Camilla Borgna, University of Turin, Italy, is an Assistant Professor of Sociology at the Department of Cultures, Politics and Society at the University of Turin, Italy. She is also an Affiliate of the Collegio Carlo Alberto and a Fellow of the College for Interdisciplinary Educational Research. Her research lies at the intersection of social stratification, sociology of education and migration.

Giovanni Cellini is an Assistant Professor, Department of Cultures, Politics and Society, University of Turin, Italy. He teaches Social Work and Professional Innovation at the Master in Social Politics and Social Services. His main research topics include social work in the welfare system, helping professions between professionalism and managerialism, social work education, innovation in social work and social services, digitalisation in the social work profession. In the international debate on digitisation in social work education, he published: Cellini, G. & Dellavalle, M. (2024). Rethinking Social Work Education in Italy in Light of the Pandemic: An Overview and a Focus on Fieldwork Education. In: Latzer, Y., Shklarski, L. (Eds.), *Social Work and Education and the COVID-19 Pandemic* (pp. 69–82). Routledge.

Javier Fernández-Albás is the Product Manager of Kampal Data Solutions in charge of the collaborative tool based on Collective Intelligence Kampal Collective Learning. He has participated in the latest developments of this online platform and managed many experiments, both in the field of education and citizen participation.

Enea Fiore is a PhD candidate specialising in comparative politics, with co-supervision at the Laval University in Canada and the University of Geneva in Switzerland. His research investigates the relational dynamics between political parties and social movements. Concurrently, he is involved in a project at the University of Turin, examining online political advertising in EU election campaigns. Fiore's main research interests include political behaviour, electoral campaigns, political parties and social movements. His work aims to deepen the understanding of political interactions and the impact of digital media on electoral processes.

Tatiana Íñiguez-Berrozpe, PhD in Sociology, is a Full Professor at the Faculty of Education in the University of Zaragoza. She is also the Vice-Dean of Information and Communication Technologies in her Faculty. Her research in Sociology of Education focuses on school coexistence, cyber coexistence among adolescents, school inequalities and adult education. She has coordinated European, national and regional research projects and published several articles in high-impact journals on those topics.

Pedro Jerónimo is an Assistant Researcher at LabCom, Department of Communication, Philosophy and Politics at the University of Beira Interior, Portugal. He is a PI of MediaTrust.Lab – Local Media Lab for Civic Trust and Literacy, a member of Observatory of Online Journalism at University of Oporto, the co-chair of IAMCR' Media Production Analysis WG and an assessor of the European Fact-Checking Standard Network. He was the Founder and Chair of SOPCOM' Local and Community Media WG and worked as a local Journalist. His research interests primarily focus on local journalism, digital journalism, media production disinformation and media literacy.

Anna Lo Prete is Associate Professor of Economics at the University of Torino, Italy. She is also Research Associate at G53 Financial Literacy and Personal Finance Network and Research Fellow at the Centre for Research on Pensions and Welfare Policies. Her research interests lie in financial and economic education, public choice, e-government and democracy. Her publications include academic articles in refereed journals, textbooks, contributions to volumes, national newspapers and online information platforms.

Antonio Martella is an Assistant Professor at the Department of Cultures, Politics and Society at the University of Turin, Italy. He is a member of the Observatory on Political and Public Communication at the same department and an Associate Researcher at MediaLaB | Big Data in Social and Political Research Lab at the Department of Political Science, University of Pisa. He serves on the board of the Italian Association of Political Communication. His research interests primarily focus on digital journalism and innovation in the production, dissemination and consumption of information through platform analysis, data science and artificial intelligence.

Carlotta Mozzone is a Research Fellow at the Department of Cultures, Politics, and Society at the University of Turin, and a Lecturer in the Bachelor's program in Social Work at the same university. She is also a doctoral student at Roma Tre University in Sociology and Social Work. Her primary research areas include the history of social work (particularly professionalization, education, and professional supervision), as well as policies and social interventions in migration processes.

Daniela R. Piccio is an Assistant Professor at the Department of Cultures, Politics and Society of the University of Turin. Her research has focused primarily on political parties, gender politics, party and political finance regulation and processes of political representation.

Antonella Seddone is an Associate Professor at the Department of Cultures, Politics and Society of the University of Turin. Her main research interests include political party organisation, party membership, digital environment and social media and political communication.

Luísa Torre is a PhD student in Communication Sciences at the University of Beira Interior (PT) and a member of the Observatory of Online Journalism at University of Oporto. Her research interests are disinformation, news deserts, journalism and power. She has a Master's in Communication Sciences from the University of Oporto (Portugal), and she worked as a Multimedia Journalist for about 10 years in local newsrooms in Brazil.

Acknowledgements

This book is one of the outcomes of the research project *The Risks of the Platform Society: Inequality, Discrimination, Manipulation*, which has been funded by the University of Turin under the framework of the Call for proposals 'Grant for Internationalisation – GFI' for collaborative research projects with international partners. Most of the colleagues participating in the project are part of the UNITA – Universitas Montium network, a European network funded by the European Commission through the Erasmus+ European Universities initiative programme.

We are grateful to the Department of Cultures, Politics and Society of the University of Turin for supporting to the project, including hosting the two international workshops organised in 2023 which are at the origin of this book.

We thank the numerous colleagues who actively contributed by participating in workshops, visiting periods and conferences organized as part of the project.

Introduction: Mapping the Evolution of the Platform Society

Cecilia Biancalana and Valentina Goglio

University of Turin, Italy

1. Why the Platform Society Needs Re-mapping

Every minute of our everyday lives is now dominated by digital platforms, whether we are at work, on vacation or caring for others. While writing this introduction – on a shared file hosted by a cloud storage service platform – the smart watch of one of the authors reminded her to take a break and walk to reach the daily target of her personalised exercise plan. During the break, she scrolled a social network to get the latest news about the Democratic Party's candidate at the next US election; and while waiting for the bus on the way home, she listened to music and podcasts on a streaming platform. The list could go on for pages, and each reader could add numerous other examples. Our social life is tightly linked to multiple digital platforms; platforms, in turn, shape and are shaped by the social structure from their onset to their everyday functioning.

This is the sense of the term 'platform society', which was coined by van Dijck, Poell and de Waal in their seminal work (2018) to denote an interconnected ecosystem in which platforms have penetrated the core of society. Platforms no longer only mediate among services, people and goods; they are so closely bound up with society that the aforementioned mutual relationship extends beyond the economy to the culture and the institutions of society. Their work throws light on an inherent conflict between the optimistic narrative painted of techno-evangelism by Silicon Valley leaders, who tend to highlight the benefits of the digital transformation while downplaying the private returns and, on the other hand, the social implications at collective level (Selwyn, 2014).

The term 'platform' was borrowed from the tech industry and soon became a new organisational, economic and social paradigm extending well beyond the tech sector, changing the organisation of people's everyday lives (Casilli & Posada, 2019). Despite presenting themselves as 'neutral', platforms are so tightly linked to society and able to impact on the social structure that their implications cannot be overlooked. Indeed, the sociological literature on the platform society has reflected upon the several domains in which the transition to the platform paradigm generates concerns.

The seminal work of Zuboff (2019) highlighted the impact of platforms on supporting capital to generate new forms of power, which are less visible and act deceitfully to extract value from users' information and behaviour. Another extensive body of empirical literature has explored the impact of platforms on the transformation of labour. It has not only analysed the risks and perils of the gig economy but also investigated the changing organisation of work, including that in the qualified professions (Arcidiacono & Sartori, 2024; Armano et al., 2022; Pais et al., 2021; Schor et al., 2023; Schor & Vallas, 2023; Stark & Pais, 2021). Numerous authors have shed light on the risks of exacerbating inequalities behind the promise of democratising education by means of ed-tech dominated platform education (Decuypere et al., 2021) and behind the growing presence of platforms in the care sector (Arcidiacono et al., 2022; López Peláez & Kirwan, 2023).

It would fall outside the scope of this book to compile an encompassing overview of the state of research on the platform society. However, given the rapid pace of technological advancement and the pervasive influence of these platforms, we believe it is imperative to constantly reassess and map the evolving landscape of the platform society. Our book arrives at a crucial juncture in 2024, a time when the implications of platformisation, as we have seen, are more pronounced than ever. The essays included in this book try to add some new items of knowledge to this burgeoning literature.

The urgency of this endeavour stems from the acknowledgement that several crucial issues, in our opinion, demand closer scrutiny and are partially overlooked by extant literature. One of the most pressing of these issues is the role of digital literacy and skills. As the digital landscape evolves, so does the necessity for individuals to possess the competencies required to navigate it effectively. Without a robust endowment of digital skills, large segments of the population risk being excluded from the benefits of digitalisation, with the consequent exacerbation of existing social inequalities. This is not merely a matter of personal empowerment but a critical issue of equity, since those without adequate digital skills are often left behind in an increasingly digital world.

Moreover, the book aims to highlight how the online world often mirrors – and sometimes amplifies – existing offline disparities. While digital platforms offer new opportunities, they also have the potential to deepen social divides, particularly when access to digital tools and skills is unevenly distributed. The digital divide remains a significant barrier, with disparities in access and participation frequently reflecting broader socioeconomic inequalities (Hargittai, 2021). Addressing these disparities is essential if we are to ensure that the benefits of digital platforms are shared equitably across all segments of society.

In addition to these concerns, this book challenges the notion that technological progress inherently leads to positive outcomes. The evolution of digital platforms is not a straightforward path to societal improvement; instead, it presents a complex landscape where the potential for both positive and negative outcomes exist. The diversity among platforms and the varied ways in which they impact users underscore the importance of avoiding simplistic, deterministic views of technology. Each platform operates differently, fostering unique behaviors and outcomes that require careful, context-specific analysis.

The impact of the COVID-19 pandemic has further complicated these dynamics by acting as a catalyst for digital transformation across various sectors. The accelerated shift towards digital platforms during and since the pandemic has fundamentally altered how we interact, work and access services. This rapid digitalisation has brought both challenges and opportunities, making it imperative to reassess our understanding of the platform society in this new context.

2. Structure of the Book

This book originates from two international workshops organised by the editors at the Department of Cultures, Politics and Society of the University of Turin within the framework of the research project 'The risks of the platform society: inequality, discrimination, manipulation', funded by the University of Turin ('Grant for Internationalization – GFI' for collaborative research projects with international partners 2022). The project examined the evolution of the challenges and opportunities presented by the platform society through a multidisciplinary lens within the realm of social and political sciences. The scholars who participated in the workshops had diverse backgrounds within the social sciences and not only brought to the discussion new evidence for the analysis of established topics (such as education, journalism and politics) but also explored emerging challenges, including e.g. those related to social work and the environment. Another added value of the workshops consisted in the fact that they did not merely identify the risks associated with the platformisation of society and politics; they also explored potential solutions and best practices to navigate the digital transformation. By encompassing case studies and analyses at the EU level as well as from countries and regions traditionally less represented in the literature (e.g. Italy, Spain and Portugal), the project offered a global perspective on the evolving opportunities and challenges posed by the platform society.

Coherently with the multidisciplinary lens that characterised the project, this book comprises nine chapters divided into five sections that seek to chart the evolution of the platform society across various domains. The five sections are education, discrimination, media, institutions and environment, an emerging new field of conflict for the platform society.

Section 1 (*Education*) provides novel evidence on the potential of platforms in the education and lifelong learning sector. The chapters in this section, *Collective Learning: Exploring the Educational Benefits of Collective Intelligence* by Pablo Bautista, Javier Fernández and Tatiana Iñiguez Berrozpe and *A Better Skilled Workforce for the Digital Transformation: What Role for Platform Education?* by Valentina Goglio, highlight the benefits of collaborative learning and examine the landscape of online training across Europe.

In the chapter *Collective Learning: Exploring the Educational Benefits of Collective Intelligence*, the authors analyse a successful practice that leverages collective intelligence to develop digital competences and manage the potential risks associated with social networks, such as fake news, sexting, cyberbullying and hate speech. The concept of collective learning is based on the principle that the average performance of a group working collectively is superior to the individual performance of each of its members. The online environment further enhances this process by significantly increasing the number of participants in groups.

The chapter introduces a collective learning tool called the 'Collective Learning Platform'. This platform is designed to generate quality solutions to complex problems or tasks by harnessing collective intelligence through successive digital social interactions. Its aim is to equip students with the skills and competencies needed to navigate and mitigate digital risks. The chapter recounts that, by participating in various sessions on the platform, Spanish students were able to engage in collaborative problem-solving and critical thinking exercises that enhanced their understanding and management of digital challenges.

The chapter by Valentina Goglio provides an overview of the distribution of online lifelong learning, encompassing online courses and learning materials, among the European working-age population. We know that workers' skills significantly influence macroeconomic prospects at the country level, while at the microlevel, a lack of the skills needed to keep pace with the rapid evolution of productive systems can adversely affect workers' job market opportunities and career trajectories. Within this context, digital tools have increasingly made online courses and learning materials accessible. But is this accessibility universal and equitable? The chapter examines the distribution of participation in online learning across different countries and investigates whether traditional social cleavages that affect participation in lifelong learning persist in the digital age. The findings indicate that better-educated individuals have greater chances of utilising these resources. At the macrolevel, the distribution of online lifelong learning across countries mirrors the traditional patterns of participation in adult and lifelong learning, suggesting that existing educational inequalities are reproduced in the digital learning landscape.

Section 2 (*Discrimination*) confronts the challenges and risks faced by marginalised communities in the digital realm. It dissects the use of digital devices and platforms in social work and explores online hate speech targeting gender-normative defiance in popular media events. This section includes *The Use of Digital Devices and Digital Platforms in Social Work: Challenges and Risks* by Giovanni Cellini and Carlotta Mozzone and *Made in Italy: Online Hate Speech Targeting Gender-Normative Defiance at the Sanremo Music Festival* by Camilla Borgna and Antonio Martella.

With respect to social work, we know that ICTs have a significant impact on it, influencing both professional practices in relationships with clients and broader processes of social exclusion and inclusion. In his chapter, Giovanni Cellini addresses the definitions of digitalisation in social work, its applications in various contexts of professional practice as well as the advantages, challenges and ethical implications associated with it. On the one hand, digitalisation poses risks such as privacy and security concerns, the potential loss of the emotional and physical dimensions of the helping relationship, increased discrimination against vulnerable individuals who may not receive necessary in-person interventions and the risk of neglecting the importance of maintaining an adequate number of social workers in direct contact with the community within the welfare system. On the other hand, it has the following benefits: enhancing access to social work services that are otherwise unavailable due to geographical distance, clients' disabilities or illnesses; enabling the real-time monitoring of clients' status, and rapid response when appropriate; providing more cost-effective delivery of social work services; facilitating communication and reducing the need for clients to travel to obtain services. Underpinning these considerations is the ongoing challenge of the digital divide, which social work must address in order to ensure equitable access to digital resources.

The chapter *Made in Italy: Online Hate Speech Targeting Gender-Normative Defiance at the Sanremo Music Festival* examines a specific risk of the online environment: online hate speech. This can be defined as a form of communication, including text, videos and photos, that expresses hatred or degrading attitudes towards individuals or groups based on their gender identity, sexual orientation, body shape, race, ethnicity, religion, national origin or other social identity factors. Against this backdrop, the chapter explores an under-researched area in the literature: comparison among social media platforms of online behaviours. It highlights that platforms differ in at least three factors that may affect the amount of online hate speech and counter-reactions to it: their typical content and usage, users' demographics and moderation and censorship policies. Through a case study involving a public figure (a singer) who challenged traditional gender norms during a mainstream televised event in Italy and subsequently became the target of violent attacks both online and offline, the chapter demonstrates that social network platforms are not all the same. The analysis focuses on online reactions to the event across three social media platforms where the singer was active, revealing significant differences among these platforms in the nature and extent of online hate speech. This study underscores the importance of understanding platform-specific dynamics to effectively address and mitigate online hate speech.

Section 3 (*Media*) ventures into the evolving landscape of news dissemination. This section provides insights into the future of journalism in the digital age by unpacking the TikTokisation of news production and addressing cases of local journalism gaps and disinformation. It comprises two chapters: *Can I Have Some News? Local Journalism Gaps and the Role of Platforms* by Pedro Jerónimo and Luísa Torre and *TikTokisation of the News: News Media Content Production Strategies in Portugal* by Antonio Martella and Pedro Jerónimo.

In their chapter, Jerónimo and Torre discuss the phenomenon of 'news deserts' which are communities where residents have very limited access to critical and credible local news and information essential for grassroots democracy and social cohesion. The rise of news deserts is closely linked to platform competition. As platforms increasingly position themselves as intermediaries between audiences and the information they seek, regional media face stronger competition, losing their centrality as news and information providers. As a consequence, in the last decade platforms have become key actors also in the local information ecosystem, often prioritising low-quality content over journalistic information that serves as a watchdog of local authorities. This shift carries significant risks. At a local level, the lack of journalism coverage leads to decreased scrutiny of local institutions, increased vulnerability to disinformation, hate speech, and populism on social media and a growing sense of suspicion and confusion among the public. However, the chapter also notes that in the absence of traditional media, information still circulates through other means. In municipalities without journalists, much of the local information is disseminated through social media platforms like Facebook pages and groups. These platforms provide content that helps build communities: they share critical local information and encourage community members to take actions that benefit society. In summary, social media platforms can also play a central role in the context of news deserts, facilitating citizens' access to information about their immediate environment.

The theme of the platformisation of journalism is also central to the chapter *TikTokisation of the News: News Media Content Production Strategies in Portugal*. The platformisation of journalism has compelled news media to adapt to network media logic, thereby affecting journalistic practices and norms. This shift has reinforced or introduced several challenges for media outlets, including heightened competition for attention, increased news avoidance and – as anticipated – the rise of social media as primary news sources. Moreover, media organisations must produce content according to algorithmic curation practices to intercept niche audiences' newsfeeds across various platforms, and the gatekeeping function performed by the interaction between algorithms and audience preferences creates a highly unbalanced power relationship between platforms and media outlets. Against this backdrop, the chapter makes the first attempt to statistically identify the production strategies adopted by major Portuguese media on TikTok.

Section 4 (*Institutions*) shifts the focus to the digital transformation of governments and democracies. The chapters *E-Government, Digital and Financial Literacy: Insights From Cross-Country Data* by Anna Lo Prete and *Turning the Tables Again? Paid Social Media as a New Campaign Environment* by Enea Fiore, Daniela R. Piccio and Antonella Seddone examine through a comparative lens the intersection among e-government, digital literacy and financial literacy and the emergence of paid social media as a new political campaign environment and its implications for democracy.

The development of government initiatives that leverage digital platforms to deliver public services is a significant feature of the platform society. On the one hand, civic engagement through e-government platforms provides citizens with new opportunities to participate in the social and political life of their community. On the other hand, digital citizenship and the digitalisation of public services can raise barriers against individuals with lower digital competence. The chapter by Anna Lo Prete presents descriptive evidence on the relationship between e-government development across countries and levels of digital and financial literacy. The results indicate that e-government is most prevalent in countries with higher digital and financial literacy. Given, however, that the average level of digital literacy remains quite low, many citizens often struggle to navigate e-government platforms. E-government is not always aligned with the cognitive skills required for individuals to navigate online independently and understand policy trade-offs, and this misalignment can significantly hinder the development of inclusive and critically independent e-citizenship through online platforms.

At the same time, digital platforms owned by private firms have become prominent actors within contemporary democracies. Their potential to compromise the integrity of electoral processes is significant because the accessibility of the personal data of users engaging on these platforms has facilitated the design of highly advanced political advertising tools: indeed, digital advertising strategies can utilise personalised information about individuals to devise micro-targeting strategies. The growing use of big data technologies and microtargeting tools by political parties and leaders to influence voters' perceptions, particularly in the run-up to significant electoral events, has prompted inquiries into the manipulation and integrity of the electoral process, intensified political polarization and enabled the spread of misinformation. The events surrounding Cambridge Analytica, Brexit and the 2016 US elections have catalysed the demand for the European Union to develop regulatory instruments to tackle the risks associated with the abuse of online political advertising. In the chapter *Turning the Tables Again? Paid Social Media as a New Campaign Environment* the authors examine the Transparency and Political Advertising Regulation (TTPA), a significant change in the relationship between EU institutions and platform services. The TTPA acknowledges the role and responsibility of institutions in addressing specific dysfunctional mechanisms that may threaten democratic processes. It introduces transparency provisions in political advertising and states that targeting techniques involving the processing of personal data are permitted only with explicit consent and when such techniques do not involve profiling.

Finally, Section 5 (*Environment*) charts a research agenda that assesses the risks of the platform society for the environment. In an era defined by environmental challenges, this section conducts a pioneering examination of the environmental implications of the digital age. It includes *Environmental Challenges in the Platform Society: Insights From the Mobilizations Against Data Centers* by Cecilia Biancalana. This chapter analyses mobilisations against data centres, large edifices that house the servers driving the digital realm. These mobilisations and conflicts, situated at the intersection between digital and environmental realms across various geographical and sociopolitical contexts, highlight several key issues. Specifically, the chapter discusses questions related to data nationalism and data colonialism, illustrating how the digital world is intricately tied to issues of territorial sovereignty. More broadly, the chapter encourages study of the environmental impacts of ICTs, a field still underexplored in political science but increasingly important because the ICT sector accounts for approximately 2.1%–3.9% of global GHG emissions. Political intervention will be crucial in mitigating these emissions.

3. Platform Society: Key Topics for a Research Agenda

The chapters of the book highlight several crucial issues. One recurring theme is the role of **digital literacy and digital skills**, emphasising their importance for navigating the digital world effectively and equitably. The objective of the Collective Learning Platform described in the chapter *Collective Learning: Exploring the Educational Benefits of Collective Intelligence* was to enable young students who participated in various sessions to acquire skills and competencies with which to manage digital risks more appropriately. However, cultivating digital skills is crucial not only for the young but also for the elderly, who are most susceptible to the digital divide. These skills are also essential in the training of social workers, as Giovanni Cellini discusses in his chapter.

Valentina Goglio's chapter highlights as a key policy area the need for a more skilled workforce and the upgrading of workers' qualifications with both technical and adaptive skills. Among these latter, digital and ICT skills are essential for the future workforce and can be provided by platform education. However, digital skills are not only vital in the workplace. Anna Lo Prete emphasises in her chapter that basic competencies needed to use e-platforms should be strengthened through educational and training programs in order to share the benefits of digitalised public services and civic engagement without incurring the dangers posed by digital technologies. Otherwise, the innovations brought by e-government will be useless. Moreover, transparency regulations for political advertising on social media, such as those outlined in the TTPA, are ineffective without a corresponding increase in digital skills. Similarly, as Jeronimo and Torre remind us, the effective use of social media platforms by citizens to fill the information void in news deserts depends on their technical skills and prior experience in using such platforms to navigate these information ecosystems properly.

The book also demonstrates how online inequalities often reflect offline disparities, impacting access and participation. Valentina Goglio's chapter shows that traditional social cleavages affecting participation in lifelong learning persist in the online world, as better-educated individuals have greater chances of using online learning resources. Similarly, Anna Lo Prete's chapter indicates that higher values of e-government are recorded in higher-income countries and that the digitalisation of public services can represent a barrier for less competent individuals. Additionally, news deserts are often found in peripheral and marginalised communities, exacerbating information inequality. Also, the choice of locations for installing digital infrastructures, such as data centres, often reproduces pre-existing inequalities. This is exemplified by the Chilean case presented in the chapter by Cecilia Biancalana, which introduces the concept of data colonialism.

More broadly, Giovanni Cellini reminds us that technological innovation does not automatically guarantee progress towards social justice and that social work has an ethical duty to ensure that technological evolution is inclusive and does not amplify existing inequalities. The digital gap and online divisions perpetuate power imbalances and privileges both within and beyond the realm of social work.

Moreover, the **diversity among digital platforms** and the importance of **avoiding technological determinism** – where technological innovation is presumed to lead to a specific outcome – are key focuses of the book. Platforms are not homogeneous, and analysing their specific affordances is essential for understanding their unique impacts and functions. For instance, in the chapter *Made in Italy: Online Hate*

Speech Targeting Gender-Normative Defiance at the Sanremo Music Festival, it is shown that hate speech is much more prevalent on Facebook than on other platforms. Conversely, TikTok emerges as the least 'hateful' environment, with most of the negative sentiment expressed being related to sadness or disappointment. Furthermore, the chapter *TikTokisation of the News: News Media Content Production Strategies in Portugal* illustrates that media must produce content according to algorithmic curation practices, which vary from platform to platform.

Another important argument advanced in the book challenges the assumption that a particular characteristic of the platform society will necessarily lead to a particular outcome, such as the notion that anonymity always fosters negative behaviour. For instance, students involved in the Collective Learning Platform appreciated the opportunity to express their ideas and feelings anonymously. They valued being able to give their opinions without restrictions and to find others who agreed with their arguments on the platform. The ability to express themselves without being negatively affected by their relationships was highly valued. In contrast, Borgna and Martella highlight that the online context facilitates the expression and spread of negative behaviour by making it easier to maintain anonymity and to access broader audiences. This is particularly the case of social media platforms, where individuals can connect with each other while avoiding face-to-face interactions, especially on platforms that strongly support anonymity.

Finally, the book addresses the **changes brought about by the COVID-19 pandemic**, detailing how it has accelerated digital transformation and altered the dynamics of online interactions and services. For instance, several chapters show that the use of the internet for online courses and learning materials in Europe exhibits a marked increase corresponding with the pandemic period, thus highlighting the critical role of digital platforms in education. The acceleration of digitalisation during the pandemic has also been significant for the welfare system and social professions by acting as a catalyst for the digitalisation of social services. This transformation has reshaped the manner in which social workers interact with clients and deliver services, emphasising the need for digital competencies in the profession. In some local newsrooms, the pandemic has prompted journalists to adopt a digital-first mindset that has fundamentally changed news production and dissemination practices. E-government initiatives also received further impetus during the COVID-19 pandemic because lockdowns and movement restrictions induced governments to devise effective digital solutions to ensure the provision of public services. This reinforces the need to update the literature on the platform society in the post-COVID-19 era, acknowledging the profound impact of the pandemic on digitalisation across various sectors.

References

Arcidiacono, D., Pais, I., & Zandonai, F. (2022). Plat-firming welfare: Examining digital transformation in local care services. *GBR*. https://publicatt.unicatt.it/handle/10807/214484

Arcidiacono, D., & Sartori, L. (2024). Algorithmic management: Invisible boss or ghost work? In M. Béjean, J. Brabet, E. Mollona, & C. Vercher-Chaptal (Eds.), *Disruptive digitalisation and platforms* (1st ed., pp. 77–99). Routledge. https://doi.org/10.4324/9781032617190-8

Armano, E., Leonardi, D., & Murgia, A. (2022). Algorithmic management in food delivery platforms: Between digital neo-Taylorism and enhanced subjectivity. In E. Armano, M. Briziarelli, & E. Risi (Eds.), *Digital platforms and algorithmic subjectivities* (pp. 87–96). University of Westminster Press. https://doi.org/10.16997/book54.g

Casilli, A. A., & Posada, J. (2019). The platformization of labor and society. In M. Graham & W. H. Dutton (Eds.), *Society and the internet* (pp. 293–306). Oxford University Press. https://doi.org/10.1093/oso/9780198843498.003.0018

Decuypere, M., Grimaldi, E., & Landri, P. (2021). Introduction: Critical studies of digital education platforms. *Critical Studies in Education*, *62*(1), 1–16. https://doi.org/10.1080/17508487.2020.1866050

Hargittai, E. (2021). *Handbook of digital inequality*. Edward Elgar.

López Peláez, A., & Kirwan, G. (2023). *The Routledge international handbook of digital social work*. Routledge. https://www.routledge.com/The-Routledge-International-Handbook-of-Digital-Social-Work/LopezPelaez-Kirwan/p/book/9780367499945

Pais, I., Borghi, P., & Murgia, A. (2021). High-skilled platform jobs in Europe: Trends, quality of work and emerging challenges. *SOCIOLOGIA DEL LAVORO*, *2021*/*160*. https://doi.org/10.3280/SL2021-160010

Schor, J. B., Tirrell, C., & Vallas, S. P. (2023). Consent and contestation: How platform workers reckon with the risks of gig labor. *Work, Employment and Society*. https://doi.org/10.1177/09500170231199404

Schor, J. B., & Vallas, S. P. (2023). Labor and the platform economy. In B. Heydari, O. Ergun, R. Dyal-Chand, & Y. Bart (Eds.), *Reengineering the sharing economy: Design, policy, and regulation* (pp. 83–94). Cambridge University Press. https://doi.org/10.1017/9781108865630.007

Selwyn, N. (2014). *Digital technology and the contemporary university: Degrees of digitization*. Routledge.

Stark, D., & Pais, I. (2021). Algorithmic management in the platform economy. *Sociologica*, 47–72. https://doi.org/10.6092/ISSN.1971-8853/12221

van Dijck, J., Poell, T., & de Waal, M. (2018). *The platform society* (Vol. 1). Oxford University Press.

Zuboff, S. (2019). *The age of surveillance capitalism: The fight for a human future at the new frontier of power* (1st ed.). PublicAffairs.

Section 1

Education

Chapter 1

Collective Intelligence Online Experiments: A Learning Method and Its Pedagogical Applications Through Online Collaborative Work Platforms

Pablo Bautista-Alcaine[a], *Tatiana Íñiguez-Berrozpe*[a] *and Javier Fernández-Albás*[b]

[a]University of Zaragoza, Spain
[b]Kampal Data Solutions, Spain

Abstract

Collective intelligence is a novel construct which posits that a large number of people can work together to come up with better answers to various problems in less time than would be spent individually or in groups. Based on this premise, the University Institute for Biocomputing and Complex Systems Physics Research (BIFI) of the University of Zaragoza and the company Kampal Data Solutions created the collective intelligence platform named 'Collective Learning.' This chapter presents the various experiments that have been carried out in the educational field with this platform, and it highlights how the results obtained have enhanced our knowledge about the generation of collective intelligence and its impact on the possible learning of digital skills and online risk management competencies by the participating students.

Keywords: Collective intelligence; online experiments; collaborative online platforms; adolescents; children; education

1. Introduction

In the current platform society analysed in this book, educational possibilities have expanded considerably, increasing the resources available to address the

---

Mapping the Evolution of Platform Society, 13–26
Copyright © 2025 Pablo Bautista-Alcaine, Tatiana Íñiguez-Berrozpe and Javier Fernández-Albás
Published under exclusive licence by Emerald Publishing Limited
doi:10.1108/978-1-83608-028-220251002

training of children and adolescents in skills and values. At the same time, the digital society to which we refer raises a series of challenges for minors that range from the need to develop information and digital abilities for optimal educational, work and social performance to the management of the possible risks that the internet and social networks entail.

In this sense, and given the purpose of this book, in the following chapter, we not only address the identification of the possible risks involved in the platformisation of society and, therefore, of children and young people, but we also provide an analysis of a good practice based on collective intelligence for the development of the aforementioned digital competences and the management of the potential risks of social networks.

2. Collective Intelligence

The application of collective intelligence in group learning can generate collective learning in which more people, regardless of their profile within the collective learning group, can gain experience and benefit the rest of the group through their skills and ideas (Woolley & Aggarwal, 2020).

Thus, Woolley et al. (2010) defined collective intelligence ('c') as a construct that emerges to explain the performance of a group of people engaged in collaborative group tasks of different types, the basic idea being that the average performance obtained with this format is better than the individual performance of each member. On formulating this definition, Woolley et al. (2010) mentioned that, over the last century, the field of psychology has made great advances in identifying and measuring the individual intelligence of people, as well as the ability of workgroups to effectively perform the tasks they face.

Woolley and colleagues then pointed out that the performance of these workgroups has not been measured in the same way as that of individuals, i.e. while information obtained from an individual can be used to predict future performance, the same does not apply to workgroups, and there is no method with which to predict the performance of a workgroup on the basis of its current performance (Wooley et al., 2010). Given this situation, they hypothesised that groups, like individuals, have certain characteristic levels of intelligence, what they called collective intelligence 'c', that can be measured and used to predict the performance of such workgroups.

To identify and define the 'c' factor, which statistically defines collective intelligence as a characteristic property of groups *per se* and not of individuals, Woolley et al. (2010) drew an analogy with the 'g' factor of general cognitive ability, which is extracted from the analysis of individual intelligence. This analogy was helpful because the g-factor of individual intelligence can be measured in one hour or less, and it is a very reliable predictor of performance on a wide variety of tasks and situations across the lifespan, such as academic qualifications, job success and even life expectancy (Woolley et al., 2010).

Once the definition of collective intelligence was established, in a first study Woolley et al. (2010) randomly divided 120 participants into 40 groups of 3 people to work together for 5 hours on several simple and one more complex task. In order to compare the hypothesised group performance, 'c', with individual performance 'g', the latter factor was measured at the beginning of each session. Tasks included solving visual puzzles, brainstorming, collective moral judgements in various situations as well as negotiation over limited resources and a game of draughts against a standardised digital opponent. In the same way as the first study, a second one was carried out with 152 groups of 2–5 participants per group but with 5 further tasks added to those just mentioned.

The results obtained through factor analysis in the first study supported the hypothesis that there was a collective intelligence factor 'c' in the groups that strongly and significantly preceded group performance in the different tasks but did not correlate significantly with the individual intelligence scores of the group members ('g'). Moreover, the results obtained in the second study, with a larger number of groups and tasks, yielded the same conclusions as those of the first study, thus confirming that collective intelligence, and the statistical factor 'c' that identifies it, exists. Finally, Woolley et al. (2010) were able to identify the first three factors that favour the emergence of collective intelligence: the social sensitivity of the group members, the fluency and respect of the conversation among all group members, and the existence of women within the group.

Replications of the Woolley et al. (2010) study have been carried out with some of the more complex tasks used in that study, such as playing chess against an artificial intelligence (AI) programme, negotiating in the face of conflicts or resolving various moral dilemmas (Engel et al., 2014; Hjertø & Paulsen, 2016). The results of each of these studies were similar to those obtained by Woolley et al. (2010), demonstrating the existence of a statistical factor 'c' that represents group intelligence and is not directly related to the 'g' factor of individual intelligence, as found by Woolley et al. in their first study (2010).

However, the possibility of confronting large groups with ill-defined problems to solve is present in another construct close to collective intelligence, so-called 'crowd intelligence' (Bernstein et al., 2018). The possibility of finding solutions to these problems in this type of large group context is conditioned by various factors that emerge during the interaction, such as the lack of collaboration of some participants, the lack of originality due to excessive reproduction of responses or the dispersion of responses. The conditioning of these factors is very similar to the variables that are closely related to the emergence of collective intelligence as mentioned by Woolley et al. (2010) in their study, with the social sensitivity of the group and the fluency and respect of the conversation among all its members being the two factors that most resemble the conditioning factors identified by Bernstein et al. (2018).

However, over the years it was decided that, because the existence of collective intelligence was proven in groups whose level of interaction was face-to-face, it was necessary to move the interaction processes by which the 'c' factor was generated into other environments with greater possibilities and which allowed for a greater number of participants. Thus, both the first research team of Woolley et al. (2010) and another group of researchers independent of this first team incorporated the novelty of moving from environments where interaction took place face-to-face to an online environment, allowing the latter format to significantly increase the number of participants in the groups (Engel et al., 2014; Woolley & Aggarwal, 2020).

Bernstein et al. (2018), in their work on 'crowd intelligence', determined that there are certain conditioning factors that prevent or minimise a group's ability to obtain optimal answers to complex problems in face-to-face collaborative environments. Similarly, Toyokawa et al. (2019) stated that the same can occur with online interaction processes to reach effective solutions to the problems proposed to large working groups. This is due to several factors that emerge during the interaction, such as the dispersion of responses, the lack of collaboration and the lack of originality due to the excessive reproduction of responses.

However, an important idea emerges when studying these contexts and the conditioning factors that surround them and influence the emergence of original and quality responses depending on them. This idea revolves around the need that, in all collaborative work, there must be a moderator or a leader who manages the interaction among participants in order to reach an effective agreement on the resolution of the problem (Salganik et al., 2006). This notion of a moderator or leader was not considered as a possible conditioner of the circulation of information in the first study carried out by Woolley et al. (2010), but it has been taken into account in subsequent studies.

Bigham et al. (2018) analysed the process of dispersing ideas in the 'crowd intelligence' study conducted by Bernstein et al. (2018), pointing out the existence and presence of a role very similar to that of the moderator or leader whose role consists in facilitating the spread of ideas. They decided to call this person a 'facilitator' ('crowd fertilisation') who distributes ideas within the group without the need to moderate the responses but to ensure that they arrive appropriately, thereby generating high productivity in the group. Therefore, the presence of facilitators in collective intelligence studies demonstrates the importance of social interaction in groups (Bigham et al., 2018). Thus, besides the dimensions to be addressed as first mentioned by Woolley et al. (2010), now to be added are the 'crowd intelligence' described by Bernstein et al. (2018) and the 'crowd fertilisation' described by Bigham et al. (2018). This shows that the dimensions to be addressed are diverse. They range from the modelling and copying of ideas to the study of facilitation roles or the role that leadership can play in the dispersion of ideas that would affect both the emergence of quality responses in collaborative environments where participants interact face-to-face (Bernstein et al., 2018) and in online environments (Toyokawa et al., 2019).

Apart from 'crowd intelligence', 'crowd fertilisation' and the variables first described by Woolley et al. (2010), which are related to the emergence of collective intelligence, in the most recent research reported by Woolley and Aggarwal (2020), the aim was to determine what other variables at a theoretical level are conducive to the emergence of collective intelligence. To this end, these researchers conducted a comprehensive review of the following factors that could favour this emergence: the link between intelligence and learning, learning in groups, tacit learning in coordination games, explicit learning in academic tests, the role of socioemotional processes and cognitive diversity. Assuming all these factors, two levels of analysis were finally proposed: the first was based on the interaction processes arising within the group ('top-down'); the second considered the characteristics of the group members ('bottom-up').

Research on top-down factors focuses mainly on interaction variables among group members in both face-to-face settings guided by a facilitator (Bigham et al., 2018) and virtual settings (Toyokawa et al., 2019). These include the duration of the task, the number of speaking turns, the diversity of the answers given, the time spent on consensus building and the heterogeneity of the group. At the bottom-up level, some of the variables analysed have been gender, cognitive diversity (Aggarwal et al., 2019), emotional intelligence (Hjertø & Paulsen, 2016), social sensitivity or individual intelligence (Woolley & Aggarwal, 2020). However, research on the conditions under which quality or more limited responses may appear in online environments is still very limited, and so is the possibility of testing whether large groups of people can interact to solve problems and avoid some of the problems that arise in these models (Toyokawa et al., 2019).

3. Collective Learning, the Collective Intelligence Platform

To generate collective intelligence through large groups in online environments, researchers at the University Institute for Biocomputing Research and Physics of Complex Systems (BIFI) of the University of Zaragoza and the Kampal Data Solutions company devised a collective learning tool based on the idea of collective intelligence propounded by Woolley et al. (2010). The 'Collective Learning Platform' is designed to create quality solutions to complex problems or tasks using collective intelligence by means of a model of successive digital social interactions, trying to avoid problems common in these contexts (Toyokawa et al., 2019).

When designing the platform, BIFI and Kampal Data Solutions considered that, when a large number of people are involved, collective work presents significant problems in terms of achieving an orderly discussion that correctly promotes the construction of ideas. Among these problems, the following stand out:

- Noise: The dissemination of ideas that have not been filtered at any point creates confusion and hinders both reflective and personal work.
- Disruption: This occurs when some of the people involved in the task seek not to generate the solutions and confuse the participants.
- Influence: This is when an opinion obtains greater consensus when it is proposed by a person with social power within the group, a fact that is independent of the quality or validity of the opinion itself.

However, just as collective work itself presents various problems and complications so does individual behaviour within the group to achieve the constructive participation of a large number of people, mainly due to the following factors:

- Isolationism: This occurs when many individuals choose to disconnect from the group, either by choice or because they feel that they do not fit in with the group and therefore disengage from it.
- Dispersion: This describes when there is a tendency for there to be as many solutions as there are people present in the collective or group.
- The Leadership Syndrome: This is when a percentage of people prefer to lead or participate in a small group with their ideas rather than join a different (usually larger) group with better ideas.

These are some of the difficulties encountered within the BIFI in studies that have attempted to test how large groups of up to 30 people must collaborate to accomplish a task (Toyokawa et al., 2019). The social learning strategies that emerge during the process become key factors in achieving agreement among the group and producing a solution of higher quality than individual ones. Within the group, there appear phenomena such as the herd effect, i.e. an initial tendency to conformism that limits the group's creativity or a large dispersion of alternatives that must be unified and coordinated (Toyokawa et al., 2019) or the decrease in creativity due to the appearance of copy effects (Lorenz et al., 2011) or the excessive influence of leaders (Iyengar et al., 2011). However, in order to take advantage of the collective effort to address problems through the exchange of ideas, cross-fertilisation requires the presence of a system that performs the role of 'facilitator', i.e. it controls and manages the work of the group as proposed by Bigham et al. (2018).

On these premises, it continues to be argued that the type of interaction among members and the type of demand or task posed are very important in understanding emergent behaviours. For example, more open tasks generate a greater dispersion of responses and a reduction in copying, which is more frequent in the case of more closed tasks (Toyokawa et al., 2019). Also, the type of interaction or the prestige of the participants may influence copying behaviours. For example, Bernstein et al. (2018) found that an intermittent interaction model versus an individual work model improves creativity and the quality of responses to ill-defined tasks. In addition, Lorenz et al. (2011) found that social prestige acts as a convergence mechanism but without implying better response quality.

3.1 Operation and Resolution of Interaction Problems

Every project or experiment conducted within the Collective Learning online platform starts with a large number of people involved in it. Each individual (his/her responses within the project or experiment) is considered a node of the platform's network. Individuals within it can work on their solution and, where possible, can see their neighbours in the network or copy from them.

Every project or experiment carried out within the Collective Learning Platform is divided into seven phases that always start from strictly local interactions that evolve within the project towards more global ones. Throughout these phases, various mechanisms used to minimise the problems outlined above are introduced within large group interactions (Iyengar et al., 2011; Lorenz et al., 2011; Toyokawa et al., 2019). In the different phases of the project or experiment where interaction is possible, each participant interacts with his/her four neighbours, who in turn interact with their other four neighbours, allowing for effective long-range interaction. Thus, the ideas generated by the participants are seen, copied or discarded by those they have as neighbours. In this way, during the evolution of the project, these ideas also evolve until those responses that have not been sufficiently copied are forced to die out in the system, which is somewhat like the social consensus of face-to-face groups.

Therefore, the general functioning of the platform devised by the BIFI is as follows: Each user owns his/her solutions and can create or modify them. The only possible interaction with other users consists in viewing or copying from accessible neighbours. Thus, even with local interaction, information is propagated throughout the entire network only if elements are copied by successive users. In Phase 1, participants cannot yet see any other solutions, but as they move into Phase 2, they can already see and copy the solutions that their neighbours proposed at the end of Phase 1. In Phases 3 and 4, the visible solutions are continuously updated each time any neighbour presses the 'save' button, maintaining geometry and thus local interaction until the end of Phase 5, and allowing the propagation of information in the network without saturating it (Toyokawa et al., 2019). When Phase 6 starts, the process assumes to a global geometry (non-local interaction in physical language), and users are shown the best 10 solutions (Top 10), defined as the solutions with the greatest 'popularity'. Users can copy elements from the Top 10 to their own solution and can still propose new solutions until the last phase begins, Phase 7, in which users can no longer edit and can only copy from the existing Top 10 solutions.

Within the latter two phases, there are mainly two effects. The first one corresponds to social influence, one of the factors that affect the type of response to any test (Bernstein et al., 2018; Lorenz et al., 2011). The second corresponds to the large amount of information to be evaluated: it is precisely this amount and the multiple options and opinions displayed that provide cognitive diversity and, therefore, help the emergence of collective intelligence (Aggarwal et al., 2019). However, a higher cognitive demand must be compensated with task mastery in the later stages. Thus, through the Top 10 answers generated by the participants, with the platform acting as a facilitator, a 'forced' consensus can be reached, although this facilitator is created by the group itself, without external intervention.

Another key issue is the popularity of the answer (prestige effect), which is executed in the background by AI acting as a moderator or facilitator (Bigham et al., 2018) between Phases 2, 3, 4 and 5, resulting in the creation of a top 10 of answers for each question in Phases 6 and 7. While in Phase 6 the participants can perform the same actions as in the previous phases, in Phase 7 they can only copy answers from the top 10 or keep their own. This popularity or prestige effect makes it possible to reduce and select information in favour of a consensus, thus acting as a facilitating element, but accepting that this can lead to lower quality and less diverse answers endorsed by less competent leaders (Bernstein et al., 2018;

Lorenz et al., 2011). Thus, Collective Learning Platform generates this popularity or prestige factor according to the frequency of appearance within the network of the same answer to each of the questions, the origin of which may be in the personal or common elaboration of the answer.

This popularity system, in addition to being a great facilitator of consensus, modulates the heterogeneity of the responses through a progressive process of extinction of responses by the AI from Phase 6 onwards. Finally, it should be noted that this process of controlling the heterogeneity of the responses through extinction helps the AI to act as a virtual moderator of the collective, assuming the essential role of the group's moderator or facilitator described above (Bigham et al., 2018). To summarise, to achieve this interaction model, collective learning uses the different means previously described (visualisation of other responses, permutation of users, copying, modification and extinction of responses) through seven phases, starting with a first individual response phase followed by six phases of interaction among users.

4. Experiences of Collective Intelligence Through Collective Learning

Since the first collective intelligence experiment was conducted on the Collective Learning Platform, 5 years have passed in which more than 50 collective intelligence sessions have been carried out. This section briefly describes the main results and conclusions that have been drawn from the use of the Collective Learning Platform.

4.1 CI Experiment 2019: Adolescent Moral Development in the Face of Cyberbullying

In this first experiment, a collective intelligence session was carried out in which students attending the first year of the baccalaureate (pre-university studies in Spain) were confronted with a case of sexting. In total, 793 students aged between 16 and 17 from 21 schools participated synchronously to find a solution to the case proposed to them by answering 3 open-ended questions. The first problem with using the tool for research purposes was the amount of data that it generated for analysis. When we realised that more than 10,000 open text responses had been generated in 1 hour of work, which was an amount of data very difficult to analyse, we randomly selected a sample of 100 participating students, whose responses to each question were analysed using a previously validated category system based on Kohlberg's (1976) theory of moral development.

To determine whether students had improved their level of moral development through their participation in the experiment, we compared the outcomes made between the first and the last phase, observing how ideas and moral reasoning evolved throughout their participation. The results obtained showed that only in one of the three questions were there significant differences between the first and seventh phases, where participants reached a level of moral development higher than expected for their age through collective work. Thus, it was found that, whilst improvements could be made to the platform, it was still necessary to delve deeper into how collective intelligence was emerging within it.

The results made us aware that both the case and the questions needed to be better adapted to the construct and the methodology. Therefore, the decision was taken that, in subsequent experiments with collective intelligence, the case should be more complex and closer to the participants' experience. Moreover, it should generate questions with a high level of complexity that would allow the multiple responses issued within the platform to be enriched. Also, the duration might be too long for the students, and the platform needed to be fine-tuned in terms of its internal programming, providing a better response to the 'top-down' variables described by Woolley and Aggarwal (2020).

4.2 CI 2020 Experiment: Developing Skills to Address Cyberbullying in Trainee Teachers

The experiment carried out in 2020 was again related to cyberbullying. However, the context was very different. On this occasion, a case of cyberbullying in the classroom was presented to a group of trainee teachers ($n = 221$) attending the second year of the Teaching Degree in Primary Education, where they were put in the shoes of a classroom tutor who had to respond to a complex case of cyberbullying. The purpose of this experiment was to find out whether, through participation in the Collective Learning Platform, future teachers improved their ability to identify, deal with and prevent cases of cyberbullying.

The main difference with respect to the first collective intelligence experiment carried out in 2019 concerned how the top-down and bottom-up variables were adapted (Woolley & Aggarwal, 2020). Regarding the top-down variables, AI functioned as a more finely tuned moderator or crowd fertiliser (Bigham et al., 2018), adequately solving most of the problems of working in large groups online (Toyokawa et al., 2019). In addition, the duration of the session was reduced so that students felt less tired during their participation. To respond to the bottom-up variables, the case developed was more appropriate to the context. It went deeper into the situation presented both professionally and emotionally. Similarly, the questions were more complex and graded multiple-choice in format (each question could be scored between 0 and 10 points), which made it possible to quantify the evolution of the students within the platform.

With the changes made to the platform, the case and the questions, the results were much better than those obtained in the 2019 experiment (Bautista Alcaine et al., 2022; Orejudo et al., 2022). On this occasion, because the questions were multiple choice, it was possible to analyse the evolution of each student's score in each phase and question through repeated measures ANOVAs. Significant differences were obtained between the first and last phases in all the questions asked, and improvements could be observed in both the identification of, and coping with, cyberbullying by future teachers. These improvements began to occur in the first phases of participation; however, the more complex the question, the greater the improvement in the first phases.

However, although the results were very positive, the improvements implemented in the tool should be tested in new educational contexts and with cases that respond to new competencies to be developed or improved among the participants. Similarly, although the multiple-choice questions provide a much better understanding of the participant's evolution on the platform, they require open answers that make it possible to know the reasons for the options selected.

4.3 CI 2022–2023 Experiments: Developing Digital Risk Competencies Among Primary and Secondary School Pupils

After the first two sessions, the advances made in the platform in terms of its programming and AI made it possible to adapt the dynamics to the educational context in which the following experiments would be conducted. Thus, the 'top-down' level was adapted so that collective intelligence could emerge more easily. Likewise, having improved the cases and questions presented to the participants, it was possible to opt for a mixed model within the questions, with both multiple-choice and open-ended questions, which would provide a better response to the bottom-up level, together with the implementation of better cases.

The experiments in collective intelligence during this period were carried out in three of the educational stages in Spain: primary education (from 10 to 12 years old), secondary education (from 12 to 16 years old), baccalaureate (from 16 to 18 years old) and vocational training (from 16 to 18 years old). On this occasion, primary school pupils would have specific cases appropriate for their age (four different ones) and unlike those that would be worked on in secondary education, baccalaureate and vocational training (eight different ones). Regardless of the educational stage, the cases were intended to work on digital skills and risks derived from social networks such as identification of fake news, sexting, cyberbullying, hate speech, social comparison, eating disorders (anorexia) or popularity on networks.

Considering the collective intelligence paradigm, two levels of participation were organised. The first corresponded to synchronous sessions in which several schools participated in the resolution of the cases depending on the educational stage on a day and at a time pre-established by the research team. The main objective of this level was to bring together as many different pupils as possible to find out how collective intelligence emerged in large heterogeneous groups made up of more than 200 participants. The second level of participation was based on a single school carrying out the different sessions with its pupils on the day and at the time that they decided. This level of participation allowed us to see how collective intelligence could appear in groups of less than 40 people.

Accordingly, 20 synchronous sessions were carried out at the first level with a total of 35 educational centres (14 primary education and 21 secondary education/baccalaureate/FP), with the participation of 2,502 pupils. At the second level of participation, 34 different sessions were carried out with 5 educational centres (1 primary education and 4 secondary education/high school/baccalaureate/FP), with a total of 1,498 pupils taking part.

Of the 54 sessions carried out during this period, 13 were analysed to delve deeper into how collective intelligence emerged within the platform and whether competence learning was taking place. First, one of the large sessions, on fake news, was analysed to check whether secondary school students had improved their ability to identify fake news. The results were positive and significant in all the multiple-choice questions, as in the 2020 experiment although they were not as good as in that experiment. After learning that, when changing the educational stage, significant improvements were still observed in the skills to be worked on during the use of the tool, a comparison was made between a large group ($n = 247$) and two small groups ($n = 58; n = 69$).

The educational stage chosen was primary education, with pupils aged between 10 and 12 years old worked with a case of social comparison in networks, a stage in which their performance on the platform had not been previously analysed. After comparing the evolution of the answers to the multiple-choice questions among the three groups, it was observed that the large group obtained significant results, while the same did not occur in the small groups, which, although they obtained good scores, remained stagnant in the phases of cooperation between participants, there being a possible ceiling effect when multiple-choice questions were used.

To find out whether this occurred in other cases, this comparison was made again, but with the secondary education stage versus a case of digital popularity, taking one large ($n = 173$) and two small groups ($n = 32; n = 24$) of second and third-year secondary school students (aged between 13 and 14 years old). The results obtained when comparing the three groups in the multiple-choice answers were the same as those obtained in the primary education stage, with significant results obtained in the large group, but not in the small group, which again showed a ceiling effect.

These results motivated analysis of the open-ended responses to the qualitative questions. The results were analysed by measuring the length of the answers given and their complexity. It was observed that, unlike the multiple-choice questions, the results were positive and significant regardless of whether the group was large or small, and improvements were found in all the groups analysed.

Thus, after carrying out the different analyses of the open and closed questions in both small and large groups, it was concluded that the multiple-choice questions could be generating a ceiling effect in pre-university stages (an effect not produced in the 2020 experiment), preventing students from going deeper into some of the issues raised while the open-ended questions allowed them to express themselves freely and make their answers more complex, giving rise to more enriching interactions and outcomes for the groups.

At this point, it was still necessary to know how the students perceived the use of this tool, as well as to know if its use was generating learning. Due to the difficulty of finding out if students learn on the platform, a brief self-report was administered so that students could give their opinion on the use of the platform, as well as to find out if we were adjusting to the 'top-down' and 'bottom-up' levels. In general, the activity was evaluated very well by the participating students, who highlighted:

- The ability to express their ideas and feelings, thanks to anonymity: to be able to give their opinion without restrictions and to find other students who agreed with their arguments within the platform. Such anonymity was valued, not to make jokes but to be on an equal footing with others. Thus, being able to express themselves without being negatively affected by their relationships was highly valued.
- To be able to know the opinions of others on issues that affected them and their immediate environment, to improve their ideas and to devise new responses that can help others. They highlighted the positive aspect of being able to compare their ideas with others to learn or modify their attitude to the case they were working on.
- Participation with other schools: because this type of activity is not usually carried out, it allowed pupils to get to know other pupils from different schools, enabling them to work together and find out what they thought.
- The closeness of the cases to their reality because the students considered that the cases on which they had been able to work on the platform were very close to their daily lives and that they and other classmates could be affected by them. That made them reflect on their attitudes and how they handle different situations.
- The general dynamics of the activity because, in general, the dynamics of the platform related to being able to copy the ideas of others or modify one's own to achieve a better response throughout their participation in real-time are valued positively.

5. Discussion and Conclusion on the Potential of Collective Intelligence

The three experiments on collective intelligence through the Collective Learning Platform were very promising. The different results obtained in each of them made it possible to generate substantial progress in how to work on each of the subsequent experiments that were conducted. Through collective intelligence, the aim was to enable the students who participated in the various sessions to acquire skills and competencies on digital risks that would help them deal with them more appropriately.

However, although the results were positive, it should be noted that in all the experiments there were certain limitations. The first of these consists in the fact that because the Collective Learning Platform must be accessed via a PC, laptop or tablet, connection failures may result in some students not completing the sessions properly, thus losing a small part of the total sample of participants. Likewise, the coordination and organisation of synchronous sessions reduces the possibility for more schools to join the experiment, thereby losing potential samples. Finally, although many experiments in collective intelligence have been carried out in which possible improvements in the skills and competencies of students have been observed, the results cannot be generalised because we have only worked with a sample from a specific region of Spain (Aragon). Likewise, at present, we cannot say for certain that learning was taking place on the platform.

New modifications are planned within the platform that will allow us to know if students are learning through its use. To this end, first, the 12 new experiments conducted with another 45 new educational centres during 2023 and 2024 only have open-ended questions so that students can express themselves freely and provide more complex answers that favour the emergence of collective intelligence. In the same way, the cases will be redesigned and adapted to the social context of the participating students. We will try to analyse the total set of outcomes from each of these new sessions, using new methods of analysis that will allow us to know how the students may be evolving during their participation, as well as to check if they are learning thanks to the appearance of collective intelligence within the platform. Being able to check learning would allow this new methodology based on the Collective Learning platform to be used in educational centres in each of the educational stages to develop specific skills and competencies, regardless of the size of the group and in short periods.

Finally, it is essential to highlight that collective learning is currently stabilised and fully functional, developing new tools that will allow us to advance and improve its use. Among the improvements under development is the temporal segmentation of users. This will enable us to know how collective intelligence is generated according to the variable we want (such as gender or age). In addition, the platform will allow the introduction of bots controlled by the administrator of the case in which students are participating so that they can enter answers within the session and find out how the students interact with them without knowing that they are generated by AI. This would allow the teacher to use the tool to propagate good answers through the network, supporting the students' creation process.

References

Aggarwal, I., Woolley, A. W., Chabris, C. F., & Malone, T. W. (2019). The impact of cognitive style diversity on implicit learning in teams. *Frontiers in Psychology, 10,* 112. https://doi.org/10.3389/fpsyg.2019.00112

Bautista Alcaine, P., Cano Escoriaza, J., Vicente Sánchez, E., Cebollero Salinas, A., & Orejudo Hernández, S. (2022). Improving adolescent moral reasoning versus cyberbullying: An online big group experiment by means of collective intelligence. *Computers & Education, 189,* 104594. https://doi.org/10.1016/j.compedu.2022.104594

Bernstein, E., Shore, J., & Lazer, D. (2018). How intermittent breaks in interaction improve collective intelligence. *Proceedings of the National Academy of Sciences of the United States, 35,* 8734–8739. https://doi.org/10.1073/pnas.1802407115

Bigham, J. P., Bernstein, M. S., & Adar, E. (2018). Human-computer interaction and collective intelligence. In T. W. Malone & M. S. Bernstein (Eds.), *Handbook of collective intelligence* (pp. 57-83). The MIT Press.

Engel, D., Woolley, A. W., Jing, L. X., Chabris, C. F., & Malone, T. W. (2014). Reading the mind in the eyes or reading between the lines? Theory of mind predicts collective intelligence equally well online and face-to-face. *PLoS One*, *9*(12), e115212. https://doi.org/10.1371/journal.pone.0115212

Hjertø, K. B., & Paulsen, J. M. (2016). Beyond collective beliefs: Predicting team academic performance from collective emotional intelligence. *Small Group Research*, *47*(5), 510–541. https://doi.org/10.1177/1046496416661236

Iyengar, R., Van den Bulte, C., & Valente, T. W. (2011). Opinion leadership and social contagion in new product diffusion. *Marketing Science*, *30*(2), 195–212. https://doi.org/10.1287/mksc.1100.0566

Kohlberg, L. (1976). Moral stages and moralization: The cognitive-development approach. In T. Lickona (Ed.), Moral development and behavior: Theory and research and social iIssues (pp. 31–53). Holt, Rienhart, and Winston.

Lorenz, J., Rauhut, H., Schweitzer, F., & Helbing, D. (2011). How social influence can undermine the wisdom of crowd effect. *Proceedings of the National Academy of Sciences*, *108*(22), 9020–9025. https://doi.org/10.1073/pnas.1008636108

Orejudo, S., Cano, J., Salinas, A. B., Bautista, P., Clemente, J., Rivero, P., Rivero, A., & Tarancón, A. (2022). Evolutionary generation of collective intelligence in very large groups of students. Pendiente de publicación. *Frontiers in Psychology*, *13*, 848048. https://doi.org/10.3389/fpsyg.2022.848048

Salganik, M. J., Dodds, P. S., & Watts, D. J. (2006). Experimental study of inequality and unpredictability in an artificial cultural market. *Science*, *311*, 854–856. https://doi.org/10.1126/science.1121066

Toyokawa, W., Whalen, A., & Laland, K. N. (2019). Social learning strategies regulate the wisdom and madness of interactive crowds. *Nature Human Behaviour*, *3*(2), 183–193. https://doi.org/10.1038/s41562-018-0518-x

Woolley, A. C., Chabris, C. F., Pentland, A., Hashmi, N., & Malone, T. W. (2010). Evidence for a collective intelligence factor in the performance of human groups. *Science*, *330*, 686–688. https://doi.org/10.1126/science.1193147

Woolley, A. W., & Aggarwal, I. (2020). *Collective intelligence and group learning*. Oxford University Press. https://doi.org/10.1093/oxfordhb/9780190263362.013.46

Chapter 2

A Better Skilled Workforce for the Digital Transformation: What Role for Platform Education?

Valentina Goglio

University of Turin, Italy

Abstract

The claim of the Fourth Industrial Revolution for a better and more skilled workforce points to an unmet demand of qualified workforce. Indeed, human capital indicators (e.g. Digital Economy and Society Index) highlight some weaknesses across EU member states with respect to digital skills and ICT-skilled workforce, which are considered key assets in the context of the digital transformation. How to tackle this issue? Educational platforms are often cited as easy, flexible and convenient resources with which to address an increasing demand for reskilled or upskilled workers. In the aftermath of the COVID-19 pandemic, these resources enjoyed even greater attention and expectations. However, research reports mixed evidence on the opportunities of access to and the benefits of online training. Free and flexible digital education could be seen as a substitute for training provided by employers, but not all individuals can fully benefit from these resources, with the risk that socio-economic gaps will widen. Moreover, relying on educational platforms for the lifelong learning of workers contributes to a shift of responsibility on workers, individualising risks and neglecting socio-economic structural barriers. By providing an overview of the use of online courses and online learning materials across the EU27 and across different social groups, this study contributes to shed light on the different arrangements that the diffusion of online lifelong learning can take in different institutional contexts, in different periods (before and during the pandemic) and whether and how educational platform may reproduce or widen inequalities.

Keywords: Lifelong learning; online learning; platform education; reskilled workforce; upskilled workforce; COVID-19 pandemic

1. Introduction

A virtually uncontested claim that accompanied the onset of the Fourth Industrial Revolution was the need for a better skilled workforce (OECD, 2019, 2023), and upgrading the qualifications of workers with both technical and adaptive skills became a key policy area (Neufeind et al., 2018; OECD, 2023)

The technological transformation led by artificial intelligence (AI) systems, particularly with the rapid spread of Generative AI and Large Language Models (LLMs), has further exacerbated concern about what skills workers will need in the near future and how they will be able to acquire them (Lassebie, 2023).

Setting aside the exact kinds of skills demanded on the labour market (Stephany, 2021), there is no doubt that the overall quality of human capital has become a crucial asset for the competitiveness of countries, particularly in terms of digital and ICT skills. Human capital indicators, indeed, have become a key component of monitoring indicators such as the Digital Economy and Society Index (DESI) and the more recent Digital Decade Policy Programme at European level (Decision (EU) 2022/2481, 2022). Such indicators highlight significant heterogeneity among EU member states with respect to digital skills and an ICT-skilled workforce, with some countries showing significant weaknesses, particularly in the field of human capital. While this can affect the macro-economic prospects at country level, at micro-level the lack of the skills necessary to keep up with the rapid evolution of productive systems can also affect workers' chances on the labour market and their careers. A low level of ICT and digital skills in a country may also suggest that there is an unmet demand for training among workers, a potential basin of reskilling and upskilling demand that can (or must, depending on the standpoint) be addressed by some form of training.

While scholarly attention has mostly focused on the consequences of the digital transformation on labour, much less attention has been paid to the needs and strategies of workers to cope with the skill demand.

In this regard, educational platforms are often cited as easy, flexible and convenient resources with which to upskill or reskill workers. In the aftermath of the COVID-19 pandemic, these resources – and especially Massive Open Online Courses (MOOCs) – enjoyed an even greater amount of attention and expectation, with the persistence of a certain faith in a 'technological fix' for social problems (Shah, 2020a). However, empirical research has shown that although on the one hand, there is some positive evidence about the flexibility and convenience of such educational platforms, at least for lifelong learning purposes, for a certain category of workers (Castaño-Muñoz & Rodrigues, 2021), on the other hand – in line with studies highlighting the strengthening of inequalities associated with the diffusion of the internet (White & Selwyn, 2012) – it has also shown that opportunities for access and returns are not equally distributed among different social groups (for a review see Goglio, 2022). Moreover, relying on educational platforms for the lifelong learning of workers contributes to a shift of responsibility to the supply side of labour, legitimising the demand of employers for job-ready workers (Brown & Souto-Otero, 2020) and ultimately increasing the individualisation of risks and responsibilities on employees (Eynon & Malmberg, 2021).

This chapter contributes to the debate by providing an overview of the spread of online lifelong learning (which includes online courses and online learning materials) across Europe. It does so by drawing on a European survey dedicated to exploring the use of the internet among households and to benchmarking ICT-driven developments at country-level. Research on online lifelong learning, in fact, is hampered by a lack of systematic data collection using large-scale surveys, by difficulties in tracking informal activities and by fragmentation among case studies or regional coverage (Eynon & Malmberg, 2021). This chapter will highlight regional differences across Europe which only partly match the findings of previous literature on the dynamics of offline adult learning and lifelong learning. It will then provide new evidence on the traditional cleavages in access to online lifelong learning, also considering the changes brought about by the COVID-19 pandemic.

2. Trends in Participation in Online Lifelong Learning

Online courses and online learning materials are part of the broader category of lifelong learning activities, which take place outside the traditional age range of schooling and separately from formal education. Following Eurostat's classification (Eurostat, 2019), the type of resources examined by this study can be considered part of informal lifelong learning: training activities which take place in informal settings. These comprise all forms of non-structured learning happening outside any institutionalised context (e.g. on the job; in the family) but which are distinguished from other cultural activities by the learner's explicit intention to acquire new knowledge. Informal learning is 'detached from any externally configured place' (Rüber & Bol, 2017, p. 765); it can occur through mentoring or be totally self-guided; and it rarely leads to recognised certification (Eurostat, 2019; Weiss, 2019).

Given the difficulty of tracking informal activities, the lack of systematic data collection by means of large scale surveys, and the lack of visible accreditation for the completion of these activities, research specifically focused on access to and the returns to online informal learning has developed only in recent years and with some methodological limitations (Eynon & Malmberg, 2021). However, an overview of the extant literature on adult education, lifelong learning and the relationship between the internet and social inequalities can provide an insightful framework for research.

The comparative study by Dammrich and colleagues (Dammrich et al., 2014) found that participation in lifelong learning activities (of all forms) was not evenly distributed across European countries. The highest rates of participation were observable in Nordic countries, moderate ones in Central European countries and much lower ones in Southern and post-socialist countries. This pattern was consistent with the different characteristics of the welfare state models adopted by these countries, which are characterised by different levels of investment, infrastructures and incentives in regard to lifelong learning. As far as individual level characteristics are concerned, regression analyses based on the Eurostat Adult Education Survey show a robust common trend across all countries whereby individuals with higher levels of education have greater chances of participating in both non-formal and formal adult education (although differences between low- and high-educated individuals are more pronounced in Southern European countries than in Nordic, Liberal and Central European ones). These results match those of previous studies showing inequalities in the distribution of lifelong learning and assuming a relative advantage of highly educated individuals in stable jobs in participating in lifelong learning activities (Biesta, 2006; Field, 2002). They therefore provide support for a 'Matthew-effect' (Merton, 1968) or a cumulative advantage mechanism (DiPrete & Eirich, 2006) as far as participation in lifelong learning is concerned.

However, online informal lifelong learning activities, like the ones which are the subject of this chapter, may differ from traditional forms of lifelong learning due to their specific mode of delivery (computer or smartphone-based). Online learning has also received a considerable boost from the COVID-19 pandemic (Cone et al., 2022; Shah, 2020b), which may have extended the audience substantially.

In this regard, it is useful to review the literature on the best-known type of online courses, i.e. MOOCs, which, despite the hyperbolic claims about their potential for democratising higher education, soon became more commonly used for lifelong learning purposes (Reich & Ruipérez-Valiente, 2019). However, research has demonstrated that the typical target audience of these courses (particularly those available on mainstream platforms such as edX, Coursera or Futurelearn) are individuals with a better socio-economic status (derived from their levels of education or occupational status), who tend to be more likely to participate but also to stay engaged and complete the courses with a certificate (Zafras et al., 2020). Already in the early days of the MOOC hype, participants tended to be white and well-educated, and living in developed, mainly English-speaking countries (Emanuel, 2013). The level of education among MOOC learners tends to be high, with an evident majority of college graduates, although the figures can vary among courses, indicating that some courses may attract a more diverse student population (van de Oudeweetering & Agirdag, 2018). Moreover, over two thirds of MOOC participants are employed: only a minority of them (from 6% to 20%, also depending on the definition of each category) are unemployed (Christensen et al., 2013; Ho et al., 2015; van de Oudeweetering & Agirdag, 2018). The prevalence of individuals with jobs in highly specialised or prestigious sectors (mostly ICT, education, business and management) indicates that the student body largely consists of individuals from privileged backgrounds who have already had access to (or are currently in) education (van de Oudeweetering & Agirdag, 2018). These individuals are likely to start with both specific and soft skills acquired during their educational pathway that make it easier for them to navigate self-directed learning as it is in the case of online courses or educational materials. As regards individual employment status, the study by Castaño-Muñoz et al. (2017) added a more nuanced perspective, highlighting that, although unemployed learners represent one third of the MOOCs student body, they tend to enrol on a higher number of MOOCs than do their employed peers. Among employed learners, workers who do not receive any support for training from their employer tend to enrol on more courses. Likewise, Goglio and Parigi (2020) found that unemployed individuals (enroled on a limited subset of MOOCs) have better chances of concluding them with a certificate. This suggests that learners in less advantaged work situations use MOOCs for their own professional development, trying to compensate for their employer's lack of support. At the same time, these studies highlight that MOOCs are better suited to an upper segment of smart and dedicated professionals, who start with a high level of specific and soft skills which enable them to devise a consistent strategy of personalised lifelong learning (Goglio, 2022).

A similar conclusion has been drawn in a recent work on online learning in the British context. The study by Eynon and Malmberg (2021) highlighted that the benefits of online learning are not equally distributed and that social structure plays a crucial role in both accessing and benefitting from online learning. Indeed, younger individuals with high educational levels and residing in advantaged areas have better chances of participating and benefiting from the online learning experience than do older and less socially advantaged individuals. This confirms a context of unequal lifelong learning policies in which 'the rich continue to get richer in relation to learning online' (Eynon & Malmberg, 2021, p. 579). A similar conclusion has been drawn by Stephany (2021), who confirmed that only high-skilled platform workers have the ability necessary to manage complex strategies of personal reskilling by combining complementary skills from different domains and fields of study, as required by the fast-moving platform economy.

2.1 Research Questions and Hypotheses

Building on this background, this study aims to provide an overview of the degree of participation in online informal lifelong learning at European level (EU27) by investigating two aspects. The first research question concerns the macro-level. The distribution of participation in online learning across countries is analysed in order to determine whether the use of online lifelong learning reveals some variations based on the institutional context, which in this case is proxied by the type of welfare regime. The second research question concerns the micro-level and entails analysis of whether the traditional social cleavages affecting participation in lifelong learning still persist and if there are differences between the use of structured (online courses) and unstructured resources (online learning materials). Finally, the analyses conclude with a comparison between the situation before the pandemic and during the pandemic (or its immediate aftermath because the latest available wave is 2021).

Consistently with the above research questions, the next, empirical, section will be guided by the following hypotheses:

H1. One observes a greater use of online lifelong learning resources in the Social-Democratic cluster compared to the others, with the Southern European and the Post-socialist countries recording the lowest percentages;

H2. One observes a greater likelihood that better-educated and employed individuals use online lifelong learning resources. Moreover, individuals employed in the ICT sector may be more familiar with online resources and may be more likely (compared to workers in other sectors) to use online courses and online learning materials;

H3. One observes some differences in the use of online courses vs online learning materials, with a greater likelihood that unemployed individuals use online courses rather than unstructured online learning materials because the former provide more specific training for the future career and may potentially receive greater recognition on the labour market.

3. Data and Method

The analysis reported in what follows relied on data taken from the survey 'Access to and use of information and communication technologies (ICT) by households and individuals' conducted by (Eurostat, 2021). Use was made of the latest available wave, 2021, which can be considered a period characterised by the persistence of measures to combat the COVID-19 pandemic in some European countries or its immediate aftermath for others (Mathieu et al., 2020). The sample consisted of working-age individuals in the 16- to 74-year-old age group, in the labour force and inactive. In some preliminary exploratory analyses, students were found to be overrepresented in the use of such resources; therefore, for the purpose of this study, students were excluded.

The two dependent variables were proxied by two dummy variables coded 1 if the interviewee replied 'yes' to the following questions 'Have you conducted either of the following learning activities over the internet for educational, professional or private purposes in the last 3 months? (a) Doing online courses; (b) Using online learning material other than a complete online course (e.g. audio-visual materials, online learning software, electronic textbooks, learning apps)'. The question was asked only if individuals declared that they had used the internet within the last 3 months. A shortcoming of the Eurostat survey is its lack of differentiation between professional and recreational purposes in the use of online courses or materials, which limited our ability to focus on truly work-related training purposes.

The independent variable at macro-level was the type of welfare state regime that characterised the country. This was proxied by a categorical variable created by grouping the EU27 countries into six clusters based on the classic welfare regime typologies developed by Esping-Andersen (1990) and Ferrera (1996) and then updated by Bohle and Greskovits (2012) for post-socialist countries.

Although not exhaustive of the complexity of a country's characteristics in terms of education and training system, as well as labour market regulation, the variable is a first informative piece of information, and it is commonly used to convey information about the institutional context. It is operationalised as a categorical variable grouping countries as follows:

- Social-democratic cluster: Denmark, Finland and Sweden.
- Liberal cluster: Ireland.[1]
- Conservative cluster: Austria, Belgium, France, Germany, the Netherlands and Luxembourg.
- Southern European cluster: Greece, Italy, Spain, Portugal, Cyprus and Malta.
- Post-socialist 'embedded' neoliberal cluster: Czech Republic, Slovak Republic, Hungary, Poland and Slovenia.
- Post-socialist neoliberal cluster: Estonia, Latvia, Lithuania, Bulgaria, Croatia and Romania.

Finally, we also included micro-level variables corresponding to the traditional cleavages affecting participation in lifelong learning such as gender, educational level and occupational status. Finally, all models also included a control for age. Table 2.1 summarises the characteristics of the sample.

Table 2.1. Sample Characteristics.

N	181,753
	%
Female	52.04
Age	
16–24	3.82
25–34	12.44
35–44	17.60
45–54	21.42
55–64	22.96
65–74	21.75
Education	
Low	22.22
Medium	47.19
High	30.59

(Continued)

---

[1]The United Kingdom is excluded from the survey.

34 Valentina Goglio

Table 2.1. *(Continued)*

N	181,753
Occupational status	
Employed	59.38
Unemployed	6.88
Inactive	33.74
Country cluster	
Social-democratic	5.33
Liberal	0.68
Conservative	26.01
Southern-EU	32.04
Eastern-EU (embedded)	13.96
Eastern-EU (neoliberal)	21.99

Source: Own elaboration on Eurostat survey 'Access to and use of information and communication technologies (ICT) by households and individuals', 2021.

4. Results

4.1 Overview of Cross-Country and Individual Level Differences

A first overview on the use of internet to do online courses or use online learning materials across years in Europe shows a rapid and recent increase corresponding to the pandemic period (2020–2021). This is particularly visible for online courses, which increased by 12.5% points (Fig. 2.1), while the use of unstructured online learning materials was already relatively more common in the pre-pandemic period and increased by about 6.5% points. During (or after) the pandemic period, therefore, the use of online courses or learning materials involved about 20% of the EU27 working age population.

To focus on the most recent wave (year 2021, Fig. 2.2), a first difference concerns the use of online unstructured learning materials and online courses: in the majority of EU27 countries, unstructured learning materials are more often mentioned than online courses, with Finland, Spain and Ireland leading in terms of the use of learning materials (about 35% of the sample). The only exceptions are the Netherlands and Slovenia (17 p.p. difference in favour of online courses) and, to a lesser extent, Belgium, Greece (about 6 p.p. in favour of online courses), Malta (+4 p.p.) and Italy (+2 p.p.), where structured online courses are more frequently mentioned. The popularity of online unstructured materials may stem from their ease of use since there are no constraints in terms of enrollments, sequenced lectures or even assignments compared to online courses.

A second divide runs across the geographical distribution of the use of such learning resources, which shows significant differences among EU27 countries

A Better Skilled Workforce for the Digital Transformation   35

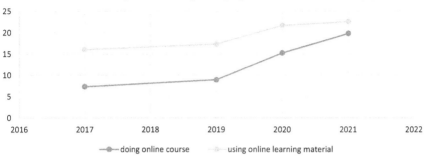

Fig. 2.1. Percentage of Use of Online Courses and Online Learning Material Over Time. *Source:* Own elaboration on Eurostat survey 'Access to and use of information and communication technologies (ICT) by households and individuals', 2017–2021. *Note:* The question is not included in the 2018 wave of the survey.

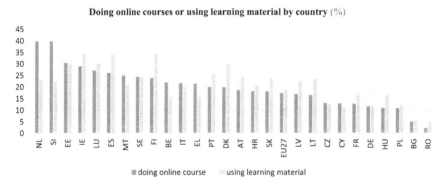

Fig. 2.2. Percentage of Use of Online Courses and Online Learning Material by Country. *Source:* Own elaboration on Eurostat survey 'Access to and use of information and communication technologies (ICT) by households and individuals', 2021.

but, at first sight, does not seem to match the typical country groupings based on welfare state or labour market regulation models (Bohle & Greskovits, 2012; Esping-Andersen, 1990; Ferrera, 1996).

Countries with the highest percentage of working age population doing an online course or using online learning materials (≥30%) belong to all the categories defined in the typologies of welfare states (e.g. Finland, Denmark and the

Netherlands for the Social-Democratic group; Eastern European countries such as Slovenia and Estonia; Ireland, belonging to the Liberal model; Spain in the Southern European cluster and Luxembourg). Other examples are Denmark and Portugal, representative of the Social-Democratic and Southern European clusters, which record similar proportions in the use of online courses (about 20%). Similarly, at the bottom of the distribution lie Eastern European countries such as Bulgaria and Romania (about 5%) but also Germany and Hungary (about 10%) in the use of online courses.

A preliminary attempt to group countries by welfare state models (Fig. 2.3) shows that the Liberal cluster (composed of Ireland alone because the United Kingdom is not covered by the Eurostat survey) leads in terms of use of both online material (35%) and online courses (30%), followed by the Social-Democratic and Southern European clusters, which do not show substantial differences, at least for the diffusion of online courses, while much lower percentages are registered in the Conservative and Post-socialist countries (respectively slightly above 15% and below 15%).

As far as micro-level variables are concerned, descriptive statistics show a substantial divide in the use of such online training resources based on the educational level and labour-market situation (Table 2.2). Indeed, more than 30% of highly educated individuals (with university-level qualifications) use these resources while the percentage decreases to 11% among individuals with medium education and then to 7% among low-educated ones. Likewise, the use of such online training resources prevails among employed individuals (about 23%), followed by unemployed individuals with about −6 p.p. differences, but it diminishes significantly to less than 10% among inactive individuals. Contrary to what was hypothesised, for employed individuals there are no differences between those employed in ICT-related professions and non-ICT professionals in the use of online courses, but the use of unstructured learning materials is slightly higher

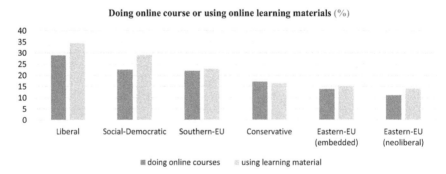

Fig. 2.3. Percentage of Use of Online Courses and Online Learning Material by Country Cluster. *Source:* Own elaboration on Eurostat survey 'Access to and use of information and communication technologies (ICT) by households and individuals', 2021.

Table 2.2. Summary of Descriptive Statistics for Individual Level Variables.

Using the Internet for …		Doing Online Courses (%)	Using Online Learning Materials (%)
Education	Low	6.31	7.57
	Medium	11.26	11.93
	High	30.85	33.34
Labour market situation	Employed	22.27	23.17
	Unemployed	16	19.51
	Inactive	5.41	7.49
Occupation	Non-ICT professional	22.27(*)	22.77
	ICT professional	21.56(*)	27.73

Source: Own elaboration on Eurostat survey 'Access to and use of information and communication technologies (ICT) by households and individuals', 2021.

Note: Percentage are computed by row per each dependent variable; differences are statistically significant at $p > 0.05$, with the only exception of (*).

for ICT professionals (+5 p.p.), arguably due to the abundance of such resources on ICT-related topics but also to the ease of access and consultation for professionals in the sector.

This preliminary overview calls for further investigation of both country-level differences and the role of individual-level factors that might be associated with the use of online structured and unstructured learning resources. The next sections explore these aspects further and discuss the results that emerged from logistic regression models run separately for the two dependent variables of interest (Table 2.3).

Table 2.3. Logistic Regression Estimates.

	2021		2019	
Using the Internet for …	Doing Online Courses	Using Online Learning Materials	Doing Online Courses	Using Online Learning Materials
Country Cluster (ref = Social-democratic)				
Liberal	0.300***	0.161**	0.00872	−0.167***
	(0.0739)	(0.0704)	(0.0539)	(0.0464)
Conservative	−0.352***	−0.807***	−0.560***	−0.602***
	(0.0300)	(0.0284)	(0.0414)	(0.0346)

(Continued)

Table 2.3. *(Continued)*

Using the Internet for ...	2021 Doing Online Courses	2021 Using Online Learning Materials	2019 Doing Online Courses	2019 Using Online Learning Materials
Southern-EU	0.176***	−0.186***	−0.226***	−0.335***
	(0.0295)	(0.0277)	(0.0405)	(0.0342)
Eastern-EU (embedded)	−0.604***	−0.861***	−0.938***	−0.947***
	(0.0339)	(0.0319)	(0.0484)	(0.0397)
Eastern-EU (neoliberal)	−0.882***	−0.971***	−1.161***	−0.600***
	(0.0325)	(0.0300)	(0.0462)	(0.0359)
Female	0.242***	0.0911***	−0.0316	−0.0627***
	(0.0147)	(0.0142)	(0.0198)	(0.0159)
Occupational Status (ref = Employed)				
Unemployed	−0.365***	−0.129***	−0.312***	−0.199***
	(0.0300)	(0.0281)	(0.0428)	(0.0335)
Inactive	−1.083***	−0.726***	−0.863***	−0.592***
	(0.0289)	(0.0261)	(0.0411)	(0.0294)
Education (ref = Low)				
Medium	0.696***	0.566***	0.626***	0.620***
	(0.0293)	(0.0273)	(0.0410)	(0.0315)
High	1.869***	1.823***	1.635***	1.699***
	(0.0289)	(0.0269)	(0.0400)	(0.0310)
Age	Y	Y	Y	Y
Constant	−1.551***	−0.979***	−2.150***	−1.372***
	(0.0480)	(0.0449)	(0.0655)	(0.0516)
Observations	153,215	153,202	143,603	143,597

Source: Own elaboration on Eurostat survey 'Access to and use of information and communication technologies (ICT) by households and individuals', 2021.
Note: Standard errors in parentheses, ***$p < 0.01$, **$p < 0.05$, *$p < 0.1$.

4.2 Institutional and Individual Dynamics: Results From Logistic Regression Models

In order to gain a clearer picture of the associations exerted by predictors, and to compare estimates for the two types of online learning identified, it is helpful to refer to the average marginal effects of the predictors of interest in order to grasp actual probabilities per each group (Leeper, 2018). The average marginal effects plotted in Fig. 2.4 indicate the difference in percentage points in the likelihoods of experiencing the outcome of interest (e.g. having used the internet to do an online course), given the fact of belonging to a certain country cluster (represented on the x-axis). Values above the line (equal to 0) indicate a higher likelihood compared to the reference category (for example, the Social-Democratic cluster), while values below the line indicate a lower likelihood. For example, the first dot in the left-hand panel of Fig. 2.4 indicates the difference (in percentage points) in the likelihood of doing an online course for individuals living in Ireland (the country representative of the Liberal cluster) vs those residing in Scandinavian countries (the reference category), given a 95% confidence interval (the vertical bar).

4.2.1 Differences Across Institutional Contexts and Individual Level Factors

The average marginal effects plotted in Fig. 2.4 (third column for the year 2021) confirm with greater clarity the distribution across country clusters that emerge from the descriptive statistics presented in the previous section. Indeed, taking the Social-Democratic cluster as the reference category, working-age individuals in Ireland (representative of the Liberal cluster) and in the Southern European countries are more likely to use the internet to do online courses, although to a limited extent (+4 and +2.5 p.p. respectively), while individuals in the Conservative (−5 p.p.) but especially the Eastern European countries are much less likely to do so (between −8 and −10 p.p.). The picture is slightly different for online learning materials (bottom panel of Fig. 2.4), which appear to be less popular in all country clusters than in Social-Democratic countries and Ireland. Therefore, Hypothesis 1 is only partially confirmed. Indeed, contrary to what was hypothesised on the basis of the trends in traditional adult and lifelong learning, the use of online courses is not most popular in the Social-Democratic cluster. Rather, it is most popular in the South-EU cluster – where participation is traditionally low – and in Ireland, which the literature locates half-way. On the other hand, the result for Post-socialist countries is in line with what was hypothesised and so too are those for countries of the Conservative cluster, which are also located mid-way after the Social-Democratic cluster. Nonetheless, when unstructured online learning is considered, Hypothesis 1 remains confirmed, with Social-Democratic countries leading, together with Ireland.

As far as individual-level factors are concerned (fourth column), the results are mostly in line with those in the literature on adult learning and training, and they support Hypothesis 2. Indeed, the use of internet to do online courses is confirmed as being far more common among individuals with higher levels of education (+22 p.p.) while unemployed (+5 p.p.) and particularly inactive individuals (−11 p.p.) are less likely to use the internet to do online courses. However, the difference between employed and unemployed individuals decreases significantly to an almost non-observable gap (−1.8 p.p.) when considering online learning materials. Moreover, introducing an interaction term between being employed and working in the ICT sector does not show any significant results. Therefore, Hypothesis 2.a is not confirmed because the analysis reveals the opposite trend: unemployed individuals

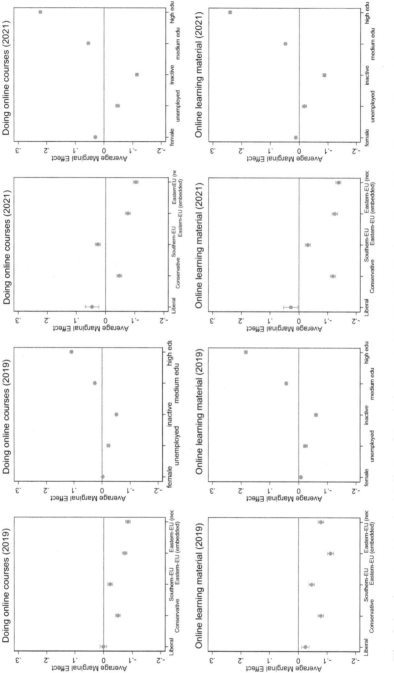

Fig. 2.4 Average Marginal Effects of Logistic Regression Models. *Source*: Own elaboration on Eurostat survey 'Access to and use of information and communication technologies (ICT) by households and individuals', year 2021.

tend to behave similarly to their employed peers as far as unstructured online learning materials are concerned while they tend to use online courses less than employed individuals. The result for gender shows a slightly higher likelihood for women (+3 p.p.) of using the internet to do online courses, but this is almost unobservable in the case of online learning materials (+1 p.p.).

4.2.2 A Comparison Between Before and During the Pandemic

In light of the strong impetus imparted by the COVID-19 pandemic to the spread of online educational activities (Cone et al., 2022), it can be appropriate a comparison between the use of such online training resources before and after the first wave of closures due to the pandemic. As seen in the descriptive statistics, the overall use of the internet for training increased significantly in the period considered (Fig. 2.1). Therefore, it can be interesting to explore whether that increase also brought changes in the distribution of online training across different groups. The particular timing of the latest available wave of the survey (2021) and the variation that occurred across countries in terms of the strictness of lockdown measures prevents a neat distinction being drawn between a pre- and a post-pandemic phase; however, it can provide some significant preliminary insights.

Comparison between the average marginal effects for the year 2019 (left-hand panels of Fig. 2.4) and 2021 (right-hand panels) shows that some small variations did indeed occur. Comparing the use of the internet for learning purposes across country clusters, it is observable that individuals in Ireland and the Southern European countries increased (compared to those in the Social-Democratic countries) their use of the internet to do online courses (and to a lesser extent online learning materials for Ireland alone) while those in the Eastern European countries instead further decreased their use. Therefore, it seems that the pandemic impacted on the traditional cleavages observed for lifelong learning trends: Hypothesis 1 receives support in the pre-pandemic period but not in the subsequent 2021 wave. The unexpected results observed in 2021 may be due to higher level of strictness of COVID-19-related lockdown measures in some countries. As reported by the COVID-19 stringency index (Mathieu et al., 2020), those measures seem to have impacted more strongly in some Mediterranean countries such as Italy but also in Ireland.[2] Alternatively, the changes observed in 2021 may in some way have been due to changes in the organisation of labour consequential on pandemic restrictions (e.g. greater use of remote working arrangements, growth of online sales and services), which may have increased the demand for skills.

On an individual level, the advantage of highly-educated individuals was further reinforced (+10 p.p. compared to 2019), accompanied by a small increase (+3 p.p.) in the use by women of online courses in the immediate aftermath of the

---

[2]For a dynamic visualisation of the COVID-19 Containment and Health Index, see the webpage https://ourworldindata.org/covid-stringency-index#containment-and-health-index.

COVID-19 pandemic period, which was not observable in the pre-pandemic period. This result can be read in light of the particular situation experienced during the pandemic by women, who were disproportionately affected by the consequences of lockdown measures (Maestripieri, 2021) and may have seen online courses as providing an opportunity to keep themselves trained in a context of uncertainty and competitiveness in the labour market. Further exploration of the model by introducing an interaction term between gender and occupational status, in fact, shows that employed women were more likely to have done an online course. It is reasonable to argue that online courses were seen by women as opportunities to keep themselves trained and updated in order to cope with greater pressure on the labour market during the pandemic period.

5. Conclusions

Online tools for informal lifelong learning have been available for more than a decade as the success of MOOCs demonstrates. But, undoubtedly, the great transformation brought about by the COVID-19 pandemic has significantly accelerated the spread of such online educational and training resources. Indeed, workers tend to be increasingly under pressure to keep themselves updated and skilled (or reskilled) in the context of a rapid technological evolution of the economy, which requires higher levels of skills for all occupations (OECD, 2023) and which ultimately increases their level of demand for learning. Such demand is often catered to by educational platforms providing various forms of online training, from MOOCs to single educational pills. This results in a progressive shift of lifelong learning activities to the online environment (Stephany, 2021), and a growing market share held by edu-tech companies (Statista Market Forecast, 2023). It fosters processes of individualisation of the responsibility for learning which tend to neglect socio-economic structural barriers (Eynon & Malmberg, 2021).

To address these challenges, this chapter has provided an overview of the use of online courses and online learning materials among the working-age European population (excluding students). It has recognised the potential of online resources but also acknowledged the persistence of the traditional socio-economic cleavages. Building on the opportunity provided by the Eurostat survey 'Access to and use of information and communication technologies (ICT) by households and individuals', which makes it possible to overcome the fragmentation of data that typically characterises the study of online courses and other online learning resources, the findings have highlighted some significant trends.

Indeed, the analysis of the use of online courses and online learning materials by the working-age population in the EU-27 (excluding students) confirmed a 'Matthew effect', which has been found by previous studies on lifelong learning, and whereby better-educated individuals are more likely to use such resources. Likewise at macro-level, the distribution of online lifelong learning across countries mirrors the traditional distribution of participation in adult and lifelong learning which has been found to be more frequent in the Social-Democratic countries, followed by countries in the Conservative cluster, and which is less frequent in the Southern European countries. However, the labour market situation of individuals does not univocally support a trend of cumulative advantage. On the one hand, it is true that employed individuals are more likely to use the internet for online courses than unemployed individuals are and even more than inactive individuals. On the other hand, the difference between employed and unemployed individuals is very small when online learning materials are considered while it remains high in comparison with inactive individuals. Unemployed individuals, therefore, seem to be more familiar with unstructured online resources than they are with online courses, a result which gainsays the hypothesis that online courses are more attractive for the unemployed in light of their potential greater visibility or recognition on the labour market.

Another interesting finding concerns the comparison between the pre-pandemic (2019) and the pandemic period (2021). Indeed, the analyses have revealed that the pandemic seems to have generated significant changes in the use of online courses and online learning materials. In the pandemic period (or the post-pandemic one for some countries), there is an evident increase in the probability of such resources being used in the Southern European cluster and in Ireland (the sole representative of the Liberal cluster because the United Kingdom was excluded from the Eurostat survey), one which is higher than for individuals living in the Social-Democratic cluster. Moreover, also women have recorded a small increase in their likelihood of using online resources in the pandemic period.

As mentioned, these dynamics may be affected by the level of strictness of COVID-19-related lockdown measures, which hit citizens of some European countries particularly hard but also generated a number of significant changes in the organisation of labour as a consequence of the shift to emergency remote work (and remote teaching). The use of online courses or online learning materials may have been a convenient, or in some cases necessary, strategy to cope with the transformations affecting work routines or growing uncertainty on the labour market. Likewise, the small increase observed among female workers may also be interpreted in light of the great pressure that they experienced during the pandemic period, which exacerbated the unequal distribution of care work and hit specific service sectors where women are overrepresented (e.g. teaching, clerical work).

Finally, this chapter is a first attempt to provide an encompassing overview of the phenomenon at European level, but it is not exempt from limitations. The first is a methodological limitation due to the data collection because the question used in the Eurostat survey does not make it possible to determine whether the use of the internet for doing online courses or using online learning materials is for work-related purposes or instead for leisure or educational ones. The next available wave (2022) should include a specific question with which to discriminate work-related training from recreational and educational purposes.

Second, the descriptive statistics have highlighted the emergence of a significant internal heterogeneity within each country cluster. Indeed, when taking the single countries into consideration, a clear pattern in the use of such online resources following the traditional clusters is no longer easily identifiable, particularly in the pandemic period. This calls for further exploration based on multilevel techniques and a modelling of the institutional context more fine-grained than the usual typology of welfare state models.

Lastly, the most recent wave available at the time of writing (2021) is very sensitive to the consequences of the rapid transition to online learning and the changes in the organisation of labour that characterised the pandemic period. This is a feature that requires further exploration in future research, possibly considering a longer period of time that makes a proper pre- and post-pandemic comparison possible.

Acknowledgements of Funding

This article has been funded by the University of Turin 'Grant for Internationalization – GFI' (2022) and by the MSCA-SE HESPRI project (GA nr. 101086224). Views and opinions expressed are however those of the author(s) only and do not necessarily reflect those of the European Union or the European Research Executive Agency. Neither the European Union nor the granting authority can be held responsible for them.

References

Biesta, G. (2006). What's the point of lifelong learning if lifelong learning has no point? On the democratic deficit of policies for lifelong learning. *European Educational Research Journal*, 5(3–4), 169–180. https://doi.org/10.2304/eerj.2006.5.3.169

Bohle, D., & Greskovits, B. (2012). *Capitalist diversity on Europe's periphery*. Cornell University Press.

Brown, P., & Souto-Otero, M. (2020). The end of the credential society? An analysis of the relationship between education and the labour market using big data. *Journal of Education Policy*, 35(1), 95–118. https://doi.org/10.1080/02680939.2018.1549752

Castaño-Muñoz, J., Kreijns, K., Kalz, M., & Punie, Y. (2017). Does digital competence and occupational setting influence MOOC participation? Evidence from a cross-course survey. *Journal of Computing in Higher Education*, 29(1), 28–46. https://doi.org/10.1007/s12528-016-9123-z

Castaño-Muñoz, J., & Rodrigues, M. (2021). Open to MOOCs? Evidence of their impact on labour market outcomes. *Computers & Education*, 173, 104289. https://doi.org/10.1016/j.compedu.2021.104289

Christensen, G., Steinmetz, A., Alcorn, B., Bennett, A., Woods, D., & Emanuel, E. (2013). The MOOC phenomenon: Who takes massive open online courses and why? (SSRN Scholarly Paper ID 2350964). *Social Science Research Network*. https://papers.ssrn.com/abstract=2350964

Cone, L., Brøgger, K., Berghmans, M., Decuypere, M., Förschler, A., Grimaldi, E., Hartong, S., Hillman, T., Ideland, M., Landri, P., van de Oudeweetering, K., Player-Koro, C., Bergviken Rensfeldt, A., Rönnberg, L., Taglietti, D., & Vanermen, L. (2022). Pandemic acceleration: Covid-19 and the emergency digitalization of European education. *European Educational Research Journal*, 21(5), 845–868. https://doi.org/10.1177/14749041211041793

Dammrich, J., Vono de Vilhena, D., & Reichart, E. (2014). Participation in adult learning in Europe: The impact of country-level and individual characteristics. In H.-P. Blossfeld, E. Kilpi-Jakonen, D. Vono de Vilhena, & S. Buchholz (Eds.), *Adult learning in modern societies. An international comparison from a life-course perspective* (pp. 29–53). Edward Elgar.
Decision (EU) 2022/2481, Pub. L. No. 2022/2481. (2022). https://eur-lex.europa.eu/eli/dec/2022/2481/oj
DiPrete, T. A., & Eirich, G. M. (2006). Cumulative advantage as a mechanism for inequality: A review of theoretical and empirical developments. *Annual Review of Sociology*, *32*(1), 271–297. https://doi.org/10.1146/annurev.soc.32.061604.123127
Emanuel, E. J. (2013). Online education: MOOCs taken by educated few. *Nature*, *503*(7476), 342. https://doi.org/10.1038/503342a
Esping-Andersen, G. (1990). *The three worlds of welfare capitalism*. Princeton University Press.
Eurostat. (2019, maggio 16). Adult education survey (AES) methodology—Statistics explained. https://ec.europa.eu/eurostat/statistics-explained/index.php/Adult_Education_Survey_(AES)_methodology#Basic_concepts
Eurostat. (2021). Access to and use of information and communication technologies (ICT) by households and individuals [Dataset].
Eynon, R., & Malmberg, L. (2021). Lifelong learning and the internet: Who benefits most from learning online? *British Journal of Educational Technology*, *52*(2), 569–583. https://doi.org/10.1111/bjet.13041
Ferrera, M. (1996). The «Southern Model» of welfare in social Europe. *Journal of European Social Policy*, *6*(1), 17–37. https://doi.org/10.1177/095892879600600102
Field, J. (2002). *Lifelong learning and the new educational order* (Reprinted). Trentham.
Goglio, V. (2022). *The diffusion and social implications of MOOCs: A comparative study of the US and Europe*. Routledge.
Goglio, V., & Parigi, P. (2020). The social dimension of participation and completion in MOOCs. *Educational Technology & Society*, *23*(4), 106–123.
Ho, A., Chuang, I., Reich, J., Coleman, C., Whitehill, J., Northcutt, C., Williams, J., Hansen, J., Lopez, G., & Petersen, R. (2015). HarvardX and MITx: Two years of open online courses Fall 2012–Summer 2014 (SSRN Scholarly Paper ID 2586847). *Social Science Research Network*. https://papers.ssrn.com/abstract=2586847
Lassebie, J. (2023). Skill needs and policies in the age of artificial intelligence. In OECD (Eds.), *OECD employment outlook 2023: Artificial intelligence and the labour market*. https://www.oecd-ilibrary.org/sites/08785bba-en/1/3/5/index.html?itemId=/content/publication/08785bba-en&_csp_=9f4368ffe3fc59de4786c462d2cdc236&itemIGO=oecd&itemContentType=book#
Leeper, T. J. (2018). Interpreting regression results using average marginal effects with R's margins. https://cran.r-project.org/web/packages/margins/vignettes/TechnicalDetails.pdf
Maestripieri, L. (2021). The Covid-19 pandemics: Why intersectionality matters. *Frontiers in Sociology*, *6*. https://www.frontiersin.org/article/10.3389/fsoc.2021.642662
Mathieu, E., Ritchie, H., Rodés-Guirao, L., Appel, C., Giattino, C., Hasell, J., Macdonald, B., Dattani, S., Beltekian, D., Ortiz-Ospina, E., & Roser, M. (2020).

Coronavirus pandemic (COVID-19). *Our World in Data.* https://ourworldindata.org/covid-stringency-index

Merton, R. K. (1968). The Matthew effect in science. *Science, 159*(3810), 56–63.

Neufeind, M., O'Reilly, J., & Ranft, F. (2018). *Work in the digital age: Challenges of the fourth industrial revolution.* Rowman & Littlefield International.

OECD. (2019). *Getting skills right: Future ready adult learning systems.* OECD Publishing. https://www.oecd-ilibrary.org/docserver/9789264311756-en.pdf?expires=1564152155&id=id&accname=ocid57004426&checksum=62A1140418C78117954C51884BB286DE

OECD. (2023). *OECD employment outlook 2023: Artificial intelligence and the labour market.* OECD. https://doi.org/10.1787/08785bba-en

Reich, J., & Ruipérez-Valiente, J. A. (2019). The MOOC pivot. *Science, 363*(6423), 130–131. https://doi.org/10.1126/science.aav7958

Rüber, I. E., & Bol, T. (2017). Informal learning and labour market returns. Evidence from German panel data. *European Sociological Review, 33*(6), 765–778. https://doi.org/10.1093/esr/jcx075

Shah, D. (2020a, maggio). MOOCWatch 23: Pandemic brings MOOCs back in the spotlight. *Class Central's MOOC Report.* https://www.classcentral.com/report/moocwatch-23-moocs-back-in-the-spotlight/

Shah, D. (2020b, dicembre 16). The second year of the MOOC. *Class Central.* https://www.classcentral.com/report/the-second-year-of-the-mooc/

Statista Market Forecast. (2023). *Online education: Market data & analysis.* https://www.statista.com/outlook/emo/online-education/worldwide

Stephany, F. (2021). One size does not fit all: Constructing complementary digital reskilling strategies using online labour market data. *Big Data & Society, 8*(1). https://doi.org/10.1177/20539517211003120

van de Oudeweetering, K., & Agirdag, O. (2018). MOOCS as accelerators of social mobility? A systematic review. *Journal of Educational Technology & Society, 21*(1), 1–11.

Weiss, F. (2019). Returns to adult education and inequality: A life course perspective. In R. Becker (Ed.), *Research handbook on the sociology of education* (pp. 408–426). Edward Elgar Publishing.

White, P., & Selwyn, N. (2012). Learning online? Educational internet use and participation in adult learning, 2002 to 2010. *Educational Review, 64*(4), 451–469. https://doi.org/10.1080/00131911.2011.626123

Zafras, I., Kostas, A., & Sofos, A. (2020). MOOCS & participation inequalities in distance education: A systematic literature review 2009-2019. *European Journal of Open Education and E-Learning Studies, 5*(1). Articolo 1. https://doi.org/10.46827/ejoe.v5i1.3260

Section 2

Discrimination

Chapter 3

The Use of Digital Devices and Digital Platforms in Social Work: Challenges and Risks

Giovanni Cellini and Carlotta Mozzone

University of Turin, Italy

Abstract

Social work developed using information and communication technologies (ICTs) within a techno-social sphere has been defined as 'e-social work'. It is a social work field that includes, among others, the use of digital devices and digital platforms in the professional relationship (with individuals, groups and communities), social service programs' monitoring and social work education. Through a literature review, the chapter will explore some parts of the international debate on e-social work. It seems to especially emphasise the positive aspects of digitisation in social work; at the same time, questions and ethical issues are proposed, especially about the social work clients' digital gaps and the need to protect vulnerable people. Digitalisation influences clients' behaviour and affects processes of social exclusion and inclusion. With reference to the elders, for example, the impact of digital divides is very significant; hence, social workers need to promote every tool at their disposal to reduce it to the bare minimum. At the same time, social workers face some risks of using digital devices and digital platforms in the professional one-to-one relationship, which especially during the Covid-19 pandemic have been increased in the welfare system.

Keywords: e-social work; innovation; digitalisation; professional practice; social work education; digital divides; discriminations; ethics

1. Introduction

Digitalisation, defined as the set of relationships, structures and elements involved in the adoption of information and communication technologies (ICTs) in any aspect of life (López Peláez & Marcuello-Servós, 2018), has a significant impact on social work and influences not only social work practices in the professional relationship with clients but also, from a broader perspective, the processes of social exclusion and inclusion. For example, in the case of elderly people, the impact of the digital divide is very significant; therefore, social work must promote tools to minimise it (De La Fuente Robles & Martín Cano, 2019). At the same time, social workers face some risks in using the digital devices and platforms in individual professional relationships; risks have increased in the welfare system since the Covid-19 pandemic. For instance, as will be better explained later, in dealing with children and families, there may be some critical aspects, such as those related to virtual home visits, which present risks in terms of privacy and security (Cook & Zschomler, 2020).

Moreover, digitalisation in social services must be contextualised within the panorama of digitalisation in the welfare services system, in which the social worker operates with specific skills, in a plurality of intervention areas. In this panorama, digitalisation represents a transformation process that directly influences policy implementation processes, organisational dynamics and culture in social welfare and health services. Although critical analyses on the matter have highlighted how the introduction and development of ICT have acted to institutionalise a highly managerialist and proceduralist culture (Parton, 2009), new technology platforms have emerged to improve the functioning of welfare and health care organisations, deliver social services and facilitate referrals to community social services organisations (Cartier et al., 2020; López Peláez & Marcuello-Servós, 2018).

The pandemic has undoubtedly accelerated the processes of digitalisation in the welfare system; and at the same time, it has led to unprecedented public investments. Regarding the European context, mention should be made of the Next Generation EU (NGEU) programme agreed upon by the European Union in response to the pandemic. This is a 750 billion euro package, about half of which consists of grants, agreed upon by the European Union in response to the pandemic crisis (European Commission, 2021). The main component of the NGEU programme is the Recovery and Resilience Facility (RRF), which has a duration of six years, from 2021 to 2026, and a total size of 672.5 billion euros (312.5 consisting of grants, the remaining 360 billion of low-interest loans). For instance, in Italy, one of the countries most affected by the pandemic, an increase in digital assistance to vulnerable population groups is expected, thanks to the RRF. Investments in the modernisation of home care and telemedicine, for example, reveal this trend and represent a challenge to increase the quantity and quality of interventions (Pesaresi, 2022). In this context, organisations and service providers are called upon to face processes of change based on field experiences and therefore on social work practice. In an innovative context, social workers are required to deal with the issues of 'usability' and 'acceptability' of digitalisation by playing a dual role that of both users and mediators. Professionals, in fact, transfer both the basic digital information and the skills necessary for correct interaction, as well as strengthening compliance, because their user experience conditions that of the user (Toccafondi & Vigoni, 2022).

The acceleration of digitalisation during the pandemic is widely recognised and is of great importance for the welfare system and social professions. The pandemic, in fact, has acted as a catalyst (Di Rosa & Pelaez, 2022) of the digitalisation in social services. This trend corresponds to an increase in studies and analyses on the use of ICT in the social work profession and mainly in two areas: the digitalisation of professional practices in welfare services and the experimentation of new tools in the training of students and in the continuous training of social workers. Regarding professional practices, a growing number of research studies address current issues, such as the opportunities and risks of using digital tools in communication with clients, or the processes of digitalisation in the organisations where social workers operate. Regarding social work education and the supervision of social workers, several studies have focused on the innovative and creative use of ICT tools.

However, we must not forget the digitalisation efforts made, and the challenges that existed, before the Covid-19 pandemic. Digitalisation in social work represented a significant transformation even before the pandemic, with a direct influence on the practices of social workers, and it was already a subject of interest in the international scientific literature.

This chapter proposes a literature review conducted with the aim of providing a summary of research carried out on digitalisation in social work, indicating the most current aspects of, and perspectives on, the state of the literature.

2. Literature Review and Research Questions

Considering that the task of a literature review is to build an argument, not a library (Rudestam & Newton, 2014), an exploratory methodological approach was chosen in order to facilitate the acquisition of knowledge on various aspects of digitalisation in the international scenario of social work and to highlight critical challenges and associated risks. Data collection was carried out through a literature review focused on the organisation and implementation of digital social work. The objective of this process was to gather detailed and updated information, establishing a solid foundation for the subsequent analysis.

Through the literature review, we aimed to answer the following questions:

- What are the definitions of digitalisation in social work?
- What are the applications of digitalisation in different contexts of professional practice and in social work education?
- What are the advantages and challenges of digitalisation in social work?
- What are the ethical implications?

We chose to focus on these research questions because studies on digitalisation in social work, particularly those with a critical approach, remain relatively unknown and underrepresented in the international scientific discourse. The systematic collection of scientific contributions is necessary to gain thorough understanding of the implications of digitalisation in social work. In order to contribute to the ongoing scientific debate, the article focuses on the opportunities and critical issues of digitalisation in social work as a crucial aspect of professional practice.

The following sources were used for the literature review: academic databases (Google Scholar, Scopus and Web of Science), scientific journals specialising in the field of social work, books and book chapters, websites of international professional organisations and conference proceedings.

The analysis has some limitations. The literature mostly focuses on Western countries, which are economically stronger and therefore more developed in digitalisation. Consequently, macro-themes concerning problematic issues arising from global inequalities in access to technology are less highlighted. It should also be considered that enriching the scientific debate on digitalisation in social work should be based primarily on empirical research rather than literature-based analyses, especially in the current historical phase characterised by increasingly rapid technological innovation in society, which has direct consequences on social work practice.

3. Results

3.1 Defining Digitalisation in Social Work

It is possible to affirm, following Campanini (2022), that the two expressions digital social work and e-social work both denote the use of digital technologies in the technical-social domain of social work. e-social (López Peláez & Marcuello-Servós, 2018) is a field of social work that encompasses the use of digital devices and platforms not only in the relationship between social worker and clients but also in the organisational and communitarian dimensions of social work. From this perspective, Goldkind et al. (2018) highlight the trifocal dimension of digital social work, which concerns the professional relationship with individuals, the involvement of social workers within welfare system organisations and community work.

Internationally, the scientific debate on the use of technology in professional practice has been ongoing for several years. In clinical social work, for example, it has focused on the therapeutic value of digitalisation in the helping relationship. Especially in North America, research shows that the use of cyber communication in clinical social work is practical, efficient and good practice (Mishna et al., 2012). Moreover, it highlights the potential to reach clients in geographically remote and underserved communities, thereby enhancing and extending the therapeutic relationship and improving treatment outcomes (Mattison, 2012). The potential of digital social work has been discussed, but also the risks (Mattison, 2012) and, as will be seen later, so too have the ethical problems and challenges (Reamer, 2013, 2015, 2024).

Digital social work is an expanding sector that utilises digital technology to enhance social work practice (Waitling & Rogers, 2012). It can include the use of online tools for assessment, intervention and communication, as well as the use of social media to connect with clients and communities. There are various definitions of digital social work, but most agree that it is an approach to social work practice that uses digital technology to improve access to services and their effectiveness and equity. In this regard, there are various possible benefits of providing social work services by electronic means: enhancing access to social work services that are unavailable in person because of geographical distance, clients' disabilities or illnesses; real-time monitoring of clients' status, when appropriate being able to respond to clients rapidly; providing more cost-effective delivery of social work services; ease of communication and reducing the frequency of clients' travel to obtain social work services. Moreover, the use of digital technologies and social media can enhance not only social work practice but also research, education and policy (NASW, 2017).

The pandemic has accelerated the debate and study of digitalisation in social work, but it would be incorrect to assert that the concept of digital social work is a new one that has developed from the Covid-19 health emergency. Even before, in fact, several scientific studies had been devoted to digital social work. In addition to Goldkin et al. (2018), one can mention Rafferty and Waldman (2006), who explored the potentialities of virtual social work practice, and Watling and Rogers (2012), who analysed the transforming social work practice in a digital society. Moreover, Rafferty and Steyaert (2009) focused on social work in the 'digital age', analysing several issues: information systems supporting practice, professional learning, the use of ICTs to provide people with resources for independent living, the relationship among ICT, social inclusion, social exclusion and the digital divide. Also to be mentioned is the research study by Di Rosa and Pelaez (2022), conducted before the outbreak of Covid-19, which addressed very relevant issues, including the presence of social work on the internet, particularly on websites and social media. Di Rosa and colleagues (2018) focused on the Italian context and, among various themes, analysed the resources derived from digital innovation, such as accessibility and greater fluidity in communication with clients and colleagues. Furthermore, they discussed various issues concerning the use of ICT, especially in professional relationships and direct interaction with individuals. They emphasised the need to strengthen social workers' skills in using digital tools. Moreover, the use of technology and its innovations in social work training was further explored.

Among the recent studies that have analysed how social work has utilised digital tools during the pandemic, the analysis by Pink et al. (2022) is particularly relevant. The authors examine in detail the practices adopted during the pandemic, the related policy responses and the implications for the profession. Furthermore, they introduce new concepts, such as 'digital materiality' and 'digital intimacy', to explain the experiences of social workers in this unprecedented context. The central thesis is that the pandemic has led to a transformation of social work, giving rise to a hybrid practice that synergistically integrates digital interventions (video calls, instant messaging and emails) and face-to-face interactions. Although the article focuses on child protection, the authors advocate a concrete and flexible hybrid digital social work practice applicable to all intervention sectors. Despite initial resistance by institutions, which tended to relegate digital practices to a marginal or last-resort role, reality demonstrates that digitalisation has become an indispensable and irreplaceable element of social work. It is essential, therefore, to rethink the profession as a hybrid practice that harmoniously integrates different modes of interaction, both digital and in person. Looking to the future, hybrid digital social work emerges as an essential reference framework in which to address the challenges and uncertainties that lie ahead. This model must be designed so that it can flexibly adapt to new needs, enhancing the improvised and adaptive approach that has always characterised the figure of the social worker.

3.2 The Applications of Digitalisation in Social Work

To provide a comprehensive interpretation of the possible use of information technologies in social work, it may be useful to mention Riquelme (2019). This author provides an overview of the various potential applications, identifying a series of digital tools in order to understand the global scenario of social work, to facilitate successful integration (individually and collectively) and to disseminate (academically and socially) intervention on the Web. A first aspect considered is that of digitalisation for knowledge and research, which are fundamental for social work as a discipline and profession. Digital scientific publications, access to statistical data, digital tools for data collection and analysis and the world of big data are essential resources for research activities aimed at understanding the needs of the population, motivating and legitimising social work action and evaluating the impact of interventions. Virtual archives of scientific studies and technological tools to use them give easy and immediate access to research on innovations, enabling the gathering of information useful not only for academic study but also for the professional practice of social workers. A second aspect considered concerns databases and the computerisation of professional activity, for example through computerised records, which allow data extraction on user characteristics, interventions and their effectiveness. Another application of digitalisation concerns social workers' actions through technology aimed at helping people in conditions or at risk of social exclusion and integrate them into society. There are also examples of applications for specific needs. Technologies, for example, can improve communication and relationships for people with visual, auditory or intellectual impairments; they can improve mobility and accessibility for elderly and disabled people; they can help women at risk of violence. Other technology applications can facilitate the matching of labor supply and demand or socio-occupational guidance for users of social services – an important tool in the field of social intervention as a support system for social integration initiatives. Finally, Riquelme analyses the area of dissemination through the Web, in which, for example, digital platforms allow for collective petitions, make problems visible, promote reform initiatives or normative changes and social policies and, more generally, use technology for policy practice interventions. It is precisely the use of platforms that has a significant place in the social service literature that refers to the 'platform society' (Van Dyck et al., 2018), a term used to describe contemporary society, which is characterised by the pervasive use of digital platforms that mediate interactions among individuals, organisations and institutions.

There are many fields of application for digital social work, and compiling a comprehensive analysis is an extremely challenging task. Therefore, for an updated overview that considers the latest developments in e-social work, we refer the reader to the handbook edited by López Peláez and Kirwan (2023), where one finds many contributions on specific areas. Among these, we cite assistive technologies, robotics and gerontological social work practice (Kaodate & Donnelly, 2023); digital technology in statutory children's services (Mackrill, 2023); digital social work and disability services (de la Fuente Robles et al., 2023); tele-social work as a complementary intervention formula that includes teleworking, remote assistance and online home visiting (Castillo de Mesa, 2023) and the use of Facebook in social work practice with families (Beddoe & Cooner, 2023).

Separate mention should be made of the application of ICT in digital social advocacy (DSA), to which we shall return later, in the section on ethical implications. Among others, the study by Bilotti (2023) highlights that DSA is a potential resource for 'engaging' hard-to-reach individuals, such as young people, among whom the use of digital tools is particularly widespread and familiar. Alternatively, it can be used to reach a larger number of people; an example of this is provided by distance childbirth preparation courses, which have allowed for the formation of groups larger than those that could be accommodated in the limited physical spaces of services and which have enabled the participation of women unable, for health reasons, to attend in person.

One of the crucial applications of digitisation concerns social work education. On this issue, it is interesting to cite Berzin et al. (2015). This paper is part of the Grand Challenges for Social Work initiative, promoted by the American Academy of Social Work and Social Welfare, which sought to support social progress through science, calling for collaborative action by educators, professionals, and national organisations to address the most urgent social challenges, particularly in the USA. The report highlights the capacity of information and communication technology to significantly improve social work practice. The integration of technology into intervention methods and practical innovation through ICTs can give rise to transformative social change. It is essential to recognise the important role that social work can play not only in adopting technologies to improve practice but also in ensuring that such technologies are developed ethically and in compliance with the principles of social work. However, it is important to note that technological innovation does not automatically guarantee progress towards social justice values. Social work has the ethical duty to ensure that technological evolution is inclusive and does not amplify existing inequalities (Goldkind & Wolf, 2015). The American document also identifies some limitations in the USA, which, however, are also apparent in Europe. These include limited education and training of social workers in effectively incorporating technology, limited exposure to innovative technology applications in social work, lack of empirical evidence on the effectiveness of technologies in social intervention and a shortage of financial resources that hinders the adoption and experimentation of technologies in the field. The invitation is therefore to reflect and act, in both basic and continuing education, to enable a more widespread and targeted use of these technologies. Moreover, the CSWE, the accrediting body for social work courses in America, has established a specific group called the Technology Advisory Group (TAG) to assist schools in developing teaching pathways that integrate technology and in using technology in social work practice.

The body of research on social work education has undoubtedly expanded since the pandemic, which triggered innovative processes, although it should be borne in mind that, even before Covid-19, research in this field was already present in the international scientific literature (Di Rosa & Pelaez, 2022; Taylor, 2017; Taylor-Beswick, 2023; Waldman & Rafferty, 2008).[1]

Among the most recent studies, that by Barberis et al. (2023), carried out in Italy, reports some interesting findings. Among them are the need to permanently establish activities and courses, in multiple disciplinary areas, that promote digital skills; the need to expand digital relational skills with in-depth exploration of how to organise online, for example, interviews and group meetings especially with individuals in particular conditions of need (for example, people with disabilities); the need for critical reflection on the use of technological tools in social work, with particular regard to the dimensions of ethics and professional ethics, the purpose being to identify risks and advantages associated with the digitalisation of work with individuals. The study highlights that the educational curriculum of a degree programme (whether undergraduate or graduate) cannot be expected to provide all the digital knowledge and skills necessary for a social worker or for those in managerial coordination roles within social services. Rather, such knowledge and these skills are enriched and consolidated through experiential learning in the field. However, the authors emphasise that in addition to learning by doing, it is essential to acquire the ability to interact with so-called 'technical' professions. Hence, the social worker is not required to master the programming and architecture of information systems but rather to critically reflect on the limitations and opportunities of the tools and – depending on the position held – share them with colleagues, managers and political-administrative decision-makers to identify procedures functional to their work. One can find similar results in the study carried out by Hooker Jones et al. (2022) on preparing students for remote social work practice (RSWP) in the USA and in the study by Lischer et al. (2021) on the changes that took place in distance education during the pandemic in Switzerland.

3.3 Critical Aspects of Digitalisation in Social Work

While the pandemic has highlighted the positive aspects of digitalisation in social work, there is a growing need to critically examine the social consequences of ICT

---

[1] Although this study was published in 2023, it was concluded in mid-2019, i.e. before the pandemic.

and digital platforms in this field. Inequalities in technology use and client exclusion are only some of the challenges the profession must face.

The transformations resulting from digitalisation concern social work at both micro- and macro-levels. Digitalisation processes have transformed interactions with clients, their demands and needs, and the organisations where social workers carry out their professional activities. At the same time, the creation of a digital environment has redefined exclusion processes (Watling & Rogers, 2012), giving rise to new forms of inequality and discrimination, such as towards the elderly and young people. Mathiyazhagan (2021) points out how structural disparities, historical injustices, prejudice, exclusion, authority and advantage represent key human rights concerns that social workers confront in their daily work. These issues have not only persisted in traditional offline communities; they have recently become manifest in online settings as well. The digital gap and online divisions perpetuate power imbalances and privileges both within and beyond the realm of social work. Social work methodologies are evolving to encompass emerging technologies across education, research, and practice. Drawing on a decade of international social work experience and fieldwork supervision, Mathiyazhagan highlights the growing necessity to integrate technology into social work practices across various domains. He examines the obstacles against and advantages of employing technology in social work, and he proposes a potential model for tech-driven social work practice aimed at fostering safe and inclusive communities, both online and offline, to advance human rights. Among the critical researchers that have examined how remote delivery and technology affect relationship-based practice, Pascoe (2022) underscored their negative effects on relationship building and the self-care of social workers. Moreover, there are concerns that efficiency may be prioritised over future face-to-face interactions with service users. During the pandemic, the adoption of alternative communication methods via technology disrupted and challenged the fundamental principles of relationship-based practice (Mishna et al., 2021).

There follows a review of several studies that have highlighted some critical aspects of digitisation in social work with reference to specific population groups.

De La Fuente Robles and Martín Cano (2019) focused on the elderly in Spain and noted that this group of the population may feel outdated, lack knowledge or find it difficult to use technology because of its complexity and high cost. Social work is called upon to facilitate an intimate and accessible pedagogical approach to enable the elderly to become active agents in the field of technology. Considering the socio-demographic and technological landscape, new challenges need to be addressed. Specifically focussing on the elderly, e-social work underscores the potential for developing new skills and capabilities through ICTs, which are seen as powerful tools with which to ensure equal access to an enhanced quality of life. Despite progress in narrowing the digital divide, its impact on individuals aged 75 and over remains notable, emphasising the importance of utilising all available means to minimise it. Social work contributes to empowering the elderly population through the technological adaptation of interfaces for easier interaction while also promoting the use of alternative technologies in online interventions. Technology has fundamentally transformed society, prompting a new perspective on ageing, vulnerability and chronic conditions. ICTs in social intervention should serve as genuine opportunities to promote social cohesion.

Focusing on social work with young people, it is apparent that social inclusion is closely linked to digital inclusion. Policy design in social welfare must ensure the digital well-being of children and adolescents, safeguarding their increasingly assertive rights in the digital sphere (Picornell-Lucas & López-Peláez, 2022). As institutions and services become digitised, both social workers and children need to acquire the digital skills necessary to 'navigate' these systems. Moreover, due to the pandemic, social workers have had to devise ways to conduct interviews, home visits, diagnoses and interventions based on the internet and technology, and particularly for children in vulnerable situations. Virtual home visits present some advantages but also risks in terms of privacy and security, especially in cases of domestic violence. According to Cook and Zschomler (2020), transitioning to virtual home visits amid the pandemic enabled social workers to be more agile in their support for children and their families. Previously, social workers had typically travelled to conduct home visits. However, with the shift to online practice, they found themselves responding swiftly to parents' text messages by initiating brief video calls. This adaptation to a 'little and often' approach brought unexpected advantages. Many social workers reported gaining deeper insights into families' daily lives despite the physical distance. Before lockdown measures, considerable time was spent on commuting to home visits. Eliminating the need for travel made some social workers feel more invigorated and focused during their interactions with families, enabling them to be available to a larger number of families throughout the workday. Social work with children and families inherently involves mobility and physical presence. Consequently, as expressed by one social worker, there was a risk of personal and professional stagnation when operating virtually. However, virtual home visits also entailed risks regarding confidentiality and safety. In cases of domestic violence, for example, social workers were uncertain whether calls were being monitored, potentially placing callers at further risk. Moreover, social workers acknowledged that certain topics were unsuitable for discussion online.

3.4 Ethical Implications

Digital social work represents a significant change in the profession. It offers new opportunities but also raises ethical challenges, which have been subject to attention in the literature. With reference to clinical social work, Reamer (2013) highlighted that the most prominent ethical challenges concern six core, traditional social work ethical concepts that pertain to the delivery of clinical services using digital technology: informed consent; privacy and confidentiality; boundaries, dual relationships and conflicts of interest; records and documentation; and collegial relationships.

In a broader view, beyond the clinical approach, Banks et al. (2024) analyse the ethical challenges during the pandemic and the rethinking of ethics in social work practice in relation to digital working. According to these authors, consideration needs to be given to improving social workers' digital competence and widening citizens' access to virtual platforms in order to avoid creating a digital divide or increasing social inequalities. Moreover, even if social work can be developed as a hybrid system of communication with users (in-person and digital), its core values of promoting social justice and inclusion should guide these developments.

In this regard, to be stressed is the importance of the DSA approach, according to which platforms and social media can be useful in reaching certain target populations of service users more easily by facilitating access to the welfare system (Hill & Ferguson, 2014). DSA campaigns can be useful in engaging more people, especially hard-to-reach individuals, and families in a situation of social vulnerability if not social exclusion. Particularly, it is effective in engaging young people, who make increasing use of digital platforms. Furthermore, DSA emerges as a crucial resource to overcome existing digital divides. Specifically, it can be used as a tool to bridge disparities involving the elderly and other population segments that may have limited access to broadband or digital technologies (Sanders & Scanlon, 2021). This form of advocacy not only makes it possible to reach these groups, but it also contributes to facilitating digital inclusion, promoting access to and participation in services and opportunities that might otherwise be difficult to access. The need to promote DSA requires that especial attention be paid to social work education, specifically teaching in the digital age (Sanfelici & Bilotti, 2022).

Finally, considering the international perspective of e-professionalism and the ethical use of technology in social work (McAuliffe & Nipperess, 2017), it seems essential for the scientific debate to reflect on the global social work statement of ethical principles which declares that

> ... social workers must recognize that the use of digital technology and social media may pose threats to the practice of many ethical standards including but not limited to privacy and confidentiality, conflicts of interest, competence, and documentation and must obtain the necessary knowledge and skills to guard against unethical practice when using technology. (IFSW, 2018)

4. Discussion and Conclusion

Digital social work offers a range of potential benefits that can revolutionise social workers' professional practice. Among these advantages, improved access to services stands out because it enables people living in rural or remote areas, or with difficulties in accessing traditional offices, to receive support and assistance. Moreover, e-social work offers the opportunity to enhance the effectiveness of social work by enabling professionals to automate some tasks and use collected data to make more informed decisions. This technology can also contribute to improving equity in access to services, offering equal opportunities to all, regardless of their background or geographical location.

The practical applications of digitalisation in social work are varied and evolving. They include the use of digital technology for client assessment, data collection and the development of personalised intervention plans. Furthermore, digital social work can be employed to provide online therapy, virtual support groups and other types of psychosocial intervention. Communication with clients, their families and healthcare providers can be facilitated by using digital technology. Finally, digitalisation can also be useful for social work education by enabling professionals in the field to acquire the digital skills necessary to fully exploit the potential of technology in their work.

However, along with these benefits, digital social work also raises a range of practical and ethical challenges that must be addressed with caution. One of the main challenges is the digital divide because not everyone has access to digital technology or the skills necessary to use it. In addition, it is critical to address one of the most important ethical issues for social work, which is ensuring the privacy and security of client data when using digital technology. Moreover, social work professionals must commit to developing the digital skills necessary to use technology effectively and responsibly in accordance with the ethical principles of the profession.

Critical reflection, therefore, is crucial for expanding knowledge and skills in the field of digitalisation. Both in the everyday practices of social work and in academic studies on social work, there are positive assessments of the potential of digitalisation but, at the same time, attention to the risks that must necessarily be addressed. This concerns various issues highlighted by Casalini (2022): the risk of losing the emotional and bodily dimension of the helping relationship; the widening of the digital divide; increased discrimination against vulnerable individuals who do not receive necessary in-person interventions and the risk of neglecting the importance of ensuring an adequate number of social workers in the field, in direct contact with the community, within the welfare system. It is at the same time necessary to reflect on issues of a strictly political nature, and particularly on the possible inclusion of so-called 'tele-assistance' within neoliberal policies, whose main objective is not the use of digitalisation for collective well-being but rather the reduction of social spending.

We believe it is crucial to continue a constant and constructive debate on digitalisation in social services and in the social work profession. This debate could draw benefits from the contributions of both professionals and scholars, with a focus on the international dimension of the phenomenon. It could be a debate that increasingly adopts a post-pandemic perspective, recognising the 'legacy' of the pandemic and focusing primarily on innovations that can promote improved quality of professional action. In this regard, training in digitalisation becomes highly important, not only for students (university education) and social workers (continuing education, supervision) but also for trainers. The acquisition and enhancement of digital skills, in fact, are essential even in university teaching and for those who are called upon to carry out continuing education activities aimed at the acquisition of professional skills.

The role of the digital social worker requires specific skills to utilise digital technologies effectively and safely. Training in digital social work should encompass various crucial areas to ensure adequate professional practice. First, ethics in digital social work is of fundamental importance. Digital social workers must be able to navigate the complex ethical issues arising in the digital environment. They must understand, and apply, ethical principles to ensure the protection and respect of users' rights. Cybersecurity is another key area of training. Digital social workers need to be aware of cybersecurity risks and of techniques for protecting users' sensitive data. This includes knowledge of cybersecurity threats and phishing techniques, as well as the adoption of appropriate measures to safeguard themselves and users against potential security breaches. Moreover, it is essential for digital social workers to develop strong digital skills so that they can effectively utilise digital technologies in social work. This includes the ability to use digital tools for online assessment and intervention, as well as the promotion of digital literacy and inclusion among users. Dual relationships, where the digital social worker assumes two or more roles with the same user, can be particularly complex in the realm of digital social work. It is crucial for professionals to be transparent with users regarding such dual relationships, manage such relationships professionally and responsibly and avoid conflicts of interest. Moreover, digital social workers must be aware of digital disparities that may limit access to digital social work for some users. Therefore, it is necessary to develop digital social work by promoting digital education and inclusion, also working with communities, in order to overcome the digital disparities. Furthermore, new challenges are now arising regarding the conscious use of artificial intelligence (Ibrahim et al., 2023) in social work, and they require the further development of skills and experimentation in the field.

References

Banks, S., Bertotti, T., Cairns, L., Shears, J., Shum, M., Sobočan, A. M., Strom, K., & Úriz, M. J. (2024). Social work beyond the pandemic: Exploring social work values for a new eco-social world. *International Social Work, 1*(15). https://doi.org/10.1177/00208728241227062

Barberis, E., Cabiati, E., & Cacopardo, B. (2023). Digitalizzazione e Social work education: Una panoramica italiana. *Politiche Sociali, 2*, 227–244. https://doi.org/10.7389/108022

Beddoe, L. & Cooner, T. S. (2023). The use of Facebook in social work practice with families: Safeguarding or surveillance? In López Peláez, A. & Kirwan, G. (Eds.), *The Routledge handbook of digital social work* (pp. 230–239). Routledge.

Berzin, S. C., Singer, J., & Chan, C. (2015). Practice innovation through technology in the digital age: A grand challenge for social work. *American Academy of Social Work & Social Welfare, 12*, 3–21.

Bilotti, A. (2023). Quale spazio per la digital social advocacy nel servizio sociale? Risultati da una ricerca esplorativa su una pratica anti-oppressiva. *La Rivista di servizio sociale, 1*, 71–82.

Campanini, A. (2022). L'utilizzo delle tecnologie informatiche nel servizio sociale. *Prospettive Sociali e Sanitarie, 3*, 38–40.

Cartier, Y., Fichtenberg, C., & Gottlieb, L. M. (2020). Implementing Community Resource Referral Technology: Facilitators And Barriers Described By Early Adopters: A review of new technology platforms to facilitate referrals from health care organizations to social service organizations. *Health Affairs, 39*(4), 662–669. https://doi.org/10.1377/hlthaff.2019.01588

Casalini, B. (2022, July 15). Servizio sociale, tecnologie digitali assistive e innovazione sociale. *welforum.it*. https://www.welforum.it/il-punto/welfare-digitale-servizio-sociale-e-gap-formativo/servizio-sociale-tecnologie-digitali-assistive-e-innovazione-sociale-uno-sguardo-critico/

Castillo de Mesa, J. (2023). The acceleration of the implementation of tele-social work as a complementary intervention formula: Teleworking, remote assistance and online home visiting. In A. López Peláez & G. Kirwan (Eds.), *The Routledge handbook of digital social work* (pp. 276–284). Routledge.

Cook, L. L., & Zschomler, D. (2020). Virtual home visits during the COVID-19 pandemic: Social workers' perspectives. *Practice, 32*(5), 401–408. https://doi.org/10.1080/09503153.2020.1836142

De La Fuente Robles, Y. M., & Martín Cano, M. D. C. (2019). E-social work and at-risk populations: Technology and robotics in social intervention with elders. The case of Spain. *European Journal of Social Work, 22*(4), 623–633. https://doi.org/10.1080/13691457.2018.1423550

De La Fuente Robles, Y. M., Martín Cano, M. D. C., & García Cortés, E. (2023). Digital social work and disability services. In A. López Peláez & G. Kirwan (Eds.), *The Routledge handbook of digital social work* (pp. 219–229). Routledge.

Di Rosa, R. T., Musso, G., Dellavalle, M., & Gucciardo, G. (2018). Social work online: A recognition of experiences and practices in Italy. *European Journal of Social Work, 21*(6), 889–901. https://doi.org/10.1080/13691457.2018.1469473

Di Rosa, R. T., & Pelaez, A. L. (2022). I servizi socio-educativi nell'era del digitale. Sfide e opportunità. *Media Education, 13*(2), 3–7.

European Commission. (2021). Next generation EU. https://commission.europa.eu/strategy-and-policy/eu-budget/eu-borrower-investor-relations/nextgenerationeu_en

Goldkind, L., & Wolf, L. (2015). A digital environment approach: Four technologies that will disrupt social work practice. *Social Work, 60*(1), 85–87.

Goldkind, L., Wolf, L., & Freddolino, P. P. (Eds.). (2018). *Digital social work: Tools for practice with individuals, organizations, and communities*. Oxford University Press.

Hill, K., & Ferguson, S. M. (2014). Web 2.0 in social work macro practice: Ethical considerations and questions. *Journal of Social Work Values and Ethics, 11*(1), 2.

Hooker Jones, A. N., Carter, K., & Goshorn, S. (2022). MSW curriculum analysis: Preparing MSW foundation level students for remote practice. *Advances in Social Work, 22*(2), 251–269. https://doi.org/10.18060/24994

Ibrahim, A. T. H., Saleh, E. F., Al Mamari, W. S., Elsherbiny, M. M. K., & Mustafa, M. M. (2023). Understanding the role of ChatGPT in social work: What we know and what we still need to discover. *Social Issues, 1*(1), 5–13.

International Federation of Social Workers (IFSW). (2018). Global social work statement of ethical principles. *International Federation of Social Workers*. https://www.ifsw.org/global-social-work-statement-of-ethical-principles/

Kaodate, N., & Donnelly, S. (2023). Assistive technologies, robotics and gerontological social work practice. In A. López Peláez & G. Kirwan (Eds.), *The Routledge handbook of digital social work* (pp. 183–195). Routledge.

Lischer, S., Caviezel Schmitz, S., Krüger, P., Safi, N., & Dickson, C. (2021). Distance education in social work during the COVID-19 pandemic: Changes and challenges. *Frontiers in Education, 6*. https://doi.org/10.3389/feduc.2021.720565

López Peláez, A., & Kirwan, G. (Eds.). (2023). *The Routledge handbook of digital social work*. Routledge.
López Peláez, A., & Marcuello-Servós, C. (2018). e-Social work and digital society: Re-conceptualizing approaches, practices and technologies. *European Journal of Social Work*, *21*(6), 801–803. https://doi.org/10.1080/13691457.2018.1520475
Mackrill, T. (2023). Digital technology in statutory children's services. In A. López Peláez & G. Kirwan (Eds.), *The Routledge handbook of digital social work* (pp. 196–205). Routledge.
Mathiyazhagan, S. (2021). Field practice, emerging technologies, and human rights: The emergence of tech social workers. *Journal of Human Rights and Social Work*, *7*(4), 441–448. https://doi.org/10.1007/s41134-021-00190-0
Mattison, M. (2012). Social work practice in the digital age: Therapeutic E-mail as a direct practice methodology. *Social Work*, *57*(3), 249–258. https://doi.org/10.1093/sw/sws021
McAuliffe, D., & Nipperess, S. (2017). e-Professionalism and the ethical use of technology in social work. *Australian Social Work*, *70*(2), 131–134.
Mishna, F., Bogo, M., Root, J., Sawyer, J.-L., & Khoury-Kassabri, M. (2012). "It just crept in": The digital age and implications for social work practice. *Clinical Social Work Journal*, *40*, 277–286.
Mishna, F., Milne, E., Bogo, M., & Pereira, L. F. (2021). Responding to COVID-19: New trends in social workers' use of information and communication technology. *Clinical Social Work Journal*, *49*(4), 484–494. https://doi.org/10.1007/s10615-020-00780-x
National Association of Social Workers (NASW). (2017). NASW, ASWB, CSWE, & CSWA stantards for technology IBN social work practice. https://www.socialworkers.org/LinkClick.aspx?fileticket=bq9JrB-oVm4%3d&portalid=0
Parton, N. (2009). Challenges to practice and knowledge in child welfare social work: From the 'social' to the 'informational'. *Children and Youth Services Review*, *31*(7), 715–721. https://doi.org/10.1016/j.childyouth.2009.01.008
Pascoe, K. M. (2022). Remote service delivery during the COVID-19 pandemic: Questioning the impact of technology on relationship-based social work practice. *The British Journal of Social Work*, *52*(6), 3268–3287. https://doi.org/10.1093/bjsw/bcab242
Pesaresi, F. (2022). Le cure domiciliari e la telemedicina nel PNRR. *Prospettive Sociali e Sanitarie*, *2*, 5–9.
Picornell-Lucas, A., & López-Peláez, A. (2022). The digital citizenship of children and adolescents: Challenges for social work education. *Research in Education and Learning Innovation Archives (REALIA)*, *28*, 32–37.
Pink, S., Ferguson, H., & Kelly, L. (2022). Digital social work: Conceptualising a hybrid anticipatory practice. *Qualitative Social Work*, *21*(2), 413–430. https://doi.org/10.1177/14733250211003647
Rafferty, J., & Steyaert, J. (2009). Social work in the digital age. *British Journal of Social Work*, *39*(4), 589–598.
Rafferty, J., & Waldman, J. (2006). Fit for virtual social work practice? *Journal of Technology in Human Services*, *24*(2–3), 1–22. https://doi.org/10.1300/J017v24n02_01
Reamer, F. G. (2013). Social work in a digital age: Ethical and risk management challenges. *Social Work*, *58*(2), 163–172. https://doi.org/10.1093/sw/swt003

Reamer, F. G. (2015). Clinical social work in a digital environment: Ethical and risk-management challenges. *Clinical Social Work Journal*, *43*(2), 120–132. https://doi.org/10.1007/s10615-014-0495-0

Reamer, F. (2024). Social work boundary issues in the digital age: Reflections of an ethics expert. *Advances in Social Work*, *23*(2), 375–391. https://doi.org/10.18060/26358

Riquelme, S. F. (2019). Conocer, integrar y divulgar. Las Tecnologías digitales para la investigación y la intervención en Trabajo social [Learn, Integrate and Divulge Digital Technologies for Investigation and Intervention in Social Work]. *Trabajo Social Hoy*, *88*(3), 43–68. https://doi.org/10.12960/TSH.2019.0015

Rudestam, K. E., & Newton, R. R. (2014). *Surviving your dissertation: A comprehensive guide to content and process*. Sage Publications.

Sanders, C. K., & Scanlon, E. (2021). The digital divide is a human rights issue: Advancing social inclusion through social work advocacy. *Journal of Human Rights and Social Work*, *6*(2), 130–143. https://doi.org/10.1007/s41134-020-00147-9

Sanfelici, M., & Bilotti, A. (2022). Teaching social advocacy in the digital era: An experimental project. *Italian Journal of Sociology of Education*, *14*(1), 227–245. https://doi.org/10.14658/pupj-ijse-2022-1-13

Taylor, A. (2017). Social work and digitalisation: Bridging the knowledge gaps. *Social Work Education*, *36*(8), 869–879. https://doi.org/10.1080/02615479.2017.1361924

Taylor-Beswick, A. M. L. (2023). Digitalizing social work education: Preparing students to engage with twenty-first century practice need. *Social Work Education*, *42*(1), 44–64. https://doi.org/10.1080/02615479.2022.2049225

Toccafondi, L., Vigoni, G. (2022). Innovazione tecnologica e servizi sociosanitari e assistenziali, *Prospettive Sociali e Sanitarie*, *2*, 15–18.

Van Dijck, J., Poell, T., & de Waal, M. (2018). *The platform society*. Oxford University Press. https://doi.org/10.1093/oso/9780190889760.001.0001

Waldman, J., & Rafferty, J. (2008). Technology-supported learning and teaching in social work in the UK—A critical overview of the past, present and possible futures. *Social Work Education*, *27*(6), 581–591. https://doi.org/10.1080/02615470802201531

Watling, S., & Rogers, J. (2012). *Social work in a digital society*. SAGE Learning Matters.

Chapter 4

'Made in Italy': Online Hate Speech Targeting Gender-Normative Defiance at the Sanremo Music Festival

Camilla Borgna and Antonio Martella

University of Turin, Italy

Abstract

This study examines online hate speech targeting gender-normative defiance during the 2023 Sanremo Music Festival in Italy, focusing on the performance of the rapper Rosa Chemical, who faced backlash after kissing a male singer on stage. Using machine learning analysis techniques, we compare user comments across three social media platforms: Facebook, Instagram and TikTok. Results reveal significant differences in the prevalence and nature of hate speech across these platforms, with Facebook exhibiting the highest levels of hate speech (35.9%), predominantly driven by anger and disgust, while TikTok had the lowest (1.9%). Hate speech was strongly correlated with negative emotions like anger and disgust, particularly on Facebook. Moreover, while on Facebook comments characterised by negative emotions produced more reactions, on TikTok comment negativity was not correlated with the number of responses. These findings are consistent with the interpretation that older audiences on platforms like Facebook feel more threatened by gender-normative challenges and resort to online hate speech as a form of cultural backlash. Moreover, platform-specific moderation policies, content distribution mechanisms and social norms about the perceived appropriateness of negative content may influence the amount of hate speech and the degree to which users decide to engage with it. This research study contributes to the understanding of the 'supply side' of online hate speech by highlighting how platform architecture and user demographics influence the production and reaction to hate speech.

Keywords: Hate speech; gender norms; cultural backlash; Facebook; TikTok; Instagram

---

Mapping the Evolution of Platform Society, 65–86
Copyright © 2025 Camilla Borgna and Antonio Martella
Published under exclusive licence by Emerald Publishing Limited
doi:10.1108/978-1-83608-028-220251005

1. Introduction

Over the past decade, internet exposure in developed countries has grown tremendously: while in 2002 only about half of the population reported using the internet, at least occasionally, 10 years later virtually all adults had become internet users (PEW Research Center, 2022). In particular, social media have widespread not only among young people but also among older individuals. In Italy, which is the empirical context of the analyses presented in this chapter, more than half of the population aged 50 or over report using social media in their daily lives (PEW Research Center, 2022). While social media have many obvious benefits in terms of social connectivity and information sharing, they have also created more opportunities for aggressive discourse to circulate (Blazak, 2009; Hawdon et al., 2017).

Online hate speech – i.e. the expression of offensive, harassing or threatening attitudes based on some social identity factor – negatively affects its victims (Wachs et al., 2022), its bystanders (Reichelmann et al., 2021) and society at large (Bilewicz & Soral, 2020). While previous studies have prevalently focused on online hate speech detection (Fortuna & Nunes, 2018), research on the processes whereby this discourse (its 'supply side') is produced is less common. Within this emerging field, two methodological approaches prevail. The first strategy relies on self-reported behaviour measured by means of targeted surveys (e.g. Inguanzo et al., 2021): this approach makes it possible to collect rich background information on potential perpetrators, but it is prone to obvious social desirability biases. The second strategy uses social media data and applies automated content analysis techniques to identify hateful discourse. In order to circumvent the lack of background information on potential perpetrators, the extant research has compared hate speech incidence across regional contexts (e.g. Vargo & Hopp, 2017).

In this chapter, we contribute to the emerging literature on the supply side of hate speech by adopting another analytical strategy, i.e. by comparing online behaviour across social media platforms. Although this strategy has been seldom applied in the literature, partly due to methodological constraints (Schemer & Reiners, 2023; Siegel, 2020), it is promising because platforms differ in terms of at least three factors that may affect the amount of online hate speech, as well as counter-reactions to it: (1) their typical content and usage; (2) users' demographics and (3) moderation and censorship policies.

In this regard, we conduct a case study on an event where a public figure challenged traditional gender norms during a mainstream televised event in Italy and thus became the target of violent attacks, both online and offline. We analysed online reactions to the event across the three social media platforms where the victim was active.

The chapter is organised as follows. Section 2 provides the background for the case study and discusses recent research on online hate speech production, while Section 3 presents our research questions and contribution to the literature. In Section 4, we describe the case that we analysed. Section 5 details our empirical strategy, and Section 6 presents and discusses the results. Section 7 concludes and suggests avenues for further research.

2. Background and Previous Studies

Online hate speech can be defined as a form of communication (including text, videos and photos) that expresses hatred or degrading attitudes towards individuals or groups of people because of their gender identity, sexual orientation, body shape, race, ethnicity, religion, national origin or some other social identity factor (Blazak, 2009; Hawdon et al., 2017). Clearly, violent and discriminatory discourse also exists and has always existed in the offline world. Yet, the online context facilitates its expression and spread by making it easier to maintain anonymity and to access broader audiences. This is particularly the case of social media platforms, where individuals can connect with each other while avoiding face-to-face interactions. However, it is important to note that the same characteristics also create opportunities for resisting and countering hate speech (Barlińska et al., 2018; Eschmann, 2021; Inara Rodis Paulina, 2021).

Most previous research on this topic has focused on artificial intelligence tools with which to detect and thus censor hate speech (for recent reviews, see European Union Agency for Fundamental Rights, 2023; Fortuna & Nunes, 2018; Gandhi et al., 2024; Schmidt & Wiegand, 2017; Siegel, 2020), as well as on identifying the individual- and contextual-level predictors of this discourse, in order to design effective prevention and intervention measures (Álvarez-Benjumea & Winter, 2018; Hangartner et al., 2021; Munger, 2021; Stahel & Weingartner, 2024).

Less investigated are the processes whereby online hate speech is produced. Content analyses of hateful discourse reveal that typical targets are individuals who challenge the status quo by not conforming to the traditional norms associated with their group, such as minority women who work in male-dominated domains or are active in the public sphere (Martella & Pavan, 2023; Sobieraj, 2020). In fact, online hate speech can be an expression of cultural backlash against ongoing social change (Inguanzo et al., 2021). As societies become more inclusive and diverse, some individuals who feel threatened by these changes may react by attacking those that they perceive as challengers to the status quo power structure, in order to reassert their perceived superiority or dominance. Hence, online hate speech can take the form of racism, sexism, homophobia, transphobia or xenophobia, among others, and often overlaps with radically conservative views (Council of Europe, 2022).

The extant research furnishes some insights into the 'supply side' of online hate speech (Hawdon et al., 2019), i.e., the characteristics of its perpetrators and the contexts that facilitate its production. By analysing data from a United States (US) online survey and by focusing on young people (aged 15–36), Costello and Hawdon (2018) found that men are more likely than women to have produced, at some point in their life, online material that other people would likely interpret as hateful or degrading. The authors did not detect any significant differences in hate speech production by age, race, educational attainment, religion, political ideology or employment status although it is important to note that their sample was not representative of the US population. Interestingly, while the amount of time spent online is not a direct predictor of hate speech production, the use of specific social media platforms, such as Reddit, is. Inguanzo et al. (2021) adopted a similar research strategy to study the characteristics of hate speech perpetrators, i.e., they designed and implemented a survey where respondents were asked to report on their online behaviour and attitudes. However, differently from Costello and Hawdon (2018), Inguanzo and colleagues did not restrict themselves to one country but collected data on the US, Spain, Germany and the United Kingdom (UK) and employed sampling procedures that ensured statistical representativeness. Their results indicated that individuals holding hostile sexist views are more likely to generate political content online. As a consequence, although some form of political polarisation of online discourse is in place, sexist discourse prevails over countering (feminist) discourse. In the same vein are the results of similar survey-based studies, such as Kaakinen et al. (2018), Frischlich et al. (2021) and Bernatzky et al. (2022), which indicate that gender, socio-economic position and political orientation are important predictors of online hate speech production at the individual level.

Despite the informative character of these studies, self-reported measures of aggressive online behaviour are likely affected by social desirability biases, with a consequent underestimation of hate speech. In contrast, research based on social media data uses automated content analysis techniques to identify online hate speech directly. The main advantages of this strategy – i.e. the direct observation of users' online behaviour in a natural setting and the large sample sizes that can be obtained – come at the cost of very limited information about users' background characteristics. At the individual level, perpetrators of online hate speech have been found to have more short-lived profiles with fewer followers because the type of content they produce often leads to banning (ElSherief et al., 2018; Ribeiro et al., 2018). However, they tend to be very active and embedded in highly dense networks, factors that enhance their visibility (ElSherief et al., 2018; Ribeiro et al., 2018). Unfortunately, social media platforms generally do not allow researchers to systematically retrieve users' socio-demographic information except (and only partially) for gender identity.

Hence, in order to study hate speech production using social media data, researchers often compare its spread across regional contexts. For instance, Vargo and Hopp (2017) studied online political discourse during the 2012 US presidential campaign by analysing 'tweets' and found that aggressive discourse was more frequent in districts characterised by poorer socio-economic conditions, low levels of partisan polarity and high levels of racial diversity. Similarly, Rosenbusch et al. (2020) used Twitter data to test whether the level and dispersion of outgroup biases based on race and sexual orientation predict differences in social media hostility, and they found evidence of a positive association at the regional level. Denti and Faggian (2021) applied the same approach to a different context (Italy) and found that hateful discourse on Twitter was more common in localities where income inequality was greater, even net of regional differences in education. This, they argued, suggests that online hate speech is fuelled by the perceived threat of instability in social positions.

In a rare example of methodological triangulation, Stahel and Weingartner (2024) combined social media data and survey data to study the processes whereby aggressive online speech is produced. First, they applied supervised machine learning techniques to classify comments posted in response to online petitions put forward on a German platform. Second, they conducted a voluntary survey among a subsample of users that had posted aggressive or non-aggressive comments. They found that online aggression is more common among historically advantaged groups (men, older people and national citizens) who have experienced a loss of social status (in terms of education or socio-economic conditions). Moreover, many of these structural effects are mediated by political inclination, meaning that these groups lean more than others towards right-wing ideologies and use online aggression as a form of cultural backlash to defend their dwindling privilege.

3. Contribution and Research Questions

In this chapter, we contribute to the emerging literature on the 'supply side' of hate speech, which has so far mainly relied on self-reported behaviour (survey data) or comparisons of actual behaviour across geographical units (social media data). We do so by adopting another analytical strategy, i.e. comparing online behaviour across social media platforms. Although this strategy has been seldom applied in the literature, partly due to methodological constraints (Schemer & Reiners, 2023; Siegel, 2020), it is promising because platforms differ in terms of at least three factors that may affect the amount of online hate speech as well as counter-reactions to it.

Typical content and usage. Social media platforms may be primarily designed and/or used to create and share content, to discuss specific topics or trends, to connect with others both socially and professionally, to build online communities centred around shared interests, to play interacting games, etc. Depending on these features, some platforms may be more conducive to hate speech. Particularly problematic are discussion forums and chat communities where users tend to remain anonymous and where political discourse is prevalent (e.g. Reddit or 4chan). Even within mainstream social media, platforms that are mainly used to share content (be it textual, as on X/Twitter or visual, as on Instagram or TikTok or YouTube) may facilitate the expression of hate speech (as well as counter-reactions) to a greater extent than networking platforms (e.g., Facebook or LinkedIn), where users are typically not anonymous. Even among platforms that are typically used to share content, differences may exist due to the prevailing social norms. By comparing emotions disclosure, Masciantonio and Bourguignon (2024) showed that Instagram tends to foster a more positive environment compared to Twitter although it is also associated with 'low' negative emotions such as boredom and lassitude. In similar vein, Waterloo et al. (2018) evidenced that expressing positive emotions is deemed more appropriate on Instagram than on Facebook, especially among women, whereas the expression of negative emotions is considered more acceptable on Facebook than on Instagram. They also linked these findings to platforms' characteristics, such as the emphasis on self-promotion and the visual nature of Instagram. Finally, platforms differ in how content becomes visible to users. For example, on Facebook, users typically see the content posted within their social networks, while on X/Twitter and Instagram users 'follow' specific content producers. TikTok is fundamentally different in this respect because content is algorithmically proposed in the 'For you' page based on individual preferences regardless of the following/follower relationship. In other words, videos are distributed by the platform in clusters of probably like-minded individuals identified algorithmically by their behaviour on the platform (Martella & Cepernich, 2024). Nevertheless, users adopt 'corrective' practices to make sure that sensitive content (i.e. LGBTQ+ community videos) is suggested to desired/imagined audiences in a way that avoids hate speech (Karizat et al., 2021).

User socio-demographics. Partly because of their content and partly because of the historical phase in which they were created, social media platforms also differ in terms of the population they attract (Meltwater & We Are Social, 2023; Schemer & Reiners, 2023; PEW Research Center, 2024). Among mainstream platforms, Facebook is used by a wide range of social groups, but it is particularly popular among adults older than 30. X/Twitter is more common among younger adults, especially those with higher levels of education and income. By contrast, TikTok is very popular among teenagers and young adults aged under 30 who are more varied in terms of socio-economic backgrounds. Finally, Instagram is extremely widespread among adolescents, young adults and, increasingly, adults in their 30s and 40s. Since previous research has indicated that socio-demographic characteristics are significant predictors of attitudes and behaviour related to online hate speech, social platforms catering to different user populations may result in a larger or smaller amount of hateful content and counter-reactions. In particular, given that hate speech can be an expression of cultural backlash (Inguanzo et al., 2021), we may expect it to be more common in platforms with older audiences, who are more likely to feel threatened by social change.

Moderation and censorship policies. Arguably the most common institutional strategy to combat online hate speech is content moderation, which may result in the removal of content and the banning of accounts that violate platforms' terms of service or stated rules. Content moderation may reduce the diffusion of hate speech in two ways: first, by discouraging users from producing it in the first place (and possibly moving to other online communities) and second, by diminishing its visibility because, even if hateful content is produced, it is quickly removed. Since the specific rules of conduct adopted by the different platforms vary, the amount of hate speech may also vary across platforms.[1] Unfortunately, the extant research reports mixed results in regard to how these bans are actually implemented by the different platforms and how effective they are in reducing hate speech (Fortuna & Nunes, 2018; Siegel, 2020).

---

[1] Since 2016, the European Commission has promoted a voluntary Code of Conduct on Countering Illegal Hate Speech Online jointly with the most popular social media platforms. This Code of Conduct is meant to harmonise moderation and censorship strategies for online content visible in the European Union, but major differences remain among the specific platform guidelines. See for example: Facebook & Instagram: https://transparency.meta.com/policies/community-standards/hate-speech/; X/Twitter: https://help.twitter.com/en/rules-and-policies/violent-speech

Against this background, this chapter asks whether the production of online hate speech (supply side) and the reactions to this kind of discourse (demand side) vary across social media platforms. Given the emerging status of research in this field and the mixed results of previous studies, we adopt an exploratory approach and refrain from formulating precise research hypotheses.

4. Case Study

To address our research questions, we investigate a specific case that occurred during the 2023 edition of the Sanremo Music Festival, in which the rapper Rosa Chemical competed with a song, titled *Made in Italy,* which celebrated sexual freedom and gender fluidity as part of the Italian identity. During his performance on February 11th, Rosa Chemical kissed a male singer and influencer, Fedez, after twerking on him. The episode generated polarised reactions in the public debate, reaching up to the national parliament. On the one hand, conservative politicians and commentators criticised the performance as offencive, dangerous for children and 'a form of gender propaganda'.[2] Critics also questioned the genuine nature of the performance and whether the kiss was consensual. Yet another controversial issue was the fact that Fedez was married to the well-known influencer Chiara Ferragni, who was in fact one of the hosts of the 2023 Sanremo Music Festival, and may have been embarrassed, both personally and professionally, by the 'adulterous' kiss. On the other hand, Rosa Chemical and his supporters argued that the performance was inherently political, as an 'innocuous kiss among friends' successfully exposed the bigotry present in mainstream television.[3]

In the immediate aftermath of the event, Rosa Chemical posted a number of pictures and videos on the three social media platforms where he was active, namely Instagram, TikTok and Facebook.[4] The content, partially overlapping between platforms, included (1) a picture of the controversial kiss, without any accompanying text; (2) a video of his contest song, *Made in Italy,* dubbed in sign language; (3) a photo gallery of himself together with Alex Mucci, an OnlyFans content creator, where the two pose with fetish dresses in public spaces,[5] with the caption 'This is just the first step. Change has just begun'; (4) a video of himself and Alex Mucci, wearing bathrobes in a dressing room and singing the contest song *Made in Italy*; (5) a photo gallery of himself together with Rose Villain, a

---

[2] See, for example, the speech by Maddalena Morgante, a Member of Parliament belonging to the government party Fratelli d'Italia, calling for Rosa Chemical to be banned from the Sanremo Music Festival: https://www.fanpage.it/politica/fuori-rosa-chemical-da-sanremo-fa-propaganda-gender-la-richiesta-di-fratelli-ditalia-alla-rai/

[3] See https://www.fanpage.it/politica/perche-il-bacio-tra-rosa-chemical-e-fedez-sul-palco-di-sanremo-non-e-solo-spettacolo/

[4] Specifically, we restrict our analytical window to the content posted on February 11th–12th, 2023.

[5] More specifically, Rosa Chemical is dressed in latex and is held on a leash by Alex Mucci who is wearing a veil shirt that allows her breasts to be seen. The pictures were taken at daytime in everyday public places in Milan (shopping galleries, subway, etc.).

female singer also competing at Sanremo, where the two pose wearing bathrobes in a hotel room, with the caption 'Sanremo is not only the Italian Music Festival. It is also the Italian Sex Festival'. Table 4.1 summarises the content of the posts and their comparability across social media platforms.

This case study is exemplary for at least three reasons. First, it involves highly visible public figures, who are likely targets of hate (ElSherief et al., 2018; Isbister et al., 2018), especially when they challenge the norms associated with the social category they embody (Sobieraj, 2020). Second, the kiss occurred during the most important musical event and TV show in Italy, which has a crucial symbolic role for many social issues, including controversies over populistic discourse, and is widely followed across generational lines (Magudda, 2020), so that it is possible to track the reactions of younger and older individuals to the same contentious event. Importantly, many online reactions emerged immediately because Sanremo is one of the most commented television programs through 'dual-screen'. This practice, which consists in engaging with online content while watching television, often reflects the identity narratives of online audiences (Airoldi, 2016). Third, taken together, Rosa Chemical's actions (kiss performance, contest song and social media posts) constituted a kind of gender-normative defying behaviour which is often targeted by online hate speech (Butler, 2024; Ging & Siapera, 2019). This is even more relevant in the Italian context, where the so-called 'anti-gender' movements, proclaiming ultraconservative views on women's and LGBTQ+ rights, are particularly strong (Garbagnoli & Prearo, 2018; Paternotte & Kuhar, 2017; Prearo, 2024).

We exploit this case to address our research questions. To do so, we analyse the number and the type of comments that social media users posted below the visual content shared by Rosa Chemical in the immediate aftermath of the kiss, as well as the number of reactions generated by such comments, in order to investigate whether similar content posted on different social platforms provoked different degrees of hostility.

Table 4.1. Comparability of Content Posted by Rosa Chemical Across Platforms.

	Facebook	Instagram	TikTok
Kiss (picture)		X	
Song dubbed in sign language (video)			X
Feat. Alex Mucci, fetish dresses (pictures)		X	
Feat. Alex Mucci, bathrobes (video)			X
Feat. Rose Villain, bathrobes (pictures)	X	X	

5. Empirical Strategy

We manually collected users' comments to the posts produced by Rosa Chemical from the time frame February 11, 2023 to February 12, 2023. In total, we collected seven posts (two on Facebook, three on Instagram and two on TikTok) reporting about 10k users' comments. We merged the two Facebook posts because they were two identical photo galleries shared within a few minutes. We removed from the analysis four Facebook comments without text.

To study the production of online hate speech, we analysed the number and type of these comments. For this purpose, we automatically analysed the text through several deep learning techniques, trained to the Italian language, to identify (a) sentiment polarity (negative or positive); (b) basic emotions (fear, joy, sadness and anger), following Bianchi et al. (2021) and (c) hate speech (dichotomous classification), following Nozza et al. (2022). Indeed, as the literature has shown, hate speech is often accompanied by negative feelings and emotions (Siegel, 2020). We then manually checked classified comments to correct misclassification. After the manual check, we concluded that the classified emotions were joy–enthusiasm, anger–disgust and sadness–disappointment. To explore the content of comments more in depth, we preprocessed the text removing URL, non-ASCII characters, etc., and we used the R library SpacyR to perform POS tagging and identify relevant lemmas (nouns, proper nouns, adjectives and verbs).

Next, in order to study the reactions to online hate speech, we tested the association between the type of comment (as identified in the previous steps) and the number of responses to it. We did so in a multivariate regression framework, estimating a generalised linear model with negative binomial distribution to account for the highly skewed distribution of the outcome (>90% of comments produced zero responses) (Hilbe, 2011).

6. Results

Table 4.2 reports the posts collected, along with some metadata. As apparent from the last column, Rosa Chemical is more popular on Instagram than on other platforms, especially Facebook, based on number of followers. This is obviously reflected in the number of interactions (N likes; N comments) produced by the posts. It would therefore be misleading to compare the absolute number of interactions across platforms.

Within platforms, however, some interesting patterns emerge. The Kiss post produced relatively few Likes (almost 50% less than those produced by the post featuring Alex Mucci), but it was by far the one most commented on. This apparent contradiction can be explained by the different meanings associated with the two interactions: Likes express acknowledgement or approval while comments often indicate debates or arguments on topics (Martella & Bracciale, 2022).

If we calculate the ratio between comments and likes, Facebook emerges as the platform with the highest number of comments per Like to the same posts (Facebook posts ratio: 0.36 and 0.82; Kiss on Instagram: 0.03), potentially

Table 4.2. Posts and Reactions Across Platforms.

Platform	URL[a]	Post	Date	N. Likes	N. Comments[b]	Retrieved Comments	Followers
Facebook	https://www.facebook.com/RosaChemical/posts/pfbid02vHZUT5tuvmvsTTsMq58DrRL4HmHM2KyfjhLvzMiWnDWX1i22RmaBaFzsFB3KRpywl	Feat. Rose Villain, bathrobes (pictures)	Feb 11	745	270	341	22,226
	https://www.facebook.com/RosaChemical/posts/pfbid0ufQvDDyg4x97763VCvdZDgTVLEoKeyh7cvtGSAVgpTb8DTFVcjkaPKNyHuhkYhZ6l	Feat. Rose Villain, bathrobes (pictures)	Feb 11	609	498		
Instagram	https://www.instagram.com/p/CokjauWKTKY/?img_index=1	Feat. Alex Mucci, fetish dresses (pictures)	Feb 12	552,000	4,768	2,753	411,000
	https://www.instagram.com/p/CoifZqQLWAI/?img_index=1	Kiss (picture)	Feb 11	288,000	8,893	3,822	
	https://www.instagram.com/p/CogB2CGq4vk/?img_index=1	Feat. Rose Villain, bathrobes (pictures)	Feb 11	269,000	1,793	1,507	

TikTok	https://www.tiktok.com/gipsyboirosa/video/7199002417428499718	Song dubbed in sign language (video)	Feb 11	211,600	896	581	309,800
	https://www.tiktok.com/gipsyboirosa/video/7199339655605587206	Feat. Alex Mucci, bathrobes (video)	Feb 12	204,200	959	629	

[a]Unfortunately, as we are writing this chapter, the Instagram posts are not visible anymore because Rosa Chemical removed almost all the content prior to 2024.
[b]The number of comments provided by the platform include nested comments that have been not retrieved for the analysis.

indicating a larger degree of contention over the posts. Concerning the ability to engage the community in commenting (N comments/N followers), the second gallery on Facebook and the kiss on Instagram reached the highest ratio (0.02) among all posts. Finally, concerning the ability to engage the community (N Likes/N followers), Rosa Chemical emerges as more able to gain likes on Instagram and TikTok compared to Facebook, especially with the post featuring Alex Mucci (N Likes/N followers: 1.34).

Therefore, this overview of the posts seems to highlight that Facebook audiences were overall more willing to comment on Rosa Chemical's posts, while Instagram and TikTok users liked his posts the most. Furthermore, the Kiss post – which unfortunately only exists on Instagram – fueled a large number of comments, suggesting that this content was more controversial than those of the other posts.

6.1 Hate and Emotions Across Platforms: Quantitative Analyses

Table 4.3 reports the shares of comments classified in terms of their hate speech content, sentiment and prevalent emotion. Comments on the Facebook posts show the highest percentages of hate (36%), negative sentiment (65%) and anger–disgust (54%). Instagram comments are the ones that expressed most joy or enthusiasm (72%). TikTok stands out as the least negative platform (12%) and with the lowest percentage of hate (2%). In terms of emotions, joy and enthusiasm prevailed (68%) and comments were more sad or disappointed (5%) than angry or disgusted (3%). These patterns reflect the relationship between hate and emotions. Indeed, on Facebook hate is rather related to anger and disgust ($\rho = 0.55$) and slightly negatively correlated with sadness and disappointment ($\rho = -0.09$). Comments on Instagram show a similar correlation between anger and hate, but they are not associated with any specific emotion. TikTok comments, on the other hand, exhibit a less intense relationship between anger and hate ($\rho = 0.49$), which, compared to other social media, is somewhat more related to sadness ($\rho = 0.07$). Finally, moving from Facebook to TikTok shows that negative sentiment is less and less connected to hate speech, with Pearson's coefficient varying from $\rho = 0.51$ (Facebook) to $\rho = 0.45$ (Instagram) and $\rho = 0.3$ (TikTok).

Thus, generally speaking, hate is much more present on Facebook than on other platforms, and it is mainly connected to anger. Moreover, Facebook audiences express far less joy – only one third of their comments do so. On the other hand, TikTok emerges as the least 'hateful' environment, with most of the negative sentiment being related to sadness or disappointment.

6.2 Qualitative Exploration of the Content of Comments

To understand the underlying emotions expressed by individuals, we extracted the lemmas most frequently used in the comments on each post. We present the results by prevalent emotion.

Table 4.3. Hate, Sentiment and Emotion Distribution by Social Media.

Social	N	Hate Speech % of Hateful Comments	Sentiment % of Negative Comments	% of Comments Anger/Disgust	Emotion[a] % of Comments Sadness/ Disappointment	% of Comments Joy/Enthusiasm
Facebook	337	**35.9**	**64.7**	**53.7**	9.5	30.3
Feat. Rose Villain, bathrobes (pictures)	337	35,9	64.7	53.7	9.5	30.3
Instagram	8,082	7.6	27.9	16.8	7.7	**71.9**
Feat. Rose Villain, bathrobes (pictures)	1,507	3.8	12.5	7.7	3.6	85.1
Feat. Alex Mucci, fetish dresses (pictures)	2,753	8.6	30.8	16.8	11.2	67.5
Kiss (picture)	3,822	8.4	31.9	20.3	6.9	69.9
TikTok	1,210	1.9	12.1	2.8	5.5	68.0
Feat. Alex Mucci, bathrobes (video)	629	2.9	13.5	4.3	7.9	66.8
Song dubbed in sign language (video)	581	0.9	10.7	1.2	2.8	69.4

[a]Not all comments expressed the emotions under analysis; therefore, the total sum of emotions does not equal 100.

6.2.1 Anger–Disgust

On Facebook, the most common words associated with anger was the verb 'do' (fare) accompanied by the noun 'suck' (schifo), which together convey the sentiment 'you suck'. Additionally, adjectives such as 'ridiculous' and 'asshole' were prevalent. Anger was also linked to the verb 'to see', referring to the Sanremo broadcast, as well as to the general discussion on the (stolen or performed) kiss and twerking by Rosa Chemical on Fedez. Indeed, the word 'Fedez' was also quite frequent, even though the post was not about the kiss, indicating that the users visited Rosa Chemical's profile with the intention of commenting on the controversial kiss episode and gathered below the latest post.

Moreover, users' criticisms of the entire performance mainly revolved around scandal rather than music, disqualifying Rosa Chemical as a musician.

On Instagram, anger related to different issues depending on the post being referred to. Comments on the post featuring the kiss were quite similar to the ones on Facebook. Here the words 'kiss' (both noun and verb) and 'Italy' are among the most frequent lexical items, arguing that with his behaviour, Rosa Chemical does not represent the country, contrary to what his contest song claimed ('Made in Italy'). Among recurrent words, we also find 'shit' and 'wife', with the second referring to Fedez being married to Chiara Ferragni, who was hosting Sanremo. In contrast, anger in comments on the post with OnlyFans content creator Alex Mucci mostly related to the word 'change', challenging the claim, present in the post caption, that the photo gallery of the couple, wearing fetish dresses and exposing the female body in public places, actually constituted social change. In other instances, users wrote that the alleged 'change' only generated disgust. Among the most frequent words were 'woman', 'naked', 'tits', 'exhibit', 'freedom' and 'sucks' ('fare schifo'). This result highlights that almost all the anger was directed at the creator, Alex Mucci, who appeared undressed in the photos in public places showing her breasts. Many angry comments point out that this was not true freedom, and that Mucci is a 'plastic surgery woman'. Angry comments related to the post featuring Rose Villain were very few as were the frequency of words. However, some criticism of both Rosa Chemical and Rose Villain emerges here because they 'suck' and represent a 'cliché' and a 'carnival' instead of 'sex'.

Finally, on TikTok only the comments to the post featuring Alex Mucci expressed some anger, which was mainly directed at both her and Rosa Chemical. Interestingly, both criticisms seem to be motivated by an alleged violation of the social norms connected with relational monogamy. On the one hand, comments attacked Rosa Chemical for ruining the Ferragnez 'family' by kissing Fedez on stage. On the other hand, users argued that the photo gallery where Mucci had Rosa Chemical on a leash suggested that she was cheating on the Italian celebrity 'Marra' to whom she is engaged.

6.2.2 Sadness–Disappointment

On Facebook, disappointment and sadness mostly related to the 'song', the singer and 'Fedez' because they do not represent 'Italian sex', he is not an 'artist' and he sucks (fare pena). This is coherent with the caption openly referring to the contest song ('Sanremo is not only the Italian Music Festival. It is also the Italian Sex Festival').

On Instagram, starting with the Kiss post, sadness concerned the kiss not being consensual and Fedez being heterosexual and married. The most frequent words related to sadness and disappointment on the post featuring Alex Mucci were quite similar to the ones that emerged in posts expressing anger. However, here the emotional tone was more disappointed and saddened by the 'naked' 'woman' showing her 'breasts' despite the 'cold' and who did not represent any 'change'. Very few comments were sad about the Instagram post featuring Rose Villain, and they mostly claimed that she is 'boring' rather than provocative.

On TikTok, the sad comments were not necessarily critical; on the contrary, many users expressed sadness or disappointment because they were 'jealous' of Mucci or Rosa Chemical while others pointed out that the 'Made in Italy' song should have won Sanremo or would have been successful in the Eurovision Song Contest. Most disappointed comments related to what had happened with 'Fedez.'

6.2.3 Joy–Enthusiasm

Enthusiastic comments on Facebook mainly related to the 'song' 'Made in Italy', expressing appreciation ('bravo', 'bravissimo', etc.). Therefore, once again, it seems that on Facebook, emotions and users' expressions dealt with the post content to a lesser extent.

On Instagram, joyful comments on the kiss post clearly expressed 'love' of 'Rosa' Chemical and 'Fedez' also because of the 'kiss' ('kissing'; 'mouth') to the extent that there were many users tagging others to share the gallery. Many users expressed their appreciation by using online slang expressions (e.g. 'you are my father', 'mother' and 'brother'). Joy concerning the gallery featuring Alex Mucci was mainly expressed by people tagging others and commenting 'wonderful', 'good looking', 'sexy', 'hot', etc. Hence, users did not seem to follow up on the call for social change mentioned in the caption text. Comments on the gallery featuring Rose Villain expressed joy through puns on the names 'Rosa' and 'Rose' and by saying 'you are my mother', 'father', 'parent', you represent 'Italian sex' and we 'love' you.

Also on TikTok, enthusiasm was mainly expressed by tagging. Appreciation of the post where the contest song was dubbed in sign language was directed towards the 'interpreter' and the 'song'. The video with Alex Mucci is mainly commented on with the above-mentioned expressions: you are my 'mother', 'father', 'brother', 'family tree' and 'chiropodist', with this last referring to Rosa Chemical's obsession with feet.

In sum, how do these analyses respond to our first research question, the one concerning hate speech creation and its differences across social media platforms? The number of hateful comments varied dramatically among platforms, ranging from more than one third on Facebook to less than 2% on TikTok. Hate was most related to anger and disgust in every platform, but this relationship was weaker on TikTok, where hate was also related to sadness and disappointment. Television content was a driver of hate comments on Facebook, as revealed by the analysis of the most frequent lemmas, which did not relate to post content but rather to the kiss incident. However, it is worth reminding that Rosa Chemical did not post anything else on Facebook in those days.

Interestingly, the most hated post on Instagram and TikTok was the one featuring Alex Mucci, and this hate was mainly driven by sadness and disappointment. Mucci's physical appearance and the way she dresses provoked most of the hate and disappointment. However, comments on the post featuring the kiss between Fedez and Rosa Chemical (only available on Instagram) emerged as the angriest and most disgusted ones.

Taken together, these results suggest that, in the Italian context, hate speech with homophobic and sexist connotation coexist at similar rates, although their emotional drivers may differ.

6.3 The Effects of Hate and Emotions on Online Debates

In order to understand whether and to what extent hate or other emotions trigger online reactions, we built four negative binomial regression models: one for each social media and one general (Table 4.4).

Table 4.4. Negative Binomial Regression Models on the Number of Responses to Comments (Odds Ratios).

Predictors	General Incidence Rate Ratios	Facebook Incidence Rate Ratios	Instagram Incidence Rate Ratios	TikTok Incidence Rate Ratios
(Intercept)	0.45*	0.24*	0.47*	0.37***
Hate	1.47	0.89	1.54	0.54
Anger – Disgust	2.58***	5.68**	2.24*	0.56
Sadness – Disappointment	3.61***	15.43***	3.25**	0.21*
Joy – Enthusiasm	0.66	1.36	0.55	0.89
Social [Instagram]	0.89			
Social [TikTok]	0.93			
Observations	9,633	341	8,082	1,210
R^2 Nagelkerke	0.091	0.166	0.092	0.021
AIC	9,515.227	753.921	7,131.163	1,448.858
Log-Likelihood	−4,749.614	−370.960	−3,559.581	−718.429

Note: *$p < 0.05$; **$p < 0.01$ and ***$p < 0.001$.

All models show that positive emotions, namely joy and enthusiasm, do not affect the number of responses; indeed, the IRR is not significant across platforms. For Facebook and Instagram, a quite clear pattern emerges from our results, one which is largely in line with the findings of previous research. Only negative emotions increase responses to comments. Hate speech is positively correlated to the number of responses, but, somewhat surprisingly, this correlation disappears once emotions are controlled for, suggesting that negative emotions, and in particular anger, mediate the effect of hate speech on engagement.[6] Among negative emotions, sadness and disappointment in particular appear to be strongly related with responses to comments. These results confirm those of previous studies on negativity on Facebook (Bene, 2017; Martella & Bracciale, 2022) and that positive emotions do not foster commenting by Facebook users (Martella & Bracciale, 2022). However, our results extend this finding to Instagram. Moreover, our analyses disentangle the influence of various negative emotions, something which – to the best of our knowledge – has not yet been done in the literature. We show that sadness and disappointment powerfully induce users to respond to comments. Indeed, except for TikTok, IRRs of sadness and disappointment are higher than those of anger. By contrast, TikTok audiences exhibit a behaviour that is very different from that of the users of the other platforms and from what has been found by previous studies relying on traditional platforms. First, anger and disgust – which triggered more users' responses on both Facebook and Instagram – were not even significant on TikTok despite the presence of a similar post featuring Alex Mucci. More importantly, sadness and disappointment *negatively* affected the number of responses, in the sense that comments imbued with these negative emotions received about 20% fewer responses ($e^\beta = 0.2$).

7. Discussion and Conclusion

In this chapter, we have explored the processes that lead to the creation of online hate speech and its consequences by analysing a case where, during the most important Italian music festival, a male singer kissed another male singer. This act challenged traditional gender norms and produced polarised reactions in the public debate, making the singer a likely target of the hate speech which proliferates around public figures who push the boundaries of their social identity (ElSherief et al., 2018; Sobieraj, 2020). Moreover, gender norms are a particularly polarizing topic in Italy (e.g. Paternotte & Kuhar, 2017). We analysed online reactions to the event on the three social media platforms where the singer is active (Facebook, Instagram and TikTok). Specifically, we collected users'

---

[6]Due to possible multicollinearity among anger, hate and joy, we run several regression models excluding anger. Our results confirm that without anger, both hate and joy are significant ($p < 0.01$), but hate IRR is lower than anger ($e^\beta = 1.8$), and joy IRR is negative, thus showing that (1) anger is a more powerful driver than hate for commenting and (2) positive emotions decrease the number of responses ($e^\beta = 0.3$).

reactions below the five posts that the singer made right after the event, and we analysed the number and the type of comments and the number of responses.

It should be borne in mind that, among the various posts made by the singer Rosa Chemical within our selected time frame, only one, made on Instagram, was about the contentious 'kiss' episode. Yet, as evident from our exploration of the most frequent lemmas, many hateful comments on Facebook directly referred to the episode. This result has two implications. First, it highlights the importance of traditional media content in generating online hate speech through 'dual screening' (television/smartphone or computer). Second, it suggests that homophobic attitudes are a significant driver of hateful discourse. This is further backed up by the fact that the 'kiss' post, compared to the other two posted on Instagram, produced the largest share of comments characterised by anger and disgust (20.3%). Yet, the 'kiss' post and the post with the (female) OnlyFans creator were met by a similar share of hateful comments on Instagram, suggesting that, at least in Italy, sexism is just as important as homophobia in generating online hate speech (see also Martella & Pavan, 2023).

Moving to the cross-platform comparison, our findings indicate that hateful comments were definitely not common on TikTok (1.9%), rare on Instagram (7.6%) and very frequent on Facebook (35.9%). This ranking holds true also when we narrow the comparison down to identical or very similar posts that Rosa Chemical simultaneously made on various social platforms. Similarly, the general sentiment was more negative than positive on Facebook while the reverse is true for the other social platforms. More specifically, on Facebook the prevailing emotions were anger and disgust (53.7%) while on Instagram and TikTok they were joy and enthusiasm (71.9% and 68%, respectively).

The stronger presence of hateful and, more generally, negative reactions on Facebook cannot be traced back to the nature of the platform. In fact, Facebook is strongly based on users' personal networks while Instagram and TikTok are mostly designed and used as 'content communities' (Bhandari & Bimo, 2022) and, as such, offer more opportunities for aggressive behaviour to anonymous users. However, TikTok differs from other platforms in its content distribution mechanism, which is highly personalised and disconnected from the relationships between users. Therefore, one factor that may have affected the lower negativity present on the platform is that the content was seen mostly by like-minded users. Yet, distribution mechanisms do not fully explain cross-platform differences, as the content was also searched for on the platforms, as evidenced by the comments on Facebook that did not address the content of the post. Therefore, it also seems likely that Facebook audiences, who tend to be older than those of Instagram and TikTok, feel more threatened by gender-normative defying behaviours and resort to hate speech as a form of cultural backlash (Inguanzo et al., 2021).

The socio-demographic composition of the different social platforms is probably strictly intertwined with the prevailing social norms about which type of content 'belongs' to the platform, and with which one can engage, and which type of content, instead 'does not belong' and therefore should be ignored (or possibly reported as inappropriate). In fact, our analyses on second-order reactions produced a different pattern of results for Facebook and TikTok (with Instagram somewhere in between).

On Facebook, comments characterised by negative emotions produced more reactions, thus replicating the results of previous studies (Bene, 2017; Martella & Bracciale, 2022). In contrast, on TikTok, comment negativity was not correlated with the number of responses. This result is consistent with qualitative insights on adolescent online behaviour, indicating unwillingness to participate in hatred disputes in the comments section (Astuti & Partini, 2019; Borgna et al., 2024) but also, more generally, with the perceived appropriateness of positive/negative content in different platforms (Waterloo et al., 2018).

In conclusion, although recent evidence indicates that TikTok is also beginning to be slightly affected by the spread of hatred, particularly against minorities and women by far-right wingers and incel movements (Weimann & Masri, 2023), our case study centred on a gender-norm defying episode points to Facebook and, to a lesser extent, Instagram, as the social media where more hatred is expressed and generates further engagement.

From a methodological perspective, our study has sought to contribute to investigation of the 'supply side' of hate speech, which has so far mainly relied on self-reported behaviour based on survey data. As we have shown, comparing the spread of online hate speech across social media platforms is promising because they differ in their architecture (typical content, social norms and moderation policies), as well as in the prevailing socio-demographics of their users. However, an obvious limitation of our approach, as opposed to survey-based research, is that we lack direct information on users' socio-demographics. Therefore, the interpretation of cross-platform differences as indicative of different behaviours prevailing among younger vs older online audiences remains, at this stage, a speculation. In particular, as mentioned, we cannot exclude that the very low presence of hate and negativity on TikTok is due to its content distribution mechanism. Finally, our study suggests multiple avenues for further research. For instance, future studies could investigate the possible reasons why adolescents refrain from engaging in online hate speech, by exploring the role of values associated with social change (e.g. gender fluidity and sexual freedom) and the role of online social norms.

References

Airoldi, M. (2016). Studiare i «social media» con i «topic models»: Sanremo 2016 su Twitter. *Studi Culturali*, *3*, 431–448. https://doi.org/10.1405/85342

Álvarez-Benjumea, A., & Winter, F. (2018). Normative change and culture of hate: An experiment in online environments. *European Sociological Review*, *34*(3), 223–237.

Astuti, F., & Partini, P. (2019). The hate speech behavior of teenagers on social media Instagram. In *International Summit on Science Technology and Humanity (ISETH2019) Advancing Scientific Thought for Future Sustainable Development* (pp. 252–259). Kartasura, 3–4 December.

Barlińska, J., Szuster, A., & Winiewski, M. (2018). Cyberbullying among adolescent bystanders: Role of affective versus cognitive empathy in increasing prosocial cyberbystander behavior. *Frontiers in Psychology*, *9*. https://doi.org/10.3389/fpsyg.2018.00799

Bene, M. (2017). Go viral on the Facebook! Interactions between candidates and followers on Facebook during the Hungarian general election campaign of 2014. *Information, Communication & Society*, *20*(4), 513–529. https://doi.org/10.1080/1369118X.2016.1198411

Bernatzky, C., Costello, M., & Hawdon, J. (2022). Who produces online hate?: An examination of the effects of self-control, social structure, & social learning. *American Journal of Criminal Justice*, *47*(3), 421–440.

Bhandari, A., & Bimo, S. (2022). Why's everyone on TikTok now? The algorithmized self and the future of self-making on social media. *Social Media + Society*, *8*(1), 1–11. https://doi.org/10.1177/20563051221086241

Bianchi, F., Nozza, D., & Hovy, D. (2021). Feel-It: Emotion and sentiment classification for the Italian language. In O. De Clercq, A. Balahur, J. Sedoc, V. Barriere, S. Tafreshi, S. Buechel, & V. Hoste (Eds.), *Proceedings of the 11th Workshop on Computational Approaches to Subjectivity, Sentiment and Social Media Analysis* (pp. 76–83). Association for Computational Linguistics.

Bilewicz, M., & Soral, W. (2020). Hate speech epidemic. The dynamic effects of derogatory language on intergroup relations and political radicalization. *Political Psychology*, *41*(S1), 3–33.

Blazak, R. (2009). Toward a working definition of hate groups. *Hate Crimes*, *3*(1), 133–162.

Borgna, C., Charitopoulou, E., & Miglio, M. (2024). *Online hate speech and prejudice among adolescents: A field experiment on Italian schools*. [Unpublished manuscript].

Butler, J. (2024). *Who's afraid of gender?* Farrar, Straus and Giroux.

Costello, M., & Hawdon, J. (2018). Who are the online extremists among us? Sociodemographic characteristics, social networking, and online experiences of those who produce online hate materials. *Violence and Gender*, *5*(1), 55–60.

Council of Europe. (2022). *Combating hate speech*. Council of Europe. https://www.coe.int/en/web/combating-hate-speech/recommendation-on-combating-hate-speech

Denti, D., & Faggian, A. (2021). Where do angry birds tweet? Income inequality and online hate in Italy. *Cambridge Journal of Regions, Economy and Society*, *14*(3), 483–506.

ElSherief, M., Kulkarni, V., Nguyen, D., Yang Wang, W., & Belding, E. (2018). Hate lingo: A target-based linguistic analysis of hate speech in social media. *Proceedings of the International AAAI Conference on Web and Social Media*, *12*(1), 42–51. https://doi.org/10.1609/icwsm.v12i1.15041

Eschmann, R. (2021). Digital resistance: How online communication facilitates responses to racial microaggressions. *Sociology of Race and Ethnicity*, *7*(2), 264–277.

European Union Agency for Fundamental Rights. (2023). *Online content moderation – Current challenges in detecting hate speech*. Publications Office of the European Union.

Fortuna, P., & Nunes, S. (2018). A survey on automatic detection of hate speech in text. *ACM Computing Surveys (CSUR)*, *51*(4), 1–30.

Frischlich, L., Schatto-Eckrodt, T., Boberg, S., & Wintterlin, F. (2021). Roots of incivility: How personality, media use, and online experiences shape uncivil participation. *Media and Communication*, *9*(1), 195–208.

Gandhi, A., Ahir, P., Adhvaryu, K., Shah, P., Lohiya, R., Cambria, E., Poria, S., & Hussain, A. (2024). Hate speech detection: A comprehensive review of recent works. *Expert Systems*, *41*(8). https://doi.org/10.1111/exsy.13562

Garbagnoli, S., & Prearo, M. (2018). La crociata "anti-gender". In *Dal Vaticano alle manif pour tous* (pp. 1–84). Kaplan.

Ging, D. & Siapera, E. (Eds.). (2019). *Gender hate online: Understanding the new antifeminism*. Springer.

Hangartner, D., Gennaro, G., Alasiri, S., Bahrich, N., Bornhoft, A., Boucher, J., Demirci, B. B., Derksen, L., Hall, A., Jochum, M., Munoz, M. M., Richter, M., Vogel, F., Wittwer, S., Wüthrich, F., Gilardi, F., & Donnay, K. (2021). Empathy-based counterspeech can reduce racist hate speech in a social media field experiment. *Proceedings of the National Academy of Sciences, 118*(50), e2116310118. https://doi.org/10.1073/pnas.2116310118

Hawdon, J., Bernatzky, C., & Costello, M. (2019). Cyber-routines, political attitudes, and exposure to violence-advocating online extremism. *Social Forces, 98*(1), 329–354.

Hawdon, J., Oksanen, A., & Räsänen, P. (2017). Exposure to online hate in four nations: A cross-national consideration. *Deviant Behavior, 38*(3), 254–266.

Hilbe, J. M. (2011). *Negative binomial regression* (2nd ed.). Cambridge University Press.

Inara Rodis Paulina, d. C. (2021). Let's (Re)Tweet about racism and sexism: Responses to cyber aggression toward Black and Asian women. *Information, Communication & Society, 24*(14), 2153–2173.

Inguanzo, I., Zhang, B., & Gil de Zúñiga, H. (2021). Online cultural backlash? Sexism and political user-generated content. *Information, Communication & Society, 24*(14), 2133–2152.

Isbister, T., Sahlgren, M., Kaati, L., Obaidi, M., & Akrami, N. (2018). Monitoring targeted hate in online environments. arXiv.org https://arxiv.org/abs/1803.04757

Kaakinen, M., Räsänen, P., Näsi, M., Minkkinen, J., Keipi, T., & Oksanen, A. (2018). Social capital and online hate production: A four country survey. *Crime, Law and Social Change, 69*, 25–39.

Karizat, N., Delmonaco, D., Eslami, M., & Andalibi, N. (2021). Algorithmic folk theories and identity: How TikTok users co-produce knowledge of identity and engage in algorithmic resistance. *Proceedings of the ACM on Human-Computer Interaction, 5*(CSCW2), 1–44.

Magudda, P. (2020). Populism, music and the media. The Sanremo festival and the circulation of populist discourse. *PArtecipazione e COnflitto, 13*(1), 132–153.

Martella, A., & Bracciale, R. (2022). Populism and emotions: Italian political leaders' communicative strategies to engage Facebook users. *Innovation: The European Journal of Social Science Research, 35*(1), 65–85.

Martella, A., & Cepernich, C. (2024). "Dacci oggi il nostro TikTok quotidiano". Strategie di pubblicazione dei quotidiani italiani su Tik Tok. *Problemi Dell'informazione, Rivista Quadrimestrale, 2024*(1), 65–92.

Martella, A., & Pavan, E. (2023). "We hate her . . . and you too": Polarized intersectionality in Italy throughout changing political scenarios. *New Media & Society*. https://doi.org/10.1177/14614448231160706

Masciantonio, A., & Bourguignon, D. (2024). Too positive to be tweeted? An experimental investigation of emotional expression on Twitter and Instagram. *Media Psychology, 27*(2), 243–270. https://doi.org/10.1080/15213269.2023.2236935

Meltwater and We Are Social. (2023). *Digital 2023 global overview report*. https://datareportal.com/reports/digital-2023-global-overview-report

Munger, K. (2021). Don't@ Me: Experimentally reducing partisan incivility on Twitter. *Journal of Experimental Political Science, 8*(2), 102–116.

Nozza, D., Bianchi, F., & Attanasio, G. (2022). HATE-ITA: New baselines for hate speech detection in Italian. In *Proceedings of the Sixth Workshop on Online Abuse and Harms (WOAH)* (pp. 252–260). Association for Computational Linguistic.

Paternotte, D., & Kuhar, R. (2017). The anti-gender movement in comparative perspective. In R. Kuhar & D. Paternotte (Eds.), *Anti-gender campaigns in Europe: Mobilizing against equality* (pp. 253–276). Rowman & Littlefield International.
PEW Research Center. (2022, December 6). *Internet, smartphone and social media use.* Report. https://www.pewresearch.org/global/2022/12/06/internet-smartphone-and-social-media-use-in-advanced-economies-2022/. Accessed on May 5, 2024.
PEW Research Center. (2024, January 31). *Americans' social media use.* Report. https://www.pewresearch.org/internet/2024/01/31/americans-social-media-use/. Accessed on May 5, 2024.
Prearo, M. (2024). *Anti-gender mobilizations, religion and politics: An Italian case study.* Taylor & Francis.
Reichelmann, A., Hawdon, J., Costello, M., Ryan, J., Blaya, C., Llorent, V., Oksanen, A., Räsänen, P., & Zych, I. (2021). Hate knows no boundaries: Online hate in six nations. *Deviant Behavior, 42*(9), 1100–1111.
Ribeiro, M., Calais, P., Santos, Y., Almeida, V., & Meira Jr, W. (2018, June). Characterizing and detecting hateful users on Twitter. In *Proceedings of the International AAAI Conference on Web and Social Media* (Vol. 12, No. 1).
Rosenbusch, H., Evans, A. M., & Zeelenberg, M. (2020). Interregional and intraregional variability of intergroup attitudes predict online hostility. *European Journal of Personality, 34*(5), 859–872.
Schemer, C., & Reiners, L. (2023). Challenges of comparative research on hate speech in media user comments: Comparing countries, platforms, and target groups. In C. Strippel, S. Paasch-Colberg, M. Emmer, & J. Trebbe (Eds.), *Challenges and perspectives of hate speech research* (pp. 127–139). Digital Communication Research.
Schmidt, A., & Wiegand, M. (2017, April). A survey on hate speech detection using natural language processing. In *Proceedings of the Fifth International Workshop on Natural Language Processing for Social Media* (pp. 1–10).
Siegel, A. (2020). Online hate speech. In N. Persily & J. A. Tucker (Eds.), *Social media and democracy. The state of the field, prospects for reform* (pp. 56–88). Cambridge University Press.
Sobieraj, S. (2020). *Credible threat. Attacks against women online and the future of democracy.* Oxford University Press.
Stahel, L., & Weingartner, S. (2024). Can political orientation explain the social structure of online aggression? Integrating social media and survey data. *Sociological Inquiry, 94*(1), 149–169.
Vargo, C. J., & Hopp, T. (2017). Socioeconomic status, social capital, and partisan polarity as predictors of political incivility on Twitter: A congressional district-level analysis. *Social Science Computer Review, 35*(1), 10–32.
Wachs, S., Gámez-Guadix, M., & Wright, M. F. (2022). Online hate speech victimization and depressive symptoms among adolescents: The protective role of resilience. *Cyberpsychology, Behavior, and Social Networking, 25*(7), 416–423.
Waterloo, S. F., Baumgartner, S. E., Peter, J., & Valkenburg, P. M. (2018). Norms of online expressions of emotion: Comparing Facebook, Twitter, Instagram, and WhatsApp. *New Media & Society, 20*(5), 1813–1831. https://doi.org/10.1177/1461444817707349
Weimann, G., & Masri, N. (2023). Research note: Spreading hate on TikTok. *Studies in Conflict & Terrorism, 46*(5), 752–765. https://doi.org/10.1080/1057610X.2020.1780027

Section 3

Media

Chapter 5

Can I Have Some News? Local Journalism Gaps and the Role of Platforms

Pedro Jerónimo and Luísa Torre

University of Beira Interior, Portugal

Abstract

How do citizens who live in municipalities that are in 'news deserts' find out about what is happening where they live? Developed in the United States and investigated in Brazil and the United Kingdom, the concept of 'news deserts' has aroused the curiosity of scholars and agents involved in the development of public policies in Europe, with the mapping of such areas being the target of a European Commission Call for Proposals to support local media in news-poor communities. The phenomenon of news deserts results from a systemic and wide-ranging crisis that journalism as a whole is facing, with profound effects on the local media. A 'news desert' is defined as a community without a local newspaper and also a community whose inhabitants face significantly reduced access to news that feeds the foundation of local democracy. One of the first mappings carried out in Europe, the *News Deserts Europe 2022: Portugal Report*, revealed that 25.3% of Portugal's municipalities did not have media outlets based in the municipality about which they produced contents, a phenomenon linked to more isolated communities with lower economic activity and smaller. But people somehow obtain information in these news deserts. Studies show that much of the local information in those regions is accessed through social media, such as Facebook pages and groups, which can be sources of disinformation and manipulation. When there is no media covering local affairs, communities are left without a point of reference.

Keywords: News deserts; local news; local media; news consumption; social media platforms; disinformation

1. Introduction

Research on 'news deserts' has grown over the last decade, with more systematic investigation of them in the United States and Brazil (Abernathy, 2016; Atlas da Notícia, 2017; Ferrier et al., 2016). However, there are still several gaps to be filled, in regard to both research questions and defining the concepts that develop within this field (Abernathy, 2023; Gulyas et al., 2023). In Europe, for example, research has been conducted only in recent years (Gulyas, 2021; Jerónimo, Ramos et al., 2022).

According to Mota (2023), the rise of news deserts, the collapse of the traditional business models and platform competition and the erosion of proximity in journalistic practices are the main issues studied in the field of local journalism.

News deserts are defined as 'communities where residents have very limited access to the sort of critical and credible local news and information that nurtures grassroots democracy and social cohesion' (Abernathy, 2023, p. 290) either as the result of closures of local news outlets or when local news content declines until it almost disappears (Gulyas, 2021).

In Europe, academic interest in the topic has been growing and especially since a call by the European Commission (2022) to fund a consortium set up to support local, regional and community news media. Led by the European Federation of Journalists, the Local Media for Democracy project also provides a theoretical basis for understanding the phenomenon of news deserts in Europe (Blagojev et al., 2023; Verza et al., 2024), deepening research in this field after the studies conducted in Portugal (Jerónimo, Ramos et al., 2022; Ramos, 2021). As a result of this project, the first mapping of news deserts in Europe was published (Verza et al., 2024).

'News desert' is a concept that arouses academic and non-academic interest. However, it can have different meanings in 'different settings and contexts, and is interpreted differently depending on what perspective the researcher takes' (Gulyas et al., 2023, p. 287). In the European context, while in the Nordic countries local media play a fundamental role and are well established, in countries like Malta national media often fulfil the local information needs of citizens due to proximity and population size (Blagojev et al., 2023).

Thus, considering the great cultural, political and social diversity that exists in Europe, the Local Media For Democracy project defines a news desert as 'a geographic or administrative area, or a social community, where it is difficult or impossible to access sufficient, reliable, diverse information from independent local, regional and community media' (Verza et al., 2024, p. 5).

Accordingly, more research should be conducted to determine different approaches to this investigation topic. As suggested by Gulyas (2021), research has adopted different focuses in an attempt to address this issue: outlet-focused studies; content-focused studies and media-ecology-focused research.

2. Growing Research on News Deserts

In districts like those in the interior of a country, local journalism has been affected by economic crisis after economic crisis, and there are more and more cases of local media outlets that 'cannot sustain themselves' or attract 'new ventures in the sector'

(Jerónimo, Ramos et al., 2022, p. 10). In such districts, residents may see the closure of the sole newspaper or radio that used to provide them with local news. The result is that they have very limited access to credible news and information, which 'worsens political, economic, digital and cultural divisions in (the) country, threatening the stability and viability of democracy' (Abernathy, 2022, p. 12).

The flight of advertisers to digital platforms, the younger generation's lack of interest in print journalism, the successive economic crises experienced in the world since 2008 and the lack of digital infrastructure will contribute to this phenomenon – the emergence of news deserts increasingly investigated in journalism studies (Abernathy, 2022).

In the United States, newspapers have been the primary, and sometimes the sole, source of local news and information for people that live in small urban and rural communities far from the metropolises. When a newspaper disappears, it is rarely substituted by a digital one, leaving the community without any alternative local news outlet (Abernathy, 2023).

News deserts are frequently found in areas distant from big cities, where there is low economic activity and where the population tends to be smaller, less educated and older than the average in the country (Abernathy, 2022; Furlanetto & Baccin, 2020). In these areas, cities, towns and villages experience a contradiction: they have access to reliable journalistic information about events in other states and countries, but they do not have a credible journalistic source of information about their own community; however, this does not mean that nothing happens there (Furlanetto & Baccin, 2020; Ramos, 2021).

At a local level, the lack of journalism coverage results in a decrease of scrutiny of local institutions, an increase in vulnerability to disinformation on social media, hate speech or populism and a growing sense of suspicion and confusion (Ardia et al., 2020; Barclay et al., 2022; Torre & Jerónimo, 2023). The absence of local journalistic coverage and the concentration of media outlets in urban, densely populated areas exacerbates inequalities and unbalances democratic processes, impacting community representation (Bisiani & Heravi, 2023).

3. Local Media and the Move to Digital First

News deserts result from a systemic and wide-ranging crisis that journalism as a whole is facing, with profound effects on local media. A 'news desert' is defined as a community without a local newspaper, and also as one whose inhabitants have significantly reduced access to news that feeds the foundation of local democracy (Abernathy, 2018).

Traditional newspapers have been experiencing a readership drop since the second half of the 20th century, and many of them, especially the smaller and less structured ones that report local news, have struggled to make the transition to digital media and address revenue decline (Anderson, 2014; Anderson et al., 2012; Costa, 2014).

The emergence of new digital media has had a strong impact on the business models of regional media because their main source of revenue has begun to migrate to large digital platforms (Anderson, 2014). In 2020 in the United States, for example, advertising revenues for regional daily newspapers fell below circulation revenues for the first time in history (Matsa & Worden, 2022). Many companies, including those that want to reach local audiences, saw social media and other platforms, to the detriment of newspapers and native digital journalism outlets, as more effective means to reach their target (Hindman, 2015). Small newspapers, local radio and regional TV stations also face challenges due to their limited geographic range, which hinders the growth of their audience (Hindman, 2015). In addition, the services that local media traditionally provided for their communities, such as public service announcements, sports results and weather forecasts, are now offered on the platforms and websites of local organisations (Jerónimo & Sanchéz Esparza, 2023).

Because local news plays an essential role by promoting the democratic participation of citizens in proximity contexts (Jerónimo, Correia et al., 2022), 'building a sustainable digital revenue model also has wider societal implications' (Olsen & Solvoll, 2018, p. 174).

As platforms increasingly position themselves as intermediaries between audiences and the information they seek, regional media are now facing stronger competition with these entities, losing their centrality as news and information providers (Jerónimo & Esparza, 2023). Platforms have become key actors in the information ecosystem, prioritising low-quality content to the detriment of journalistic information that serves as a watchdog of local authorities (Bell et al., 2017).

On the local media side, business structures are not always professional, and newsrooms are generally made up of small teams with few journalists (Jerónimo, Correia et al., 2022). Local newspapers remain attached to a traditional production culture, often disregarding the potential that online journalism could give them. They are subject to frequent financial constraints, dependence on state support and the need to adapt to new formats despite paying low salaries (Jerónimo, 2015; Jerónimo, Correia et al., 2022). Moreover, some of those media outlets still rely, to a great extent, on revenues from print products (Jenkins & Nielsen, 2020). Despite this scenario, there are some signs of change. In some local newsrooms, the Covid-19 pandemic has induced the journalists to adopt a digital-first mindset (Jenkins & Jerónimo, 2021). On the other hand, recent studies show that regional journalists in Portugal believe that being present on digital platforms is essential for publishing and distributing content (Jerónimo, Correia et al., 2022).

Changing consumer habits have also impacted local newsrooms because audiences prefer to get their information on mobile devices like smartphones and do not want to pay for news (Quintanilha, 2018). In Portugal, only 11% of respondents to a survey conducted in 2023 said that they had paid for news in digital format in the previous year, compared to a global average of 17% (Cardoso et al., 2023), showing difficulties in identifying the purchase of access to news over the internet as a product to be paid for (Christofoletti, 2019).

As regards local media in Portugal, their audiences believe that the approach taken by journalists still needs to include more multimedia elements, consolidating a real transition to digital means with optimisation of the content produced (Morais et al., 2020). In a world marked by speed, the audiences also put pressure on journalists to publish information as quickly as possible, so that verifying content is very challenging in newsrooms with few journalists, as is the case of local newsrooms, which can lead to errors that calling journalistic authority into question (Morais & Jerónimo, 2023).

4. Researching From a European Perspective

In Portugal, Spain, United Kingdom, Croatia and Turkey, research has advanced to a geographical mapping of where there are local media and where there are not. The criteria used to do so have varied according to the national context, considering the media regulatory framework and information available (HND, 2023; Jerónimo, Ramos et al., 2022; Kızılkaya & Yılmaz, 2021; Mitchell et al., 2023; Negreira-Rey et al., 2023).

While in the Iberian Peninsula, the mapping was carried out within university-linked research centres, in the United Kingdom it was developed by the Public Interest News Foundation and in Croatia and Turkey, respectively, by the Croatian Journalists' Association and the Trade Union of Croatian Journalists and by a journalistic magazine that reports on the media, namely Journo.

At the European level, Verza et al. (2024) carried out, as part of the Local Media for Democracy research project, an extensive mapping of local and community media in Europe, identifying areas that can be considered news deserts and communities experiencing challenges in accessing diverse and good-quality information. The study evaluated the risks for local and community media on the basis of six indicators: granularity of the infrastructure of local media; market and reach; safety of local journalists; editorial independence; social inclusiveness and best practices and open public sphere.

The study also plotted a geographical map of local media in 13 European countries. It relied on previous research by country partners, highlighting areas in which news deserts are concentrated and outlining the 'diversity and heterogeneity of European countries in terms of geography, history, economy and governance structures' (Verza et al., 2024, p. 197). As in larger countries, e.g. France and Spain, areas with lower population density are vulnerable to news desertification, so in small countries such as Malta, Luxembourg and Cyprus local news almost overlaps with national news. While in Northern and Western European countries, public service media are more present, in Eastern European countries media markets tend to be more concentrated, in part due to the heritage of the Communist media system.

Other topics that do not include mapping have also been explored in the European context: news desertification at a content level in Switzerland (Vogler et al., 2023); the so-called 'zombie papers', which are published without a local staff, in Germany (Assmann, 2023) and the lack of skilled local journalists in Norway (Olsen & Mathisen, 2023).

Despite having a different focus, it is impossible not to highlight that the existence of local media – a theme that goes hand in hand with the idea of news deserts – has also been previously monitored in Sweden, Finland, Netherlands, Spain and Italy (Brogi et al., 2016; Negreira-Rey et al., 2018; mediestudier, 2015; SVDJ, 2021; Virranta, 2021).

5. Mapping News Deserts in Portugal

One of the first mappings carried out in Europe, the *News Deserts Europe 2022: Portugal Report* revealed that 25.3% of Portugal's municipalities did not have media outlets based in the municipality about which they produced content. Out of these 78 municipalities, 17.5% were in a 'total desert', that is, they did not have any media outlets, and about 8% were in a 'semi-desert', that is, they only had infrequent news or unsatisfactory news coverage (Jerónimo, Ramos et al., 2022). The phenomenon of news deserts is linked to more isolated communities, with lower economic activity and smaller populations, and it is more prevalent in the regions of Trás-os-Montes, Alentejo and Centre (Jerónimo, Ramos et al., 2022).

In Portugal, a first study of news deserts was carried out by Ramos (2021); and in 2022, a comprehensive mapping of news deserts was carried out in the country to determine in which municipalities there were no media outlets (Jerónimo, Ramos et al., 2022). This mapping, developed as part of the MediaTrust.Lab – Local Media Lab for Civic Trust and Literacy project, carried out at the University of Beira Interior, was based on an ERC (the Portuguese media regulation entity) database of May 31, 2022.

In terms of publications, both print and digital, the following were considered: only publications classified as regional/local; those not owned by public organisations; only those with journalistic content, excluding doctrinal publications, scientific journals and magazines from trade associations and tourism promotion organisations. In terms of radio broadcasters, only local generalist radio stations were considered, excluding exclusively musical or doctrinal operators, transmitters of national or non-regionalised content and specialised radio stations (e.g. sports radio stations).

The study evaluated the presence or absence of media and the frequency of broadcasting. It did not evaluate the characteristics of the news broadcast in the media. For print media, satisfactory news coverage was considered to be the existence of dailies, weeklies and fortnightlies; for the digital media, media with daily or at most weekly updates. Digital media without updates for more than 90 days were discarded. For radio broadcasters, radio stations with professional journalists located in the municipality for which they were licenced (or in a neighbouring municipality) and local news were considered to have satisfactory news coverage.

Jerónimo, Ramos et al. (2022) defined a 'news desert' as a Portuguese municipality without news outlets and a news 'semi-desert' as a Portuguese municipality with less frequent or unsatisfactory news coverage. The other category that arouses some alarm regarding news coverage was 'threatened', which is a Portuguese municipality with a single medium that produces local news. Municipalities with two or more media producing local news were considered to be 'outside the desert'.

According to the findings of Jerónimo et al., in 2022 about half of the Portuguese municipalities presented some degree of risk regarding local news coverage, ranging from the lowest ('threatened') to the highest ('desert'), passing through intermediate situations ('semi-desert'). This means that over half (53.9% or 166) of the 308 municipalities in Portugal already were or were on the verge of becoming news deserts. About 17.5% of them, 54 municipalities, were considered news deserts because they did not have any media outlet, while another 7.8% (24) were considered semi-deserts because, although there were media outlets based in the area, they were not satisfactorily producing local news – because there were no journalists in the municipality and the local coverage was conducted at a distance or because local news reports were released less frequently than fortnightly. There were also 88 municipalities (28.6%) at risk of entering the desert because they had only one medium with regular news production (Jerónimo, Ramos et al., 2022).

According to Jerónimo, Ramos et al. (2022), the North, Centre and Alentejo regions, particularly the parts of those regions that are in the interior of the country, concentrate more than 80% of news deserts and semi-deserts in Portugal. The districts of Beja, Bragança, Évora, Portalegre and Vila Real are those with the largest share of municipalities considered news deserts.

Bragança, a district in the north-east of the country, on the border with Spain, has over half of the municipalities (58.3%) in news deserts or semi-deserts. Portalegre, a district in the Alentejo region that also borders on Spain, has 60% of its municipalities in some kind of news desert. Vila Real, in the North region, has half of its municipalities in the same situation. Évora, in the Alentejo region, has 4 out of 14 municipalities (28.6%) in news deserts and 7 threatened; and Beja, the only district that extends to the coast, in the South of Portugal, has 5 out of 14 municipalities (35.7%) in news deserts and 6 threatened ones.

6. The Role of Platforms as Information Sources in News Deserts

As we mapped the areas, many questions arose. How do citizens living in communities considered news desert find out about what is happening where they live?

Some scholars have begun to address these questions, notably in the United States, the United Kingdom and Brazil. In the absence of media, information finds a way to circulate in other forms (Deolindo, 2013). When there are no journalists in the municipality, much of the local information in these areas is reached through social media platforms, such as Facebook pages and groups (Barclay et al., 2022; Collier & Graham, 2022; Deolindo, 2013; Duarte, 2023; Furlanetto & Baccin, 2020; Furlanetto & Baccin, 2021; Javorski & Bargas, 2020; Smethers et al., 2021), but also through alternative solutions such as community and student initiatives (Ferrucci & Alaimo, 2020; Finneman et al., 2022; Javorski & Bargas, 2020).

In the United States, researchers have found that people in news deserts still gain access to news but not in the traditional, journalistic manner. The research study by Collier and Graham (2022) found that people in news deserts in the United States resort to Facebook pages and groups for local information and that these pages provide content that helps people build their communities, with shared misinformation being almost irrelevant.

Non-traditional sources of news include local Facebook pages, chambers of commerce, community bulletin boards, email blasts, and word of mouth. In Collier and Graham's study, respondents who agreed that their community was a news desert attributed this to its small population or rural location, often referring to the idea that nothing happens in such places. Although they obtained a lot of information through social media, and some respondents said that it is impossible not to see what is happening locally on such platforms, others stated that they did not get a lot of information about their local communities, only some information on specific topics (Collier & Graham, 2022).

Social media were the most widely used source of local information, accessed daily by most of the study's participants. As regards the content that people in news deserts consume on Facebook pages, Collier and Graham's study examined 3,010 Facebook posts shared by local pages. It concluded that they share information that is critical to local communities, engaging less in self-promotion and more in encouraging community members to take actions that benefit society, with misinformation making up a small proportion of the posts (Collier & Graham, 2022).

When a newspaper closes, leaving a news void in an area, the local community organizes to transmit information to the outside, but it does not reach everyone as journalistic news did. Smethers et al. (2021) observed in a case study that when a traditional newspaper closes, community leaders resort to creating individual social media networks to disseminate information specific to some organisations.

In the case of Baldwin City, organisation-specific listservs, Facebook pages, Twitter feeds, newsletters, websites and city hall became sources of news, much of it based on social media platforms, which can foster community fragmentation (Smethers et al., 2021). As a result, people rarely know what is happening outside their peer communication networks. The community's newspaper, The Baldwin City Signal, was seen as a community institution that affected not only the social fabric of the community's citizens but also the local economy as it was 'essentially a one-stop directory of important community services and professional businesses for older professionals looking to move to Baldwin City' (Smethers et al., 2021, p. 393).

In the United Kingdom, the local reality is no different. Through 72 interviews and 8 focus groups in news deserts, Barclay et al. (2022) found that social media platforms were the dominant sources for local news and information systems, not only for peer-to-peer communication but also for accessing regional news websites. Facebook pages and groups were by far the most important for local news and information.

Individuals obtained information from the pages of local institutions, including local government, local police and local businesses. Groups, in turn, provided information ranging from job postings to crime reports and links to news websites. Group administrators boasted about their speed of publication, but they admitted that this agility meant they did not check information before posting (Barclay et al., 2022). Individuals did not typically access regional news websites directly but reached them through social media posts when other peers shared such content.

The issue has also been studied in Brazil. Furlanetto and Baccin conducted two studies in four cities in different states of the Southern Region, two in Rio Grande do Sul (Furlanetto & Baccin, 2020) and two in Paraná (Furlanetto & Baccin, 2021). They concluded that there was a role for community radio in the country's news deserts, but that social media platforms also played a very important role in disseminating information in those areas.

In the first study, Furlanetto and Baccin (2020) looked at the cities of Bossoroca and São Miguel das Missões, in the state of Rio Grande do Sul, and found that both had initiatives to address the lack of local news, either through a blog or a community radio with a website. However, after analysing the content published and broadcast by these media, the authors concluded that the existing coverage was still unsatisfactory for the context of the two cities, with a strong dependence on the production of the City Hall Press Office and very little original content. Local issues and the local development of national issues were not well covered (Furlanetto & Baccin, 2020).

Facebook groups and pages were also very important sources of information in those contexts. Group members shared advertisements, live broadcasts on social media and products for sale among members, and they promoted local businesses and events, but they did not produce or share news or information about the city (Furlanetto & Baccin, 2020).

In the cities of Pato Bragado and Francisco Alves, in the state of Paraná, Furlanetto and Baccin (2021) used questionnaires that showed that people in news deserts are interested in news about their cities, and in the absence of local journalistic coverage, they turn mainly to digital social media, such as Facebook pages and groups, and WhatsApp groups, which may limit their perception of what is happening in their localities.

Despite the lack of professional news outlets in the cities considered, Furlanetto and Baccin found that community radio stations, portals run by bloggers or amateurs, digital social media groups and local municipal administrations were news sources that residents turned to when they wanted to be informed about local affairs. It was also common to consult the official portals of municipal administrations, which cannot be classified as news sources. The majority of respondents said they felt well informed, but those who felt they were not well informed were aware that the news they received about their local reality was not enough and lacked depth (Furlanetto & Baccin, 2021).

Also in Brazil, but in the northern region, Javorski and Bargas (2020) studied the case of Rondon do Pará, where there are no news outlets, no locally produced journalistic content, and no journalists working in the area. Again, according to this study, the information sources of the city's inhabitants were digital media platforms, with social media platforms such as Facebook and Instagram and messaging apps such as WhatsApp standing out.

The content that circulated among citizens was mostly not original, did not offer a local approach and followed the trend of disinformation, as information of questionable quality ended up by fulfiling the role of journalism (Javorski & Bargas, 2020). Individuals read the headlines but did not follow the links, they obtained information at a superficial level without different points of view and they received information according to the logic of pre-existing social relations.

Again, in Brazil, Duarte (2023) studied the same dynamics in a city in the north-east, in the state of Bahia, called Andorinha. The study pointed out that, although Andorinha is considered a news desert, there are some media products in the municipality that circulate on social media platforms such as YouTube and Instagram, produced by influencers who assume the role of local communicators. They base their communication heavily on interacting with the audience through comments and question boxes about life, and they share information on local issues such as politics, crime and social problems, as well as national issues.

In WhatsApp groups, individuals share local information about, for instance, car accidents and animal vaccination campaigns, local business promotions, news produced by the national media, information about politics in the country, state and city and also information based on manipulated images, audio and fake, deceptive text, which is sometimes challenged by group members (Duarte, 2023). Word of mouth and cars with loudspeakers are also very traditional sources of information in the area.

A survey reported by Duarte's study found that the inhabitants of the city of Andorinha missed having a local radio station to obtain information since the municipality includes rural areas that do not have access to the Internet, and it is customary to listen to radio broadcasts from neighbouring cities (Duarte, 2023).

7. The Threat of Disinformation in Local Contexts

The question of how people obtain local, trustworthy information where there are no news outlets was raised during the Covid-19 pandemic when the presence of media outlets regained a certain centrality because receiving unqualified and unreliable information could mean a death sentence, given that it was essential to maintain basic health conditions (Javorski & Bargas, 2020).

Even in an era where digital devices are omnipresent, news deserts persist. They are linked to the phenomenon of disinformation because the lack of reliable information, the fragmentation of news and the circulation of unverified information on social media platforms can be a source of disinformation and manipulation (Ardia et al., 2020; Javorski & Bargas, 2020; Smethers et al., 2021).

Communities feel there's a big gap when something happens, and there is no media or no one to explain what is going on. In addition, the use of social media can exacerbate social division and polarisation, and 'Facebook rumours' can add to this dysfunction. Because there is no trusted information source to consult, fact-check and confirm information reported on social media, it can cause fear, anxiety or anger in those who consume it (Barclay et al., 2022). This debate could be better balanced if the public sphere was shared with journalistic information (Abernathy, 2022; Torre & Jerónimo, 2023).

This brings us to another dimension of the phenomenon: if informal information is to be understood and given the status of news by virtue of its being the only source of local information, citizens must have the skills and tools with which to determine its veracity (Javorski & Bargas, 2020). The good use of social media platforms by citizens to fill the information void they face in news deserts depends on their technical skills and prior use of such platforms to properly navigate these information ecosystems (Smethers et al., 2021).

Disinformation has great potential to damage democracy, especially at the local level. The role of regional media in countering disinformation in proximity contexts is also crucial, and this endeavour can include fact-checking routines and in-depth reporting. But responses to this issue can also emerge from the local public sphere, particularly in a collaborative relationship between journalists and other active members of the community (Jerónimo & Esparza, 2022; Torre & Jerónimo, 2023).

8. Paths Ahead and Solutions

Two main solutions to meet citizens' need for trustworthy information emerge from the literature review: the first concerns the community, which should produce its own news; the second concerns universities, which should organise graduate courses developing local media labs in news deserts.

Community journalism is the result of a collective mobilisation of citizens organised in polyphonic structures based on proximity ties, following a logic of the common good despite a lack of journalistic skills or training (Paiva, 2018). As found by studies, especially in Brazil, there are some types of community media that emerge in such areas, usually in the form of radio stations (Furlanetto & Baccin, 2020, 2021).

However, in the two studies carried out (Furlanetto & Baccin, 2020, 2021), the researchers noted that the production of original content was very limited and that such media mostly reproduced information about the region or the country, with a reduced part of the content focused on local affairs.

There are, however, some interesting experiences reported in the literature: for instance, the case of the Sopris Sun newspaper, investigated by Ferrucci and Alaimo (2020). This is published in the small town of Carbondale, in Colorado, United States, where the former local news provider, *The Valley Journal*, was permanently shut down in 2008.

The *Sopris Sun* is a weekly community newspaper produced by a nonprofit organisation, with one full-time editor and six part-time staff members and a board of directors that comprises Carbondale community members. It uses an open-system approach to journalism, embracing the influence of community stakeholders and engaging them in the news process, giving different outside institutions access to (but not control over) agenda building and story construction while maintaining editorial control and journalistic autonomy (Ferrucci & Alaimo, 2020). The relationship among journalists, audience, donors and advertisers is cultivated not only through social media but also happy hour events with an editor and a weekly radio show that make the readers feel like an important part of news production. On the other hand, journalists see boundaries get blurrier.

In addition, some university journalism initiatives have taken place in news deserts, such as in Brazil and the United States.

In the United States, Finneman et al. (2022) reported on news organisations created at three US universities: the *Triangle Tribune* and *Scope*, which provide news coverage to communities of colour in the Pittsburgh and Boston metropolitan areas and *The Eudora Times*, which covers Eudora, a rural community in Kansas that lost its newspaper in 2009. The study explored the experiences of the students involved in these startups (Finneman et al., 2022). While these outlets are shaped by the interests of the communities that develop their journalistic roles within the newsrooms, the students embrace the altruistic role of journalism, with content rooted in service roles, leaving the watchdog role on the sidelines.

In addition, Finneman et al. (2022) highlighted some of the challenges that arise when student journalists cover news desert communities: the relationship between the university-run local news project and the community, which affects trust building; the difficulty of obtaining funding to run a newsroom, which the journalism school must be able to uphold; ensuring faculty oversight and the involvement of professors and supervisors and maintaining a steady flow of content during university breaks.

It is important to highlight that the concept of the first two startups challenges the idea of news deserts tied to geographical space, which adds to the debate about new framings that can be attributed to this concept, broadening its range. Finneman et al.'s study (2022) suggests that 'conceptualizations of news deserts should take into consideration not only geography but also demographics when considering the definition of a news desert while acknowledging the historical context of journalism's exclusion of underserved populations' (p. 350).

Javorski and Bargas (2020) also reported on a university initiative, the digital news portal *Rondon Notícias*, in the municipality of Rondon do Pará. The researchers argued that the site met journalistic quality indicators, including fact-checking and plurality, but served a community unaccustomed to qualified local news content, so that it was difficult for *Rondon Notícias* to penetrate the community and consolidate itself as a news reference.

The outlet was based on the premises of community journalism and constantly developed activities to attract an audience, but the student journalists found limited support in the community and encountered difficulties in getting closer to official and professional sources (Javorski & Bargas, 2020).

9. Final Considerations

The growing body of research on news deserts shows that it is indeed a powerful concept that is attracting the interest of both academic and non-academic audiences. But there is still much to explore within this topic because it is closely linked to the specific local contexts in which this phenomenon is situated, and it can be interpreted from different perspectives (Gulyas et al., 2023).

The concept of news deserts is still in its infancy and requires further refinement and exploration on several fronts. First, methodologically, there is an urgent need to establish robust frameworks within which to identify and study news deserts with greater precision. Second, the definition of news deserts needs refinement. While the term has traditionally been associated with geographical characteristics, socio-economic factors, including gender and racial inequalities, should be explored as they may influence the manifestation of news deserts in different ways.

What seems inescapable, however, is that social media platforms play a central role in the context of news deserts, facilitating citizens' access to information about their immediate environment. As found in contexts as diverse as Brazil, the United States and the United Kingdom, when there is no journalistic information circulating in an area, its residents rely heavily on information disseminated through social media platforms for their news consumption, both in open (Facebook pages and groups) and closed (WhatsApp groups) systems. However, future research needs to address the extent to which such consumption patterns differ from those in regions that are not news deserts and the extent to which regional journalistic outlets can still mobilise their audiences. It is also important to understand which platforms citizens use to obtain the information they value.

When citizens rely on social media posts for information, they often feel that they do not obtain all the information they could about their city, in all its diversity and depth. If there are no journalists, there is no-one to investigate local government or local issues, there is no depth, and no trusted, verified explanation of what is going on in the communities where they live, as Barclay et al. (2022) found.

The key point is that the spread of disinformation poses a significant threat in environments without robust journalistic content to counterbalance it. The conspicuous absence of journalism leaves a void in the dissemination of verified information and in the monitoring of current events. Ultimately, there is no-one to check what is happening and provide truly verified information, leaving communities without a reference point (Barclay et al., 2022; Javorski & Bargas, 2020; Smethers et al., 2021).

While community journalism and academic institutions have the potential to make a meaningful contribution to solving this problem, they are constrained by inherent limitations for which remedies are still lacking.

Research on news deserts holds promise not only for scholars of community journalism but also for policymakers seeking to strengthen democracy at the grassroots level. More research is needed to understand how news consumption practices vary among geographic regions, how residents are affected by disinformation and how they build trust in the information they encounter. Further research on this topic can underpin public policies that can help redress inequalities in news provision and foster the conditions for exercising genuine citizenship.

Funding

The authors acknowledge Fundação para a Ciência e a Tecnologia (FCT): for the funding of MediaTrust.Lab (http://doi.org/10.54499/PTDC/COM-JOR/3866/2020), project whose scope gave rise to this study; the PhD scholarship of Luísa Torre (2023.05397.BD); the contract of Pedro Jerónimo (https://doi.org/10.54499/CEECINST/00016/2021/CP2828/CT0004); and LabCom (http://doi.org/10.54499/UIDB/00661/2020), the center where all authors do research.

References

Abernathy, P. M. (2016). *The rise of a new media baron and the emerging threat of news deserts*. University of North Carolina Chapel Hill: Center for Innovation and Sustainability in Local Media.

Abernathy, P. M. (2018). *The expanding news desert*. University of North Carolina: Center for Innovation and Sustainability in Local Media.

Abernathy, P. M. (2022). *The state of local news: The 2022 Report*. Northwestern Medill School Local News Initiative. https://localnewsinitiative.northwestern.edu/research/state-of-local-news/report/

Abernathy, P. M. (2023). News deserts: A research agenda for addressing disparities in the United States. *Media and Communication, 11*(3). https://doi.org/10.17645/mac.v11i3.6728

Anderson, C. W. (2014). Jornalismo Pós-industrial – Crises Permanentes, Turbulências Constantes (Interviewed by Andriolli Costa). *IHU On-Line - Revista Do Instituto Humanitas Unisinos, 14*(447), 8–10.

Anderson, C. W., Bell, E., & Shirky, C. (2012). *Post-industrial journalism: Adapting to the present: A report*. Columbia Journalism School.

Ardia, D., Ringel, E., Ekstrand, V. S., & Fox, A. (2020). *Addressing the decline of local news, rise of platforms, and spread of mis-and disinformation online: A summary of current research and policy proposals*. UNC Center for Media Law and Policy.

Assmann, K. (2023). Rise of the zombie papers: Infecting Germany's local and regional public media ecosystem. *Media and Communication, 11*(3), 360–370. https://doi.org/10.17645/mac.v11i3.6816

Atlas da Notícia. (2017). Atlas da Notícia - Desertos de Notícias: um panorama do jornalismo local e regional do Brasil. *Projor/Observatório da Imprensa/VOLT*. https://bit.ly/3wqSCX1

Barclay, S., Barnett, S., Moore, M., & Townend, J. (2022). *Local news deserts in the UK what effect is the decline in provision of local news and information having on communities?* The Charitable Journalism Project.

Bell, E., Owen, T., Brown, P., Hauka, C., & Rashidian, N. (2017). *La prensa de las plataformas. Cómo Silicon Valley reestructuró el periodismo*. Columbia University. https://doi.org/10.7916/D8B86MN4

Bisiani, S., & Heravi, B. (2023). Uncovering the state of local news databases in the UK: Limitations and impacts on research. *Journalism and Media, 4*(4), 1211–1231. https://doi.org/10.3390/journalmedia4040077

Blagojev, T., Borges, D., Brogi, E., Kermer, J., Trevisan, M., & Verza, S. (2023). *News deserts in Europe: Assessing risks for local and community media in the 27 EU member states preliminary report – Literature review and methodology*. Local Media for Democracy.

Brogi, E., van Eijk, N., Ó Fathaigh, R., Furnémont, J.-F., Gerber, O., Iacino, G., Janssen, M., Kevin, D., McGonagle, T., Ostling, A., Pellicanò, F., Selier, B., & Valais, S. (2016). *Regional and local broadcasting in Europe*. European Audiovisual Observatory, IRIS Special.

Cardoso, G., Paisana, M., & Pinto-Martinho, A. (2023). *Digital news report Portugal 2023*. Obercom.

Christofoletti, R. (2019). *A crise no jornalismo tem solução?* Estação das Letras e Cores.

Collier, J. R., & Graham, E. (2022). *Even in "News Deserts" people still get news*. Center for Media Engagement.

Costa, C. T. (2014). Um modelo de negócio para o jornalismo digital. *Revista de Jornalismo ESPM*, 9(9), 51.

Deolindo, J. (2013). Fronteiras jornalísticas: do silêncio à alteridade. In *XXXVI Congresso Brasileiro de Ciências Da Comunicação* (pp. 1–12). Intercom.

Duarte, L. da S. (2023). O que circula em um deserto de notícias: um estudo de caso em Andorinha-BA. *Revista Discente Planície Científica*, 5(2), 38–53.

European Commission. (2022, June 22). Supporting local and regional news media in face of emerging news deserts. https://digital-strategy.ec.europa.eu/en/funding/supporting-local-and-regional-news-media-face-emerging-news-deserts

Ferrier, M., Sinha, G., & Outrich, M. (2016). Media deserts: Monitoring the changing media ecosystem. In M. Lloyd & L. Friedland (Eds.), *The communication crisis in America, and how to fix it*. Palgrave Macmillan. https://doi.org/10.1057/978-1-349-94925-0_14

Ferrucci, P., & Alaimo, K. I. (2020). Escaping the news desert: Nonprofit news and open-system journalism organizations. *Journalism*, 21(4), 489–506. https://doi.org/10.1177/1464884919886437

Finneman, T., Heckman, M., & E. Walck, P. (2022). Reimagining journalistic roles: How student journalists are taking on the U.S. news desert crisis. *Journalism Studies*, 23(3), 338–355. https://doi.org/10.1080/1461670X.2021.2023323

Furlanetto, A. C., & Baccin, A. (2020). A produção noticiosa nos desertos de notícias: uma análise de duas cidades interioranas do RS. *Encontro Nacional de Jovens Pesquisadores Em Jornalismo (JPJOR)*, 10, 1–17.

Furlanetto, A. C. R., & Baccin, A. N. (2021). Desertos de notícia e fontes de informação em duas cidades do interior do Paraná. *Encontro de Jovens Pesquisadores Em Jornalismo (JPJOR)*, 11, 141855.

Gulyas, A. (2021). Local news deserts. In D. Harte & R. Matthews (Eds.), *Reappraising local and community news in the UK: Media, practice, and policy* (p. 13). Taylor & Francis.

Gulyas, A., Jenkins, J., & Bergström, A. (2023). Places and spaces without news: The contested phenomenon of news deserts. *Media and Communication*, 11(3), 285–289. https://doi.org/10.17645/mac.v11i3.7612

Hindman, M. (2015). Stickier news: What newspapers don't know about web traffic has hurt them badly - But there is a better way. *Shorenstein center on media, politics and public policy - Discussion paper series*. (Issue April). https://shorensteincenter.org/wp-content/uploads/2015/04/Stickier-News-Matthew-Hindman.pdf

HND [Hrvatsko novinarsko društvo]. (2023, April 12). Hrvatsko Novinstvo u "Medijskoj Pustinji". https://www.hnd.hr/hrvatsko-novinstvo-u-medijskoj-pustinji

Javorski, E., & Bargas, J. (2020). A informação sobre a Covid-19 nos desertos de notícias: a relevância do jornalismo interior do Pará. *Liinc Em Revista, 16*(2), e5339. https://doi.org/10.18617/liinc.v16i2.5339

Jenkins, J., & Jerónimo, P. (2021). Changing the beat? Local online newsmaking in Finland, France, Germany, Portugal, and the U.K. *Journalism Practice, 15*(9), 1222–1239. https://doi.org/10.1080/17512786.2021.1913626

Jenkins, J., & Nielsen, R. K. (2020). Preservation and evolution: Local newspapers as ambidextrous organizations. *Journalism, 21*(4), 472–488. https://doi.org/10.1177/1464884919886421

Jerónimo, P. (2015). *Ciberjornalismo de proximidade*. Editora LabCom.IFP.

Jerónimo, P., Correia, J. C., & Gradim, A. (2022a). Are we close enough? Digital challenges to local journalists. *Journalism Practice, 16*(5), 813–827. https://doi.org/10.1080/17512786.2020.1818607

Jerónimo, P., & Esparza, M. S. (2022). Disinformation at a local level: An emerging discussion. *Publications, 10*(2), 15. https://doi.org/10.3390/publications10020015

Jerónimo, P., & Esparza, M. S. (2023). Jornalistas Locais e Fact-Checking: Um Estudo Exploratório em Portugal e Espanha. *Comunicação e Sociedade, 44*, e023016. https://doi.org/10.17231/comsoc.44(2023).4553

Jerónimo, P., Ramos, G., & Torre, L. (2022b). *News deserts Europe 2022: Portugal report*. MediaTrust.Lab/LabCom.

Kızılkaya, E., & Yılmaz, E. (2021). Türkiye'nin haber çölleri: 973 ilçeden 1.1 milyon haberi taradık, 3 haritayla anlatıyoruz. *Journo*. https://journo.com.tr/haber-colleri

Matsa, K. E., & Worden, K. (2022, May 26). *Local newspapers fact sheet*. Pew Research Center. https://www.pewresearch.org/journalism/fact-sheet/local-newspapers/

mediestudier. (2015). Så många redaktioner har försvunnit i Sverige. https://kommundatabas.mediestudier.se/

Mitchell, J., Roche, M., & Milburn-curtis, C. (2023). *Deserts, oases and drylands: Mapping the UK's local news outlets*. Public Interest News Foundation.

Morais, R., & Jerónimo, P. (2023). Platformization of News", authorship, and unverified content: Perceptions around local media. *Social Sciences, 12*(4). https://doi.org/10.3390/socsci12040200

Morais, R., Jerónimo, P., & Correia, J. C. (2020). *Jornalismo na Região Centro: Trabalho, Tecnologia e Negócio*. Editora Labcom.

Mota, D. (2023). The erosion of proximity: Issues and challenges for local journalism in contemporary society. *Comunicação e Sociedade, 44*, 1–19. https://doi.org/10.17231/comsoc.44(2023).4744

Negreira-Rey, M.-C., López-García, X., & Rodríguez-Vázquez, A.-I. (2018). Los cibermedios locales e hiperlocales en España y Portugal. La fase de búsqueda de modelos. *Sur Le Journalisme, About Journalism, Sobre Jornalismo, 7*(2), 50–63. https://revue.surlejournalisme.com/slj/article/view/358

Negreira-Rey, M.-C., Vázquez-Herrero, J., & López-García, X. (2023). No people, no news: News deserts and areas at risk in Spain. *Media and Communication, 11*(3). https://doi.org/10.17645/mac.v11i3.6727

Olsen, R. K., & Mathisen, B. R. (2023). Deserted local news: Exploring news deserts from a journalistic recruitment perspective. *Media and Communication*, *11*(3). https://doi.org/10.17645/mac.v11i3.6738

Olsen, R. K., & Solvoll, M. K. (2018). Bouncing off the paywall–understanding misalignments between local newspaper value propositions and audience responses. *JMM International Journal on Media Management*, *20*(3), 174–192. https://doi.org/10.1080/14241277.2018.1529672

Paiva, R. (2018). Para Reinterpretar a Comunicação Comunitária. In R. Paiva (Ed.), *O Retorno da Comunidade: Os Novos Caminhos do Social* (pp. 133–148). Mauad X.

Quintanilha, T. L. (2018). 2029 - o fim dos jornais em papel em Portugal? Um estudo longitudinal sobre os principais indicadores de desempenho no sector da imprensa escrita tradicional portuguesa. *Observatorio (OBS*)*, *12*(3). https://doi.org/10.15847/obsOBS12320181318

Ramos, G. (2021). Deserto de Notícias: panorama da crise do jornalismo regional em Portugal. *Estudos de Jornalismo*, *13*, 30–31.

Smethers, J. S., Mwangi, S. C., & Bressers, B. (2021). Signal interruption in Baldwin City: Filling a communication vacuum in a small town "news desert". *Newspaper Research Journal*, *42*(3), 379–396. https://doi.org/10.1177/07395329211030687

SVDJ. (2021). Aantal lokale nieuwssites bijna verdubbeld: elke gemeente in Nederland telt minstens één hyperlocal. https://www.svdj.nl/nieuws/aantal-lokale-nieuwssites-bijna-verdubbeld-elke-gemeente-in-nederland-telt-minstens-een-hyperlocal/

Torre, L., & Jerónimo, P. (2023). Esfera pública e desinformação em contexto local. *Texto Livre*, *16*, 1–14. https://doi.org/10.1590/1983-3652.2023.41881

Verza, S., Blagojev, T., Borges, D., Kermer, J. E., Trevisan, M., & Reviglio, U. (2024). *Uncovering news deserts in Europe: Risks and opportunities for local and community media in the EU*. Centre for Media Pluralism and Media Freedom, European University Institute.

Virranta, R. (2021). Onko Suomessa uutiserämaata? *Suomen Lehdistö*. https://suomenlehdisto.fi/onko-suomessa-uutiseramaata/

Vogler, D., Weston, M., & Udris, L. (2023). Investigating news deserts on the content level: Geographical diversity in Swiss news media. *Media and Communication*, *11*(3), 343–354. https://doi.org/10.17645/MAC.V11I3.6794

Chapter 6

TikTokisation of the News: News Media Content Production Strategies in Portugal

Antonio Martella[a] *and Pedro Jerónimo*[b]

[a]University of Turin, Italy
[b]University of Beira Interior, Portugal

Abstract

The platformisation of journalism has compelled news media to adapt to network media logic, affecting journalistic practices and norms. Several challenges emerged for media outlets, including competition for attention, news avoidance and the dominance of social media as primary news sources. Among platforms, TikTok represents an opportunity for news media to engage with new audiences, particularly those who tend to avoid traditional news sources. TikTok's algorithm assesses content virality based on factors like sound, hashtags and content itself, prompting media outlets to develop new strategies to compete in this space.

Our study focuses on Portuguese media, which received limited attention despite TikTok's rapid adoption rate growth, rising from 13% in 2020 to 45% in 2023.

We analysed the last 58 TikTok posts of the most popular Portuguese media according to the Digital News report 2023 starting from 1 September 2023, identifying various elements, such as music, hashtags, featured subjects, topic, etc. To uncover newsroom strategies, we applied multiple correspondence analysis and hierarchical clustering on principal components to identify post clusters. These strategies have been then be correlated with the number of views to determine their effectiveness in engaging audiences.

Keywords: TikTok; journalism; media; social media; platformisation; news production strategies

1. Platformisation of Journalism

The platformisation of journalism (van Dijck et al., 2018) has compelled news media to adapt to network media logic (Klinger & Svensson, 2015), thereby affecting journalistic practices and norms (Hermida & Mellado, 2020).

Although there are differences due to countries' and audiences' particular characteristics (Nielsen & Fletcher, 2023), platformisation has reinforced (or introduced) several challenges for media outlets, including heightened competition for attention, increased news avoidance and the rise of social media as primary news sources (Freelon & Wells, 2020; Newman et al., 2023).

First, platforms are high-choice media environments in which very different contents and producers vie for users' attention and time in an exacerbated competition (Freelon & Wells, 2020). These environments not only contribute to the further fragmentation of audiences but also foster information avoidance, even among individuals who have no particular aversion to news (Skovsgaard & Andersen, 2020). Indeed, 'when it comes to news, audiences say they pay more attention to celebrities, influencers, and social media personalities than journalists in networks like TikTok, Instagram, and Snapchat' (Newman et al., 2023, p. 10). Moreover, especially, younger people prefer entertainment-oriented news (Geers, 2020) or at least news presented in an entertaining format (Costera Meijer, 2007).

Algorithms play a central role in the platformisation of information and in the case of content distribution through recommendation systems. Indeed, while the goal of platforms is to show content that is relevant to the audiences to which it is offered, those who produce the news also seek to provide specific content to the most promising audiences (Hagar & Diakopoulos, 2023). However, this intersection of aims can easily contribute to unintentional news avoidance because potential publics are not reached.

For many years, social media have become increasingly important in accessing news – often being the primary source of it – and not only for younger audiences, complicating the attempt by media outlets to engage audiences (Newman et al., 2023). Moreover, the integration of social media with mobile technologies introduces new constraints and production strategies for media organisations, which must adapt their content and formats to align with platform affordances (Hill & Bradshaw, 2018).

In this context, the above-mentioned algorithmic intervention for content distribution poses further challenges for news media. On the one hand, media have to produce content according to algorithmic curation practices in order to intercept niche-audiences' newsfeeds across various platforms (Caplan & boyd, 2018). On the other hand, the gatekeeping function performed by the interaction between algorithms and audience preferences produces a highly unbalanced power relationship between platforms and media outlets that are increasingly dependent on the former for content distribution and reaching audiences (Ekström & Westlund, 2019). Not by chance, changes in social media algorithms have given rise to significant issues in the visibility of content, especially for legacy media (Tandoc & Maitra, 2018). Consequently, the agency of newsrooms is increasingly limited: editorial teams can choose or modify organisational and production methods according to their own historical, cultural and economic context (Christin, 2020), but they have to adapt to the standards prevailing in the platform market.

In other words, platforms, and especially social media, are changing journalistic practices, blurring the boundaries between news and entertainment and forcing the adoption of different strategies according to platforms' dynamics and affordances (Vázquez-Herrero, Negreira-Rey, & Zago, 2022).

2. News Media and TikTok

TikTok is a short video app that is the fourth ranking social media platform in terms of monthly users worldwide (1 billion), 60% of whom are women.[1] Moreover, it reaches 44% of young people (aged 18–24) globally and 20% for news (Newman et al., 2023). Therefore, it represents an opportunity for news media to reach those audience segments most affected by news avoidance (Newman et al., 2023). Indeed, the engagement of new and younger audiences is a fundamental goal for media and journalists (Vázquez-Herrero, Negreira-Rey & López-García, 2021), who are currently seeking new strategies with which to adapt to the new opportunities and dynamics of TikTok (Klug & Autenrieth, 2022; Vázquez-Herrero, Negreira-Rey & López-García, 2021).

One of the main and most novel characteristics of TikTok is the For You Page, which provides a personalised feed of videos exclusively driven by algorithmic recommendations mainly based on three elements: users' preferences; content features (i.e. hashtags, sounds, etc.) and account details (i.e. language or country) (Hagar & Diakopoulos, 2023).

The first consequence is that TikTok algorithms apparently do not take into account the chronological order of the events and the date of publication of posts so that TikTok is a challenging environment for news chronicles and daily news (Negreira-Rey et al., 2022). Furthermore, unlike other social media, the flow of content on TikTok is completely disconnected from the network of followers/followings, leading to the irrelevance of online and offline popularity to content dissemination. All these characteristics seem to contribute to the development of increasingly diverse and fragmented audiences (Peña-Fernández et al., 2022), resulting in personal news feeds that are closely customised to individual preferences (Boccia Artieri et al., 2022).

Consequently, the curation of each content becomes more necessary than ever within TikTok (Martella & Cepernich, 2024), where authority is built almost from scratch through constant production that must contend with new formats, genres and actors that gain more relevance as they align more closely with

---

[1] https://www.searchlogistics.com/learn/statistics/tiktok-user-statistics/

algorithmically determined interests and audiences (García-Ortega & García-Avilés, 2023; Newman, 2022).

Thus, news producers need new strategies that fit the different logic and affordances of TikTok to gain visibility. They must take advantage of the algorithmic amplification inherent in the platform (Vázquez-Herrero, Negreira-Rey & López-García, 2021) but also overcome the apparent resistance of the algorithm to including news and information in users' feeds (Hagar & Diakopoulos, 2023).

Nevertheless, and differently from the beginning, TikTok content has become increasingly diverse, and it now includes educational, social and public health items, along with entertainment (Klug et al., 2021). Indeed, Zhu et al. (2019) found that TikTok was used to disseminate information about Covid-19 by institutional and media actors while other studies have highlighted that the platform is used for ground reporting and footage of protests and wars (Boccia Artieri et al., 2022; Cheng & Li, 2024).

Previous research on how news media approach TikTok has found that there are no precise strategies or recipes, but it has identified some general patterns. Chobanyan and Nikolskaya (2021) found that television often posts political content, sound bites and adapted formats (i.e. brief highlights and programme cuts). Other studies have underlined that informative content in media production is prevalent also on TikTok, followed by funny and humourous scenes, promotion and TikTok challenges (Vázquez-Herrero, Negreira-Rey & López-García, 2021). Klug and Autenrieth (2022) instead identified three distinct approaches employed by traditional news outlets on TikTok: first, repackaging existing news content with original audio; second, providing behind-the-scenes insights with news explanations and third, posting soft news accompanied by popular sounds and filters.

Regarding the online engagement on TikTok, some studies have found that shorter videos engage users more, along with dance and image slide shows (Li et al., 2021; Zhu et al., 2019). The same studies have highlighted that also the presence of human actors or specific subjects in videos, as well as experts or celebrities, can foster content virality.

Background music plays an important role in content diffusion. It does so for several reasons, including the peculiar origin of the platform related to lip-syncing and dancing (Boccia Artieri et al., 2022) and the searchability of soundtracks and their relation to challenges and trends spreading within the environment (Serrano et al., 2020).

Regarding technical elements, subtitles and captions foster content virality (Li et al., 2021) because they make videos easier to understand and watch also in public spaces (Mudra & Kitsa, 2022), sometimes emphasising specific speech moments (Alonso-López et al., 2021).

Finally, as on Twitter, hashtags can help content diffusion, especially when they address current events or soft news stories that could become trending topics on TikTok (Negreira-Rey et al., 2022).

3. Research Questions

Previous research on news media strategies within TikTok (Chobanyan & Nikolskaya, 2021; Klug & Autenrieth, 2022; Vázquez-Herrero et al., 2021; Vázquez-Herrero, Negreira-Rey & López-García, 2021) has rarely sought to identify strategies with statistical methods. Moreover, Portuguese media have received limited attention despite TikTok's rapid adoption-rate growth, rising from 13% in 2020 to 45% in 2023 (Newman et al., 2023). To the best of our knowledge, our study is the first attempts to identify statistically the production strategies adopted by main Portuguese media.

> *RQ1.* What content production strategies do Portuguese news media adopt on TikTok?

As already highlighted, TikTok's algorithm assesses content virality on the basis of factors like sound, hashtags and content, prompting media outlets to increasingly fit with the platform's affordances in order to gain content visibility (Vázquez-Herrero, Negreira-Rey & López-García, 2021).

> *RQ2.* What strategies prove most successful in engaging TikTok audiences across different media outlets?

4. Case Study

To answer the above research questions, we selected the most popular media (online) in Portugal (Newman et al., 2023): SIC Notícias, Jornal de Notícias, CNN Portugal, Observador, Expresso, Público, TVI News, Diário de Notícias, Rádio Comercial, RTP News and RFM online. We removed SAPO and MSN News from the original list provided in Newman et al. (2023) because they mainly serve as news aggregators. Moreover, Correio da Manhã has been inactive since 2020, and although Notícias ao Minuto is one of the most popular online news sources, we were unable to find its TikTok profile.

To be noted is that Portuguese media and journalists have developed a high degree of professionalism, moving away from the polarised pluralist model that characterised the country's media system until the 1970s (Hallin & Mancini, 2017). Indeed, Portugal 'remains one of the highest-ranking markets for trust in news [58%, overall trust], due to low political polarisation and a generalised sense of the press as free' (Newman et al., 2023, p. 93).

Regarding news consumption, about 81% of Portuguese citizens get news from social media.[2] TikTok is adopted by 26% of people, and the adoption rate is rising faster and more than those of the other social media (Newman et al., 2023).

---

[2] See https://journals.sagepub.com/doi/10.1177/02673231231189043#supplementary-materials

Table 6.1. Most Popular Media in Portugal - Reuters Digital News Report 2023.

Media	Type	Followers	Followings	n	First Post
SIC Notícias	TV	71,200	0	239	2021-11-08
Jornal de Notícias	Daily news	7,053	16	230	2023-02-10
CNN Portugal	TV	**136,000**	4	**670**	2021-11-22
Observador	Daily news	796	0	93	2020-04-23
Expresso	Weekly news	23,600	**38**	232	2022-09-29
Público	Daily news	8,793	1	151	2022-03-09
TVI news	TV	**394,200**	42	**770**	2023-01-03
Diário de Notícias	Weekly news	481	4	119	2022-11-16
Rádio comercial	Radio	**123,200**	19	139	**2016-12-09**
RTP news	TV	99,500	6	175	2020-10-12
RFM online	Radio	**135,700**	37	70	2020-12-01

Table 6.1 shows that the most followed accounts on TikTok are television and radio while daily and weekly news media are rather unpopular. As already highlighted by other studies (Klug & Autenrieth, 2022; Martella & Cepernich, 2024), also Portuguese media outlets do not follow others in social media.

Among the ones most followed, Rádio Comercial emerges as the platform's earliest adopter (2016) while others did not publish their first post until 2020. The last ones to adopt the platform were Jornal de Notícias and TVI News, both in 2023.

5. Methodology

We manually collected the last 54 posts starting from September 7, 2023 along with available data and metadata, gathering a total of 594 videos.

Three trained coders identified the presence/absence of a summary (on-screen news summary), subtitles, data/numbers, speaker identification, news media logos, hashtags related to the topic covered, hashtags related to media outlets (e.g. #TVI, #sicnoticias, etc.), journalists' names, images in the video, stickers, media fragments (TV programs, other media, etc.) and sounds (environment, voice and music).

To identify topics, we used a list of frequent themes on social media (Martella & Roncarolo, 2023).

Following Bracciale et al. (2018), we identified six main categories of actors in videos: (1) Politicians and institutions; (2) Journalists and media; (3) Sport and entertainment; (4) Citizens; (5) Civil society actors (associations, unions, professionals, etc.) and (6) Social media experts (spin doctors, social media managers, TikTok influencers, etc.).

Video duration was transformed into a categorical variable: >60s or ≤60s because a 60-second threshold represented the original limit of videos that could be published on TikTok.

Following previous studies (Martella & Cepernich, 2024), we also identified Journalistic genres/formats (Table 6.2) as well as reportage, investigation, news chronicle, etc. emerged from studies on journalism and TikTok (Ferrignolo, 2003; Moscato et al., 2023; Sorrentino, 2002; Steensen, 2018; Vázquez-Herrero, Negreira-Rey & López-García, 2021; Zhu et al., 2019).

Several training sessions made it possible to reach satisfying values (Hayes & Krippendorff, 2007) of intercoder reliability among the coders: Krippendorff's α ranged from 0.65 to 1.

We used multiple correspondence analysis (MCA) to summarise the variables identified in a limited number of dimensions. Then we applied hierarchical clustering (HCPC) on the first eight dimensions, representing 99% of the total variance re-evaluated (Benzecri, 1973), to identify clusters of videos that we interpreted as production strategies (Martella & Cepernich, 2024).

6. Production Strategies on TikTok

The hierarchical clustering on principal components (HCPC) enabled us to identify 13 consistent clusters of TikTok videos based on the variables identified. Despite some differences, it was possible to aggregate the production strategies into seven categories: Promotion, Entertainment, Interviews, Long stories, Short stories, Reports and Chronicles.

6.1 Promotion (89 Videos)

Promotion is an already-known practice by media on TikTok that often includes short excerpts from programs (Mudra & Kitsa, 2022; Peña-Fernández et al., 2022), previews and announcements (Vázquez-Herrero et al., 2021). Our results show that explicit promotion includes 89 videos (14%) and divides into two different categories: TV short clips and Short promotional clips.

TV short clips (44)

Here, promotion is represented by subtitled (89% of the cluster), short (82%), non-native videos from TV or other media (98%) focused on entertainment (95%). The main aim of these videos is to promote TV programs (87%) through the repurposing of programme fragments like Taskmaster, I Love Portugal, Dois às Dez and Goucha. Consequently, the actors featured are especially from entertainment (91%) or the media (86%).

Table 6.2. Journalistic Genres/Formats.

Genre/Format	Definition
Chronicle	Reporting of facts in chronological order. Reporting on what has happened and is about to happen or will happen.
Investigation	A report resulting from investigative activity conducted by journalists. In-depth reconstruction of a fact/event, with collection of evidence, testimonies, etc.
Reportage	A comprehensive account of a local reality, of a social phenomenon and of a historical process that aims at thematisation or in-depth analysis. Reportage therefore goes beyond mere reporting: it is a story linked to current events that seeks to highlight all aspects of a phenomenon and involves a journalistic presence in the field of study.
Interviews	Questions and answers. Between journalist and interviewee(s).
Summary or review	Summary of a fact in a few lines, e.g. small town news episodes or news summaries of the last 24 hours. Brief reviews of the most important daily news.
Commentary/editorial/excerpt	Commentary and opinions on facts expressed by the journalist, editor or a columnist.
Feature news	Narrative of an environment, an atmosphere, a mood related to an event or occasion or the simple discovery of a place or social environment. Descriptive topical article with vivid and colourful depictions of the environment/mood.
Biographies or commemorative articles	News focused on the life or death of significant people.
HowTo/Well explained	Thematic insights on facts that are not news: guides, recipes, horoscopes and 'well-explained' topics.
Humour & dance (from editorial team)	Funny content, silly situations and jokes and journalists' reactions to comic situations. People dancing in personal and professional spheres.

Table 6.2. *(Continued)*

Genre/Format	Definition
Promotion	Promotion of content or products. Editorial backstage, news announcement and brand promotion. Trailers of interviews.
TikTok challenge	TikTok challenges involving journalists or members of the editorial team.

Source: Martella and Cepernich (2024, p. 75).

This strategy is mainly adopted by RTP (75% of the cluster and 61% of its videos) and TVI (20% of the cluster).[3,4]

Short promotional clips (45)

There are two main differences with respect to TV short clips: first, some videos seem more aimed at promotion, resembling teasers. Second, programme fragments (Vázquez-Herrero, Negreira-Rey & López-García, 2021) appear less TikTokised. They lack subtitles and brand logos, and sometimes, the video format does not align with the platform's standards as already reported by other studies (Vázquez-Herrero et al., 2021).[5] Moreover, along with entertainment and gossip (63%), videos also address themes like culture and curiosity (18%). From a journalistic perspective, the main format adopted is promotion (69% of the posts).

This production strategy is mainly adopted by TVI (49% of the cluster and 61% of their videos).[6]

6.2 Entertainment (134)

Entertainment is the strategy most adopted by Portuguese media (22% of posts), and it includes Media/Newsroom fun and Radio entertainment clips. Some research studies focused on news media (Vázquez-Herrero, Negreira-Rey & López-García, 2021) have included newsrooms' backstage in promotion, considering that these videos are often made to promote a brand. We decided to identify Promotion as a specific format/genre (see Table 6.2), therefore distinguishing between videos aimed at explicit promotion and entertainment. Accordingly, we considered newsroom behind-the-scenes content as promotion, but we included scenes of humour and dancing by media members in entertainment, as in the case of Media/Newsroom fun.

---

[3] https://www.tiktok.com/rtppt/video/7226391692721540357
[4] https://www.tiktok.com/tvioficial/video/7275661544136920352
[5] https://www.tiktok.com/tvioficial/video/7270974767140785441
[6] https://www.tiktok.com/tvioficial/video/7270898452521831713

Media/Newsroom fun (41)

This strategy is mainly embodied (66% of the cluster) by videos reporting humourous scenes by media hosts and newsrooms (Negreira-Rey et al., 2022) complemented by music (90%). Consequently, the main actors in these videos are journalists and media workers (69%) or celebrities (51%). Unlike clips, these TikToks are not subtitled, and the brand is not explicitly placed on videos.

This strategy is mainly adopted by Rádio Comercial (46%) and TVI (24%).[7,8]

Radio entertainment clips (93)

Most videos in this strategy last more than 60s (75%), and the journalistic formats most adopted are interviews (47%), commentaries (11%) and newsroom/backstage scenes (12%).

The topic most addressed is entertainment (90%), and as to be expected, media hosts (88%) and celebrities (69%) are the main actors in videos.

Considering all these elements, the aim of this strategy is to propose fragments of programs adapted to TikTok (Vázquez-Herrero et al., 2021).

This strategy is mainly adopted by radio stations: RFM (37% of the cluster and 63% of its production) and Rádio Comercial (20%).[9,10] Considering the significant presence of radio in this cluster, our results confirm previous research indicating that radio stations and channels disseminate fragments of their programs on TikTok, covering various topics adopting different formats (Vázquez-Herrero et al., 2021).

6.3 Interviews (73 Videos)

Differently from what has been found by studies on other countries (Martella & Cepernich, 2024; Vázquez-Herrero, Negreira-Rey & López-García, 2021), interviews seem quite numerous and varied in the Portuguese 'TikToksphere'. Indeed, this classic journalistic genre is staged according to two strategies that differ mainly in terms of the themes addressed and the actors featured. Both strategies consist of videos that last longer than 60 seconds, with the brand logo and journalists featured in videos and in captions; and they often relate to podcast series broadcast by media outlets on TikTok.

Hard news interviews (45)

These interviews are mainly focused on Politics and Institutions (53%) and Economy and Welfare (31%). Consequently, political and institutional actors are the ones most featured in videos (76%).

Media that adopt this strategy the most are as follows: Diário de Notícias (44%), especially through the show 'Alta tensão' or 'Em alta voz', SIC Notícias

---

[7] https://www.tiktok.com/radiocomercial/video/7174465806003211526
[8] https://www.tiktok.com/tvioficial/video/7269452351935761697
[9] https://www.tiktok.com/rfmportugal/video/7272352685267979553
[10] https://www.tiktok.com/radiocomercial/video/7231985806922026266

(20%), through its video podcast 'Geração 70' and Expresso (20%), with its podcast 'Liberdade para Pensar'.[11-14]

Health interviews (28)
In this strategy, the majority of videos are subtitled (93%). They address health & healthcare (82%) featuring journalists (75%) and people from civil society (i.e. professionals, associations, etc. in 57% of the videos).
Expresso is the most involved in this strategy (75% of the cluster), and this is mainly due to its podcast devoted to mental health problems: 'Que Voz é Esta?'[15]

6.4 Long Stories (51)

This strategy is characterised by videos lasting longer than a minute (55%) that often include images (43%) and address various topics: Culture & Curiosity (31%), Economy & Welfare (14%) and Other (18%).
The most significant journalistic genres are 'How to/Well explained' (24%) and interviews (49%).
This strategy closely resembles that of explainer videos (Schneiders, 2020), already adopted by Italian newspapers on TikTok (Martella & Cepernich, 2024), in which journalists delve into specific issues using images and data.
Media outlets that adopt this strategy the most are Diário de Notícias (35%), Público (26%) and SIC Notícias (18%).[16-18]

6.5 Short Stories (49 Videos)

Differently from the findings of previous studies (Martella & Cepernich, 2024), the features that characterise 'Short Stories' in Portuguese TikTok split between two different strategies: explanation and summaries. Both strategies include short videos in which news stories are summarised through video captions (more than 95%) accompanied by images (from 68% to 89%). This category of strategies oscillated between explanation videos and scrollytelling (Schneiders, 2020), but it is adapted to platform affordances.

Short explanations (27)
This strategy is mainly characterised by the large presence of images (89%) and by the topics addressed: Politics and Institutions (41%), Health & Healthcare (22%), and Other (19%).

---

[11] https://www.tiktok.com/diario.de.noticias/video/7265255363501477153
[12] https://www.tiktok.com/diario.de.noticias/video/7236739604894797082
[13] https://www.tiktok.com/sicnoticiaspt/video/7265264696960290081
[14] https://www.tiktok.com/jornalexpresso/video/7259400412741111066
[15] https://www.tiktok.com/jornalexpresso/video/7245311072192711963
[16] https://www.tiktok.com/diario.de.noticias/video/7244828605023276314
[17] https://www.tiktok.com/publicopt/video/7254215412584434971
[18] https://www.tiktok.com/sicnoticiaspt/video/7272135024802106657

The most frequent format is the 'How to/Well explained' one (81%), thus resembling the explainer video described by Schneiders (2020), in which images, words, spoken language and data combine in narrative videos with a didactic purpose.

This strategy is constituted by videos from Observador (74%), especially through the series 'Isso é mesmo verdade?' and Público (22%).[19,20]

Data summaries (27)

Differently from Short explanations, all Data summaries condense the most important news stories of the day (100%) often featuring data and numbers (86%). This strategy is mainly constituted by video from Observador (90%).[21]

6.6 Reports (59 Videos)

The journalistic reports on the Portuguese TikTok are characterised by the strong presence of ordinary citizens on video (between 70% and 80%) and are divided according to two categories.

Feature reportage (43)

This production strategy consists of several elements that recall feature journalism (Steensen, 2018), ranging from the most significant format in the cluster, 'feature news' (58%), through the focus on entertainment, which includes sport, celebrities, etc. (58%), to short videos (84%) accompanied by music (63%) and featuring citizens (70%) and entertainment actors (51%).

There are no media outlets statically significant for this cluster. However, we found posts by Expresso, Jornal de Notícias and RFM online.[22–24]

Social issues reportage (16)

Unlike Feature reportage, videos included in this strategy are captioned (94%), last longer than one minute (75%) and often address civil rights (44%) but also social problems in a reportage-like format (56%). Along with citizens (81%), the actors most featured come from civil society (38%).

The media outlets most significant for this strategy are SIC Notícias (38%) and CNN Portugal (31%).[25,26]

---

[19]https://www.tiktok.com/observador_/video/6907245312922979585
[20]https://www.tiktok.com/publicopt/video/7249326437113613594
[21]https://www.tiktok.com/observador_/video/6841245584024800518
[22]https://www.tiktok.com/jornalexpresso/video/7255705060598893851
[23]https://www.tiktok.com/jornaldenoticias/video/7271008566302035233
[24]https://www.tiktok.com/rfmportugal/video/7265812239154810144
[25]https://www.tiktok.com/sicnoticiaspt/video/7274661971562138913
[26]https://www.tiktok.com/cnnportugal/video/7273121088471584033

6.7 Chronicles (116 Videos)

News chronicles are predominantly focused on current events, and they feature politics and institutions in videos that are often characterised by live audio. Both strategies are presented in a news chronicle format (about 90% of videos), and the main difference between the two clusters is the adoption of some features of TikTok.

Branded News Chronicle (82)

This strategy appears to be the TikTokised version of chronicle due to the presence of many of the platform's features, including video titles (48%), captions summarising the news (62%) accompanied by hashtags related to the topic (93%) and the prominent presence of the media brand on videos (96%).

This strategy consists in videos by Jornal de Notícias (34%), Público (26%) and SIC Notícias (20%).

News Chronicle (34)

A slight difference with respect to the previous strategy relates to the topics addressed (Current events: 65% and Other: 24%) and consequently to the actors featured (political and institutional: 53%). However, the most important difference consists in the absence of some technical features like titles, summary, hashtags, etc. which indicates a low engagement with the platform by the newsrooms.

This cluster consists almost entirely of videos by CNN Portugal (91%).[27]

7. Strategy Adoption

Table 6.3 shows the distribution of production strategies according to media type. First, radio production appears to be strongly focused on entertainment (73%) while televisions mainly engage in promotion (52%) and chronicle (25%). Due to their podcast programmes, weekly newspapers appear rather focused on interviews (47%) while only daily newspapers choose Short stories as a production strategy on TikTok (30%).

Fig. 6.1 shows the production strategies adopted by each newsroom on TikTok. First, some media outlets appear very focused on specific strategies. Radio stations clearly prefer to entertain their audiences (more than 70% of their production) and sometimes promote themselves and their shows (ranging from 9% to 17%). The production strategies of TVI and RTP (TV) appear to mirror those of radio stations: promotion is the most frequently adopted strategy (74%), followed by entertainment (more than 15% of videos).

Also, other media outlets appear to be quite focused on specific strategies: Observador devotes 70% of its posts to Short Stories and 19% to Entertainment,

---

[27] https://www.tiktok.com/cnnportugal/video/7270915933542108449

Table 6.3. Production Strategies and Media Type.

Media Type	Chronicle %	Entertainment %	Interviews %	Long Stories %	Promotion %	Reports %	Short Stories %	Total
Daily news	**31.5**	13.6	1.9	11.1	3.1	9.3	**29.6**	162
Radio	0	**73.1**	0	1.9	13.9	10.2	0.9	108
TV	**25**	13	8.8	4.2	**38.9**	10.2	0	216
Weekly	10.2	4.6	**47.2**	20.4	7.4	10.2	0	108

TikTokisation of the News 121

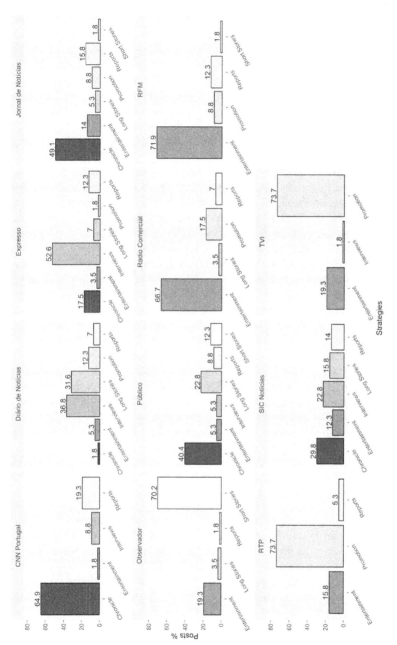

Fig. 6.1. Media Adoption of Production Strategies ($n = 54$).

while CNN Portugal focuses on Chronicle (65%) and Reports (19%). The latter also posts some interviews (9%).

The other media outlets vary their production somewhat although it is possible to discern some patterns. Weekly newspapers, namely Diário de Notícias and Expresso, invest in their podcast production in order to address TikTok audiences. Due to the platform's demographic (Meltwater & We Are Social, 2023), this could be an interesting choice for legacy media, considering that podcasts 'resonate strongly with young people because they have become integral to how they spend time on their mobile phones in general, and how they share and discuss content' (Galan et al., 2019, p. 55). Conversely, daily newspapers, namely Jornal de Notícias and Público, prefer to maintain their traditional news function in more than 40% of their videos.

If we look at the consistent adoption of strategies by the media, it is possible to highlight that only three news outlets adopt more than three production strategies: Jornal de Notícias, Público and SIC Notícias.[28] Considering that the first two are newspapers, this is a rather unexpected result. Indeed, as found by previous studies, legacy media and newspapers, in particular, struggle to adapt quickly to the changes imposed by platformisation and new media environments (Tandoc & Maitra, 2018). Moreover, Público and SIC Notícias consistently produce 'Long Stories' and 'Short Stories' that could be considered some of the most innovative formats/genres that emerged in our analysis. In this regard, also Observador and Diário de Notícias are interesting cases due to the attention given to these two strategies: Short Stories account for 70% of Observador's production (more than 80% of all posts in this strategy) while Long Stories cover a third of Diário's posts.

Therefore, our answer to RQ1 (What content production strategies do Portuguese news media adopt on TikTok?) is that news media adopt several strategies aimed at different goals including promotion, entertainment, information and insights into non-news events. The most common strategies are Promotion, Chronicle, Entertainment and Interviews, representing more than 73% of posts. However, the adoption is rather uneven, many media outlets prefer to focus on specific strategies and only a few exhibit a wide range of content.

8. The Success of Online Strategies

Fig. 6.2 shows the success of production strategies in terms of visualisation. To be borne in mind is that visualisation on TikTok strongly depends on its algorithm, which suggests content to users independently of the popularity of the accounts but on the basis of users' actions and preferences (Klug et al., 2021).

Among the categories of strategies, Promotion is the clearly the most successful one in terms of visualisation. This is mainly due to TV short clips that consist in short subtitled programme fragments mostly focused on entertainment and accompanied by thematic hashtags. As reported in the literature, all these elements seem to be drivers of engagement, especially for younger cohorts. Indeed,

---

[28]We considered to be consistent a strategy with at least five posts.

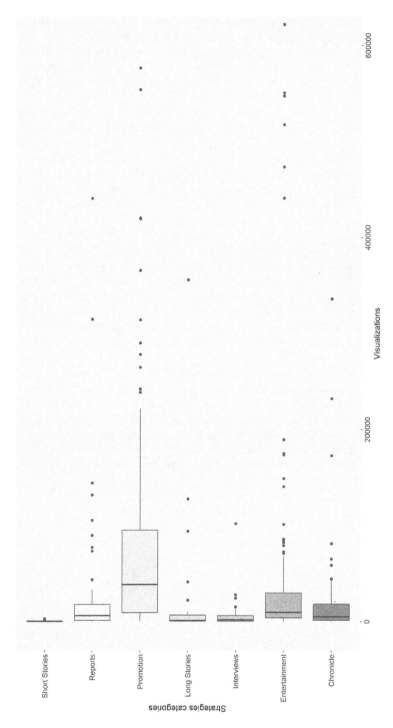

Fig. 6.2. Distribution of Visualisations for Each Strategy.

subtitles facilitate the 'perception of information' and enable the viewing of videos in public (Mudra & Kitsa, 2022). Thus along with entertainment, they are able to attract wider and younger audiences (Geers, 2020). Also hashtags, especially if related to current affairs or trending challenges, are known as drivers of content within the platform due to their searchability (Negreira-Rey et al., 2022; Vázquez-Herrero, Negreira-Rey & López-García, 2021).

The second most visualised category of strategies is Entertainment, especially due to Media/Newsroom fun videos. Besides the aspect already highlighted, i.e. entertainment, this strategy has other components useful for virality. For example, background music plays an major role in content diffusion due to both its ability to emphasise visual content and its searchability within the platform (Alonso-López et al., 2021; Boccia Artieri et al., 2022; Serrano et al., 2020). Furthermore, backstage or newsroom scenes have been considered appropriate for TikTok audiences because of their humourous and fun content often accompanied by music (Vázquez-Herrero, Negreira-Rey & López-García, 2021).

Fig. 6.2 evidences that also two traditional journalistic formats can become viral on TikTok. Indeed, the distribution of visualisations of Reports, especially of Feature reportage, shows a higher median and several outliers. This is not new: other studies have shown that short reports are being adopted by various media outlets on TikTok even with a fair amount of success in terms of visibility (Martella & Cepernich, 2024; Vázquez-Herrero, Negreira-Rey, & Zago, 2022). Moreover, Feature reportage are characterised by several elements that fit with the environment, including shortness, background music, emotionality and a prevalent focus on entertainment (Feng et al., 2019; Peña-Fernández et al., 2022; Vázquez-Herrero, Negreira-Rey & López-García, 2021). Regarding Social issue reports, to be stressed is that, although these topics are preferred by younger cohorts (Newman et al., 2022) and gain a fair amount of visualisation in Italy (Martella & Cepernich, 2024), Portuguese audiences seem to like them to a lesser extent.

Regarding Chronicle, the most successful strategy is the most TikTokised one: Branded Chronicle. This result highlights that addressing current events is not sufficient to gain visibility, but the presence of socio-technical features like captioned summaries, hashtags, etc. is probably useful to boost content in TikTok.

Differently from other studies in which interviews were mostly devoted to entertainment (Martella & Cepernich, 2024), interviews in Portuguese media divided by topic: Health and Hard news. Between these two, Health interviews were able to gain more attention. On the one hand, this was probably because the specific topic is frequently debated on social media and TikTok (Lischka & Garz, 2023; Zhu et al., 2019) and on the other hand, because it is preferred by younger audiences compared to hard news (Newman et al., 2022). Furthermore, to be borne in mind is that both interviews and strategies (Health and Hard news) mainly consist in podcasts fragments that resonate with educated and younger audiences (Newman et al., 2023). Our hypothesis is that the specific topic along with subtitles attracts the most attention of viewers.

Long Story visualisations are very close to those of interviews despite the novelty of the format, the wide range of topics covered (including soft news), the adoption of different formats as well as interviews and 'How to/well explained', which could help virality (Boccia Artieri et al., 2022; Klug & Autenrieth, 2022). However, these results are in line with those of other studies in which this strategy performed even worse (Martella & Cepernich, 2024).

In line with the findings of previous studies (Martella & Cepernich, 2024), Short Stories are not successful on TikTok. Both strategies, Short explanations and Data summaries, like Long Stories address a wide range of topics but last less time. The most frequent formats are 'How to/Well explained' or summaries of the daily news, and content is summarised by video captions. However, although these characteristics fit the TikTok aesthetic and practices – Data summaries are even accompanied by background music – our hypothesis is that the topics addressed and the specific formats recalling explainer videos (Short explanations) and Scrollytelling (Data summaries) do not meet with audience favour.

Therefore, our answer to RQ2 (What strategies prove most successful in engaging TikTok audiences across different media outlets?) is that Promotion is absolutely the most successful strategy followed by Entertainment, Chronicle and Reports, partially confirming that TikTok is strongly aimed at entertaining audiences.

9. Conclusion

Differently from other studies that have highlighted the prevalence of information in news media production on TikTok (Chobanyan & Nikolskaya, 2021; Vázquez-Herrero, Negreira-Rey & López-García, 2021), our results shows that more than 40% of posts are dedicated to Entertainment and Promotion. However, it is worth noting that (1) posts in the Chronicle category are quite frequent (20% of the database) and (2) the adoption of strategies is rather uneven, with Radio Comercial and RFM producing approximately 60% of Entertainment content, while RTP and TVI produce about 75% of Promotional content. Regarding Promotion, quite surprising is the success of TV Short Clips, which are the most visualised strategy ever. This strategy has been already adopted by other media (Vázquez-Herrero et al., 2021), and now, we can add that it seems to perfectly fit with TikTok audiences probably due to the focus on entertainment and the presence of celebrities.

Generally speaking, our analysis has revealed several 'new' or adapted (TikTokised) production strategies, as well as the repurposing of pre-existing content with minimal adaptation as emerged in other studies (Klug & Autenrieth, 2022).

Among the most innovative strategies, we identified two types of Short Stories: Short Explanation and Data Summaries, which, respectively, resemble video explanations and scrollytelling formats adapted from Instagram and other social media (Schneiders, 2020). Despite their novelty, neither strategy was successful in attracting user attention on TikTok. This finding is particularly insightful given that Short Promotional Clips strategy, although it is among the ones least suited to TikTok, was one of the most viewed strategies, along with Chronicle.

More specifically, News Chronicle lacks several feature characteristic of the platform; however, it still manages to capture more audience attention than other strategies. On the other hand, Branded Chronicle performs better, probably due to its suitability for the platform, considering that both strategies address current events.

On the contrary, Long Stories, despite incorporating images, data, sound effects, covering various topics and sometimes adopting tutorial formats, achieve limited online success.

In Portuguese 'TikToksphere', Interviews primarily involve the repurposing of existing podcast fragments, which could be an interesting choice for media outlets considering the platform's demographic (Newman et al., 2023). However, both Health interviews and Hard news interviews do not receive significant attention.

Therefore, our conclusion is that success on TikTok is very difficult to predict. Adapting formats and including platform affordances does not necessarily lead to more views. In other words, several variables affect the intersection of algorithmic logic and audience preferences that drive success in terms of views. Moreover, the same variables seem to affect the number of visualisations in a different way according to the specific ensemble of elements. Put briefly, entertainment seems to be the most important driver of success although it's not guaranteed.

Finally, unlike other research studies (Klug & Autenrieth, 2022; Vázquez-Herrero et al., 2021), we did not observe a significant adoption of typical TikTok practices, such as duets and challenges, or features like filters and effects. This suggests that we are still in the early stages of media adoption of TikTok, at least in Portugal. Therefore, we anticipate that strategies could evolve in the near future.

Acknowledgements

Heartfelt thanks go to Adriana Gonçalves, Florence Oliveira and Luísa Torre of the LabCom at the University of Beira Interior (Portugal) for their work on video coding and for discussing the results of the analyses within the research group.

References

Alonso-López, N., Sidorenko-Bautista, P., & Giacomelli, F. (2021). Més enllà de reptes i balls virals: TikTok com a vehicle per al discurs desinformatiu i la verificació d'informació a Espanya, Portugal, el Brasil i els Estats Units. *Anàlisi, 64*, 65. https://doi.org/10.5565/rev/analisi.3411

Benzecri, J.-P. (1973). *L'analyse des données, Tome 2: l'Analyse des Corrispondences.* Dunod.

Boccia Artieri, G., Zurovac, E., & Donato, V. (2022). Visibility and networked. Participation in TikTok. The Breonna Taylor trend. *Comunicazione Politica, 3*, 403–422.

Bracciale, R., Martella, A., & Visentin, C. (2018). From super-participants to super-echoed: Participation in the 2018 Italian electoral Twittersphere. *PArtecipazione e COnflitto * The Open Journal of Sociopolitical Studies, 11*(2), 361–393. https://doi.org/10.1285/i20356609v11i2p361

Caplan, R., & boyd, d. (2018). Isomorphism through algorithms: Institutional dependencies in the case of Facebook. *Big Data & Society, 5*(1). https://doi.org/10.1177/2053951718757253

Cheng, Z., & Li, Y. (2024). Like, comment, and share on TikTok: Exploring the effect of sentiment and second-person view on the user engagement with TikTok news videos. *Social Science Computer Review*, *42*(1), 201–223. https://doi.org/10.1177/08944393231178603

Chobanyan, K., & Nikolskaya, E. (2021). Testing the waters: TikTok's potential for television news. *World of Media. Journal of Russian Media and Journalism Studies*, *3*(3), 62–88. https://doi.org/10.30547/worldofmedia.3.2021.3

Christin, A. (2020). *Metrics at work. Journalism and the contested meaning of algorithms*. Princeton University Press.

Costera Meijer, I. (2007). The paradox of popularity. *Journalism Studies*, *8*(1), 96–116. https://doi.org/10.1080/14616700601056874

Ekström, M., & Westlund, O. (2019). The dislocation of news journalism: A conceptual framework for the study of epistemologies of digital journalism. *Media and Communication*, *7*(1), 259–270. https://doi.org/10.17645/mac.v7i1.1763

Feng, Y.-L., Chen, C.-C., & Wu, S.-M. (2019). Evaluation of charm factors of short video user experience using FAHP – A case study of Tik Tok app. *IOP Conference Series: Materials Science and Engineering*, *688*(5), 055068. https://doi.org/10.1088/1757-899X/688/5/055068

Ferrignolo, A. (2003). Come sta cambiando il mondo della carta stampata. In C. Sorrentino (Ed.), *Il giornalismo in Italia. Aspetti, processi produttivi, tendenze* (pp. 109–124). Carocci.

Freelon, D., & Wells, C. (2020). Disinformation as political communication. *Political Communication*, *37*(2), 145–156. https://doi.org/10.1080/10584609.2020.1723755

Galan, L., Osserman, J., Parker, T., & Taylor, M. (2019). How young people consume news and the implications for mainstream media. https://reutersinstitute.politics.ox.ac.uk/sites/default/files/2021-02/FlamingoxREUTERS-Report-Full-KG-V28.pdf

García-Ortega, A., & García-Avilés, J. A. (2023). Innovation in narrative formats redefines the boundaries of journalistic storytelling: Instagram stories, TikTok and Comic. In M.-C. Negreira-Rey, J. Vázquez-Herrero, J. Sixto-García, & X. López-García (Eds.), *Blurring boundaries of journalism in digital media. New actors, models and practices* (pp. 185–197). Springer.

Geers, S. (2020). News consumption across media platforms and content. *Public Opinion Quarterly*, *84*(S1), 332–354. https://doi.org/10.1093/poq/nfaa010

Hagar, N., & Diakopoulos, N. (2023). Algorithmic indifference: The dearth of news recommendations on TikTok. *New Media & Society*. https://doi.org/10.1177/14614448231192964

Hallin, D. C., & Mancini, P. (2017). Ten years after comparing media systems: What have we learned?. *Political Communication*, *34*(2), 155–171. https://doi.org/10.1080/10584609.2016.1233158

Hayes, A. F., & Krippendorff, K. (2007). Answering the call for a standard reliability measure for coding data. *Communication Methods and Measures*, *1*(1), 77–89. https://doi.org/10.1080/19312450709336664

Hermida, A., & Mellado, C. (2020). Dimensions of social media logics: Mapping forms of journalistic norms and practices on Twitter and Instagram. *Digital Journalism*, *8*(7), 864–884. https://doi.org/10.1080/21670811.2020.1805779

Hill, S., & Bradshaw, P. (2018). *Mobile-first journalism*. Routledge. https://doi.org/10.4324/9781315267210

Klinger, U., & Svensson, J. (2015). The emergence of network media logic in political communication: A theoretical approach. *New Media & Society, 17*(8), 1241–1257. https://doi.org/10.1177/1461444814522952

Klug, D., & Autenrieth, U. (2022). *Struggle for strategy. Presence, practices, and communicative strategies of legacy news providers on TikTok* (pp. 1–17). 12th International Conference on Social Media & Society.

Klug, D., Qin, Y., Evans, M., & Kaufman, G. (2021). Trick and please. A mixed-method study on user assumptions about the TikTok algorithm. In *13th ACM Web Science Conference 2021* (pp. 84–92). https://doi.org/10.1145/3447535.3462512

Li, Y., Guan, M., Hammond, P., & Berrey, L. E. (2021). Communicating COVID-19 information on TikTok: A content analysis of TikTok videos from official accounts featured in the COVID-19 information hub. *Health Education Research, 36*(3), 261–271. https://doi.org/10.1093/her/cyab010

Lischka, J. A., & Garz, M. (2023). Clickbait news and algorithmic curation: A game theory framework of the relation between journalism, users, and platforms. *New Media & Society, 25*(8), 2073–2094. https://doi.org/10.1177/14614448211027174

Martella, A., & Cepernich, C. (2024). Dacci oggi il nostro TikTok quotidiano. Strategie di pubblicazione dei quotidiani italiani su Tik Tok. *Problemi Dell'informazione, Rivista Quadrimestrale, 2024*(1), 65–92. https://doi.org/10.1445/113229

Martella, A., & Roncarolo, F. (2023). Giorgia Meloni in the spotlight. Mobilization and competition strategies in the 2022 Italian election campaign on Facebook. *Contemporary Italian Politics, 15*(1), 88–102. https://doi.org/10.1080/23248823.2022.2150934

MeltwaterWe Are Social. (2023). Digital 2023 global overview report. https://datareportal.com/reports/digital-2023-global-overview-report

Moscato, G., Monti, F., & Romanin, T. (2023). *Il Medium siamo noi. Manuale di giornalismi*. Mondadori.

Mudra, I., & Kitsa, M. (2022). What, how and why? Tiktok as a promising channel for media promotion. *Media Literacy and Academic Research, 5*(2), 225–237.

Negreira-Rey, M.-C., Vázquez-Herrero, J., & López-García, X. (2022). Blurring boundaries between journalists and Tiktokers: Journalistic role performance on TikTok. *Media and Communication, 10*(1). https://doi.org/10.17645/mac.v10i1.4699

Newman, N. (2022). How publishers are learning to create and distribute news on TikTok. Reuters Institute. https://reutersinstitute.politics.ox.ac.uk/how-publishers-are-learning-create-and-distribute-news-tiktok

Newman, N., Fletcher, R., Eddy, K., Robertson, C. T., & Nielsen, R. K. (2023). Digital News Report 2023. Reuters Institute. https://reutersinstitute.politics.ox.ac.uk/digital-news-report/2023

Newman, N., Fletcher, R., Robertson, C. T., Eddy, K., & Nielsen, R. K. (2022). Digital News Report 2022. Reuters Institute. https://reutersinstitute.politics.ox.ac.uk/digital-news-report/2022

Nielsen, R. K., & Fletcher, R. (2023). Comparing the platformization of news media systems: A cross-country analysis. *European Journal of Communication, 38*(5), 484–499. https://doi.org/10.1177/02673231231189043

Peña-Fernández, S., Larrondo-Ureta, A., & Moraes-i-Grass, J. (2022). Current affairs on TikTok. Virality and entertainment for digital natives. *El Profesional de La Información*. https://doi.org/10.3145/epi.2022.ene.06

Schneiders, P. (2020). What remains in mind? Effectiveness and efficiency of explainers at conveying information. *Media and Communication*, *8*(1), 218–231. https://doi.org/10.17645/mac.v8i1.2507

Serrano, J. C. M., Papakyriakopoulos, O., & Hegelich, S. (2020). Dancing to the partisan beat: A first analysis of political communication on TikTok. In *12th ACM Conference on Web Science* (pp. 257–266). https://doi.org/10.1145/3394231.3397916

Skovsgaard, M., & Andersen, K. (2020). Conceptualizing news avoidance: Towards a shared understanding of different causes and potential solutions. *Journalism Studies*, *21*(4), 459–476. https://doi.org/10.1080/1461670X.2019.1686410

Sorrentino, C. (2002). *Il giornalismo Che cos'è e come funziona*. Carocci.

Steensen, S. (2018). Feature journalism. In *Oxford research encyclopedia of communication*. Oxford University Press. https://doi.org/10.1093/acrefore/9780190228613.013.810

Tandoc, E. C., & Maitra, J. (2018). News organizations' use of native videos on Facebook: Tweaking the journalistic field one algorithm change at a time. *New Media & Society*, *20*(5), 1679–1696. https://doi.org/10.1177/1461444817702398

van Dijck, J., Poell, T., & de Waal, M. (2018). *The platform society: Public values in a connective world*. Oxford University Press.

Vázquez-Herrero, J., Negreira-Rey, M.-C., & López-García, X. (2022a). Let's dance the news! How the news media are adapting to the logic of TikTok. *Journalism*, *23*(8), 1717–1735. https://doi.org/10.1177/1464884920969092

Vázquez-Herrero, J., Negreira-Rey, M.-C., & Rodríguez-Vázquez, A.-I. (2021). Intersections between TikTok and TV: Channels and programmes thinking outside the box. *Journalism and Media*, *2*(1), 1–13. https://doi.org/10.3390/journalmedia2010001

Vázquez-Herrero, J., Negreira-Rey, M.-C., & Zago, G. (2022). Young audience wanted! Journalism looks to the future. In B. García-Orosa, S. Pérez-Seijo, & Á. Vizoso (Eds.), *Emerging practices in the age of automated digital journalism* (pp. 56–66). Routledge.

Zhu, C., Xu, X., Zhang, W., Chen, J., & Evans, R. (2019). How health communication via Tik Tok makes a difference: A content analysis of Tik Tok accounts run by Chinese provincial health committees. *International Journal of Environmental Research and Public Health*, *17*(1), 192. https://doi.org/10.3390/ijerph17010192

Section 4

Institutions

Chapter 7

Digital and Financial Literacy and the Development of e-Government Platforms

Anna Lo Prete

University of Turin, Italy

Abstract

The rapid growth of e-government platforms in the first decades of the new millennium has created both new opportunities and challenges. Digital citizenship and the digitalisation of public services can represent a barrier for less competent individuals who need to connect and process information. The present contribution offers descriptive evidence on the relationship between e-government development and the average level of competences that may be arguably related to the ability of citizens to benefit from the digitalisation of public services, namely digital and financial literacy.

Keywords: Digital literacy; financial literacy; human capital; e-government; platform society

1. Introduction

The development of government initiatives that exploit digital platforms to deliver public services is an important feature of the platform society. In the early 2000s, the first e-government platforms were introduced to strengthen the collaboration between citizens and governments online. Since the commitment of Barak Obama's Administration to an 'open government' model in 2009, governments around the world have increased the number and scope of internet-based platforms to facilitate the public engagement of citizens (United Nations, 2020), a process that received further stimulus during the COVID-19 pandemic, when lockdowns and restrictions on the free movement of people motivated governments to envision effective digital solutions to guarantee the provision of public services. According to the United Nations, between 2003 and

2018 e-government platforms recorded on average a 50% increase around the world, and a 67% increase over the slightly longer 2003–2020 horizon.

The rapid growth of e-government platforms in the first decades of the new millennium has created both new opportunities and challenges. On the one hand, civic engagement through e-government platforms can provide citizens with new means to participate in the social and political life of their community (Campante et al., 2018; Ceccarini, 2021; Khazaeli & Stockemer, 2013; McDonald, 2008). The United Nations defines *e-participation* as a new form of civic engagement that, in principle, should foster open and participatory governance through ICTs – information and communications technologies (United Nations, 2020).

On the other hand, digital citizenship and the digitalisation of public services can represent a barrier for less competent individuals who need to connect and process information and who should engage in bottom-up policymaking and in the co-production of public services. In this regard, the digitalisation of contents and services can reduce or hinder the political participation of less-educated voters, who, according to traditional theories in social sciences (Lijphart, 1997), are more likely to support redistributive policies (Fujiwara, 2015; Gavazza et al., 2019).

Thus, whether the digitalisation of governments promotes social inclusion and helps address social injustice or it widens democratic gaps is a question to address empirically by studying data on both the supply side and the demand side of digital public services. To contribute to the discussion on this topic, the present chapter offers descriptive evidence on the relationship between e-government development across countries and the average level of competences that may be arguably related to the ability of citizens to benefit from the digitalisation of public services.

Following recent studies on the digitalisation of financial services (Lo Prete, 2022), the analysis in this chapter is motivated by the idea that people need both the cognitive skills necessary for independent movement in the digital world – a known determinant of the digital divide in e-government development (see, e.g. Tomaszewicz, 2015) – and the skills necessary to understand the contents (or products) therein. Specifically, along with education at school, this chapter will consider (i) digital literacy, defined as the ability 'to access, manage, understand, integrate, communicate, evaluate and create information safely and appropriately through digital technologies for employment, decent jobs and entrepreneurship' (UNESCO, 2018) and (ii) financial literacy, defined by the OECD as 'a combination of awareness, knowledge, skill, attitude and behavior necessary to make sound financial decisions and ultimately achieve individual financial wellbeing' (Atkinson & Messy, 2012) and that the recent literature relates to better public decisions (Fornero & Lo Prete, 2019, Lo Prete, 2023).

This chapter will use graphical evidence and descriptive statistics to provide insights into the relationships of interest and to discuss the policy implications of e-government conditional on the level of competence of European Union citizens.

2. e-Government Platforms

The term 'e-government' refers to the delivery of digital public services through online platforms. According to the European Commission, the provision of effective digital public services can produce benefits including increased transparency, citizens' participation in political life, efficiency and savings for the public and the private sector and greater cross-border mobility. It also has implementation costs that cannot be ignored but are not the focus of the present chapter.

The state of development of e-government platforms has been monitored since 2003 by the United Nations. Every two years, the United Nations E-Government Development Database assesses e-government development comparatively, focusing on the development of government websites and their accessibility in terms of infrastructure development and of educational levels in each country.

Specifically, e-government effectiveness in the delivery of public services is measured by the 'E-Government Development Index' (EGDI). This is a composite index computed as the weighted average of three components, independent of each other, that measure the role of technological constraints, general competences available at the country level and online provision of public services. Some methodological changes were introduced in the 2022 Survey that this study will not consider, focusing instead on the values recorded in 2018, before the outbreak of the COVID-19 pandemic.[1]

An important caveat to bear in mind is that, by construction, the United Nations' benchmarking exercise provides information on the supply side of e-government platforms at the national level. It does not include data on the use of these platforms by citizens.

As the histogram in Fig. 7.1 shows, there are wide differences in EGDI among the European Union's 27 member states. The index ranges between zero (less developed) and one (most developed). The higher values are recorded in the higher-income countries, with the Scandinavian countries at the top of the ranking, while the EGDI values of Romania, Latvia, Croatia and other countries in the East of Europe and the Balkan region fall below the EU average. With respect to the rest of the world – not considered in this chapter – it is useful to point out that, over the past 20 years, Europe has recorded the highest average EGDI value, followed by the Asian region, the Americas, Oceania and Africa (United Nations, 2022). Moreover, among the 15 countries that are world leaders in e-government development, there are other high-income countries: South Korea, New Zealand, Iceland, Australia, the United States, the United Kingdom, Singapore and Japan.

---

[1] The time window considered reduces possible measurement issues due to the limited availability of data for cross-country comparisons on digital and financial literacy. As the next section of this chapter explains, the most recent data available at the time of writing are the data on digital literacy from the OECD-PIAAC 2018 survey and the data on financial literacy from the 2014 Standard and Poor Survey.

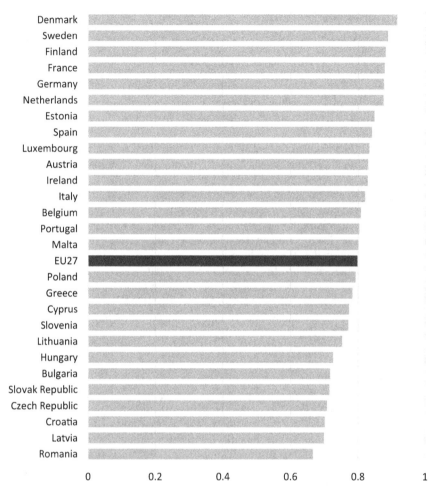

Fig. 7.1. E-Government Development Across the EU.

The EGDI provides an overall picture on the state of e-government platform development. The discussion that follows considers its components, which enter the EGDI with equal weight, in order to deepen the analysis and focus on different aspects of the digitalisation of public services.

The first component of the EGDI is the 'Telecommunications Infrastructure Index' (TII). This includes information on the proportion of internet users and of mobile subscribers, as well as on the proportion of wireless (i.e. active mobile-broadband) and fixed broadband subscriptions. It is interesting to point out that the value of the TII has remained broadly stable since the first edition of the United Nations E-Government Survey (United Nations, 2022). This can be explained by considering that, technically speaking, the TII does not measure infrastructural features of e-government platforms but rather the more general dimension of the reach of ICTs.

The second component of the EGDI is the 'Human Capital Index' (HCI). This measures the average level of human capital based on the following four components, all of which reflect information on schooling: (i) the literacy rate of adults measured by the percentage of people aged 15 years old and above that can read, write and understand a short statement on everyday life; (ii) the combined primary, secondary and tertiary gross enrolment ratio defined as the number of students enroled in all grades, regardless of their age, as a percentage of the school-age population; (iii) the total number of years of schooling completed by the adult population (defined as 25 years old and above) excluding the years spent repeating grades and (iv) the expected years of schooling, defined as the number of years that a child is expected to spend at school in the future, where the probability of being in school is based for each specific age on the current enrolment ratio at the national level.

The third component of the EGDI is the 'Online Service Index' (OSI), which measures the delivery of public services on national e-government platforms. This is what is termed 'e-government'. The index includes information on various aspects of public service provision. Technically, it is based on five components that evaluate the level of institutional quality (10% of the OSI), service provision (45%), content provision (5%), technology (5%) and e-participation (35%). Basically, it is an indicator of the ability of governments to set up national websites, policies and the strategies needed to deliver public service online.

The three indexes capture very different aspects of e-government platforms' development that can furnish a more informative picture of digital governments when considered one by one: TII, the reach of technologies, i.e. the number of users of mobile phones, broadband and internet services; HCI, the level of competence that people acquire in school, and OSI, the level of e-government development.

The graphical analysis of pairwise comparisons in Fig. 7.2 makes it possible to disentangle the dimensions of interest. In each panel, a dashed straight line represents the best fit of an ordinary least squares model that minimises the distance between the line itself and each observation. It represents the estimated linear relationship between the variables measured on the two axes and immediately provides information on whether there exists a positive, negative or null statistical association between them.

The top panel of Fig. 7.2 shows the association between TII (on the vertical axis) and OSI (on the horizontal axis). The positive slope of the dashed line indicates that countries where more people use the internet and have access to wireless and fixed broadbands are also countries with more e-government development, as measured by online public services. Estonia is at the same level of the top performing Scandinavian countries, France, Germany, the Netherlands and Luxembourg. The other ex-socialist countries occupy the bottom-left of the figure, where low levels of use and access to ICTs are associated with equally low levels of online public services' delivery, except for Poland, where large e-governments are associated with relatively low access to and use of digital technologies.

138 Anna Lo Prete

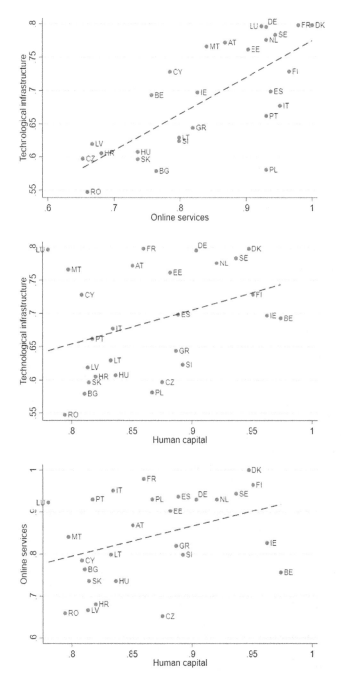

Fig. 7.2. Disentangling the EGDI in Three Dimensions.

The panel in the middle of Fig. 7.2 compares the TII (on the vertical axis) with the HCI (on the horizontal axis). These two indicators are positively associated, as the positive slope of the regression line indicates, but observations are more dispersed. There is a cloud of countries with relatively higher TII in the upper region of the scatter plot and a group of countries, including Portugal, Italy, Spain, Ireland and Belgium with average values, all associated with very different levels of human capital. However, this information is not easy to read because human capital levels are quite similar – as the close range of values on the horizontal axis shows. All the South-Eastern European countries and all the Baltic states except for Estonia are in the bottom-left region of those with lower access to and use of technologies and average or lower human capital.

Finally, the indicators of human capital and of online public services are positively associated in the bottom panel of Fig. 7.2, but the distance between many observations and the regression line indicates that there is some heterogeneity across countries in the relationship of interest, with Ireland and Belgium standing out as countries with high levels of human capital but medium-low levels of e-government development.

On comparing the panels of Fig. 7.2, it is apparent that Portugal and Italy provide online public services to a population that is relatively less active on the internet and has lower human capital. Countries like Ireland and Belgium do not invest much in e-government, notwithstanding their high levels of human capital and average use of technologies. More in general, the delivery of online public services and the reach of online technologies seem to go hand in hand while a more complex picture emerges when human capital, measured by the level of schooling, is also considered.

3. Digital and Financial Literacy

To better understand how e-platforms have developed in relation to the competences needed to reap the benefits of digitalisation, this section draws a relationship between cross-country e-government experience and less generic competences with respect to the level of attained and expected schooling in each of the countries that the HCI component of the EGDI considers. The following analysis focuses on two sets of skills: digital literacy to capture proficiency in the use of digital platforms and applications and financial literacy, which can be a proxy for the ability to understand policy content (Fornero & Lo Prete, 2023).

3.1 Digital Literacy

Digital literacy (DL) is defined by the United Nations Educational, Scientific and Cultural Organization (UNESCO) as 'the ability to access, manage, understand, integrate, communicate, evaluate and create information safely and appropriately through digital technologies for employment, decent jobs and entrepreneurship. It includes competences that are variously referred to as computer literacy, ICT literacy, information literacy and media literacy' (UNESCO, 2018).

Mapping digital competences is not an easy task. The UNESCO has developed and provides guidelines based on the examination of previous frameworks adopted by different countries, enterprises and institutions. The resulting synthesis constitutes its Global Framework of Reference on Digital Literacy Skills. The measure of digital skills that this chapter uses is the indicator that the OECD computes through its Survey of Adult Skills that is conducted as part of the Programme for the International Assessment of Adult competencies.

The OECD Survey of Adult Skills (PIAAC) measures cognitive skills of working-age adults (aged between 16 and 65 years) based on evaluation of respondents' ability to read digital and traditional print-based text, master mathematical information and ideas, use technology to solve problems and accomplish tasks (OECD, 2019). The PIAAC survey is administered every 10 years in three yearly rounds of data collection. The first cycle took place between 2011 and 2017. It covered 38 countries/economies, with data released in 2018. The second cycle is ongoing (at the time of writing), taking place in the period 2018–2024 and covering 30 countries/economies.

The PIAAC complex measurement exercise evaluates skills in the three domains of numeracy, literacy and problem-solving in a technology-rich environment (recently renamed 'adaptive problem solving'). The following discussion will focus on the last domain.

The measure of 'problem-solving in a technology-rich environment' is computed on the proportion of the population aged 16 to 65 that was able to undertake the computer-based version of the assessment, a precondition for displaying competency in this domain. That is, the target population can vary across countries. The resulting indicator is the percentage of adults scoring at the two highest levels (out of three) in problem-solving in technology-rich environments. To provide an idea of the cognitive skills required to show a basic level of digital competence, we define as digitally literate a respondent who could use both generic and specific technology applications to perform non-trivial tasks such as using a command to sort information and use a browser to navigate across pages.

In the upper panel of Fig. 7.3, the PIAAC indicator of digital skills, measured on the vertical axis, is low on average. Considering the 16 countries/economies of the European Union that participated in the survey, only three persons out of 10 can be defined digitally literate, and even in the top performing Scandinavian countries, the percentage is well below 50%, that is less than one person out of two can operate in a digital environment at a good level. The dispersion of the observations in the top panel of Fig. 7.3, which plots the (positive) bivariate association between digital literacy and human capital (on the horizontal axis), indicates that countries may have a high level of schooling because education is compulsory and people spend time studying, but the time spent at school may not be a good proxy for the skills needed to comprehend digital contents and to navigate on the internet being able at least to solve easy tasks.

Digital and Financial Literacy 141

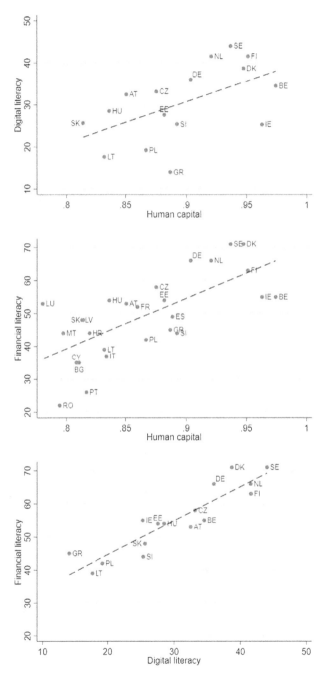

Fig. 7.3. Indicators of Competence.

3.2 Financial Literacy

Financial literacy (FL) is the set of competences in economics and finance that help people take basic personal finance decisions (Lusardi & Mitchell, 2011). Research has extensively analysed how the lack of basic economic and financial competence relates to saving and investing behaviour in individual and aggregate data (see Lusardi & Mitchell, 2023, for a review of the literature). More recently, the same indicator has served as a proxy for citizens' understanding of the content of public policies, an element needed to inform public decisions (Fornero & Lo Prete, 2019) and that is also associated with higher electoral participation (Lo Prete, 2024). The idea is that those same people that have basic knowledge about economics and finance also have a better understanding of the trade-offs that lie behind private and public intertemporal choices. They can evaluate the content of a policy proposal at a lower information cost, and, in the context of this chapter, they can make better use of e-government, as regards both the use of online public services and open participation in bottom-up policymaking.

The largest worldwide collection of data on basic economic and financial competences is the 2014 Standard & Poor's Ratings Services Global Financial Literacy Survey commissioned by the Global Financial Literacy Excellence Centre (GFLEC). The survey covered a sample of over 140 countries and, unfortunately, has not been administered again since 2014. Hence, the data considered in this chapter refer to that year, on the hypothesis that the relative position of countries and the level of financial literacy did not change much after that until 2019.[2]

The set of questions included in the survey were based on Lusardi and Mitchell (2011)'s classification and definition of financial literacy. They covered four topics: numeracy, compound interest rate, inflation and risk diversification. The survey was administered to 1,000 individuals in each country, and the indicator of financial literacy measured the percentage of respondents who correctly answered at least three questions out of four.

Around the world, only one adult out of three understands the basic notions of (simple and compound) interest, inflation and risk diversification (Klapper & Lusardi, 2020). Narrowing the analysis to the European Union, 49% of people are financially literate, with wide differences between the lowest values recorded in Romania and Portugal, both below 30%, and the highest 71% of Sweden and Denmark.

In the medium panel of Fig. 7.3, financial literacy, measured on the vertical axis, shows more cross-country heterogeneity with respect to the indicators of digital literacy and human capital. It is positively associated with human capital, measured on the horizontal axis, for the two groups of countries above and below the dashed line. Among the higher-income countries, Italy and Portugal record the lowest levels of financial literacy.

---

[2]The hypothesis that the level of financial literacy was quite stable over time is reasonable over the period considered, when specific financial education programs were missing at the school level and in training programs for adults (see the discussion in Lo Prete, 2018).

Finally, the bottom panel of Fig. 7.3 shows that digital and financial literacy are closely correlated across countries. As discussed in Lo Prete (2022), individuals who master financial literacy are also more digitally literate; and poor digital literacy is associated with poor financial literacy. Missing information on digital literacy for Italy and Portugal prevents determination of the relative positions of these countries.

4. Competence and e-Government Platforms

Recent analyses on personal finance indicate that people need both digital literacy and financial literacy to share the benefits of the digitalisation of banking and financial services (Lo Prete, 2022). This chapter explores whether the same competences relate to the use of digital public services in general.

The previous section showed that low-skilled respondents who could use only basic applications and take a few steps on digital platforms (e.g. sorting email in pre-existing folders) formed a significant fraction of the population. And that financial literacy used as a proxy for the skills that help assess the content of public policies and services is low on average, with wide differences among the 27 member states of the European Union.

Fig. 7.4 plots the two indicators of digital and financial literacy on the horizontal axis of the top-left and the bottom-left panel respectively and the level of e-government measured by the OSI on the vertical axis. The positive slope of the dashed line in both panels indicate that e-government is most widespread in countries with higher digital and financial literacy. Recalling that the level of digital literacy is quite low on average, online public services are provided to citizens that are often digitally illiterate and who may find it difficult to navigate on e-government platforms. In the top panel of Fig. 7.4, this is especially true in the case of Poland but also of Greece, Estonia and Ireland. In the bottom panel, the provision of public online services is associated with very low levels of financial literacy in Portugal, Italy and Poland while other countries in the bottom-right area do not deliver many online public services but have higher levels of financial literacy.

The close correlation between the two indicators of digital and financial literacy makes it difficult to evaluate if one dimension is more relevant to e-government than the other. To obtain insights into this regard, it is possible to focus on the relationship between one indicator of skills only and e-government, controlling for the role of the other skill indicator. By partialling out financial literacy, in the top-right panel of Fig. 7.4, it is no longer possible to detect an association between digital literacy and the provision of online public services. The same exercise conducted controlling for the level of digital literacy, in the bottom-right panel of Fig. 7.4, shows that a positive association between financial literacy and e-government still exists – at conventional significance levels if the Czech Republic is treated as an outlier and dropped from the statistical analysis. These statistics indicate that, in the small sample of European countries and economies under analysis, controlling for the level of digital literacy, the supply of

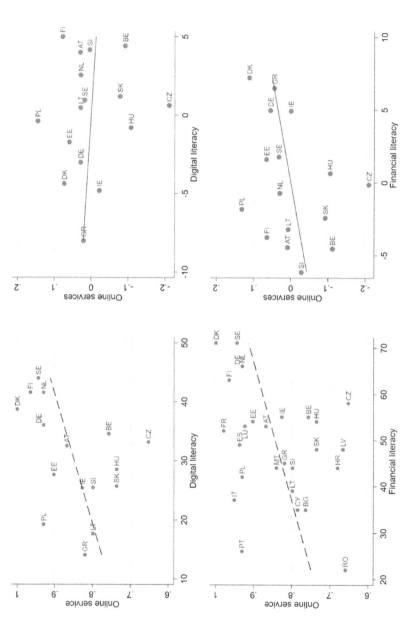

Fig. 7.4. Digital and Financial Literacy and E-Government. *Notes*: Bivariate correlations in the left panels; partial correlations in the right panels.

e-government services is higher in countries where citizens have a better understanding of the trade-offs behind personal and public finance. E-government may not be widespread in countries where citizens are digitally literate per se, raising the issue of understanding whether they can use digital platforms in the first place.

5. Conclusion

Whether citizens possess the skills necessary to access e-government platforms and use online public services – the dimension most relevant to evaluating the degree of e-democracy and e-participation – is an issue that the indicators of digital and financial literacy imperfectly capture. As the previous sections have shown, e-government is not always associated with the level of cognitive skills that enable individuals to navigate online independently and understand policy trade-offs. This can represent a severe barrier to the development of inclusive and critically independent e-citizenship through online platforms.

At present, the supply of e-participation tools seems to offer new channels of civic engagement to those citizens who are concerned about the collective costs of climate change and global warming; and in turn, it seems to have an impact on the level of government spending on redistributive functions such as welfare (Lo Prete & Sacchi, 2023). Similarly, evidence on the use of digital technologies and e-platforms by the government in China indicates that governments pay greater attention to social welfare policies, even in the absence of electoral accountability, and improve the quality of governance when citizens engage more online (Jiang et al., 2019).

However, the use of ICTs can also represent a barrier for voters who are exposed to huge amounts of information on online platforms. Gavazza et al. (2019) find that the internet can increase information costs and drain political participation, with perverse effects on government policies in terms of a decrease of public expenditures addressed to less-educated voters. Moreover, new forms of civic engagement can modify the level and composition of government spending, not necessarily increasing spending on functions that are particularly beneficial to the poor (Fujiwara, 2015).

Cognitive skills are a precondition for civic participation. The basic competences needed to use e-platforms, i.e. 'digital literacy', and the basic competences needed to understand the policy contents therein, proxied by indicators of 'financial literacy', should be strengthened by educational and training programs in order to share the benefits of the digitalisation of public services and civic engagement without incurring the dangers that digital technologies imply. This is especially necessary if the delivery of public services online substitutes, instead of complementing, the traditional in-person interaction between public servants and citizens.

To be transparent and inclusive, open government and participation should integrate all groups of citizens, without leaving the most vulnerable segments of society behind, and they should protect all citizens/users against any manipulation. Provided that traditional electoral participation does not necessarily increase the quality of policies and of politicians (Lo Prete & Revelli, 2017), it is crucial to understand how its online counterpart, e-participation, works. For instance, digital forms of e-democracy require platforms that function through algorithms that choose who sees what posts and define the salience of different topics and discussions. The legislator, at the national and European level, should also establish the rules regulating the online community, especially if public money and resources are invested in e-government platforms that may change the way in which citizens engage with and participate in political and civil life.

References

Atkinson, A., & Messy, F.-A. (2012). *Measuring financial literacy: Results of the OECD/International network on financial education (INFE) pilot study*. OECD Working Papers on Finance, Insurance and Private Pensions, No. 15. OECD Publishing.

Campante, F., Durante, R., & Sobbrio, F. (2018). Politics 2.0: The multifaceted effect of broadband internet on political participation. *Journal of the European Economic Association, 16*(4), 1094–1136.

Ceccarini, L. (2021). *The digital citizen(ship). Politics and democracy in the networked society*. Edward Elgar Publishing.

Fornero, E., & Lo Prete, A. (2019). Voting in the aftermath of a pension reform: The role of financial literacy. *Journal of Pension Economics and Finance, 18*(1), 1–30.

Fornero, E., & Lo Prete, A. (2023). Financial education: From better personal finance to improved citizenship. *Journal of Financial Literacy and Wellbeing, 1*, 12–2.

Fujiwara, T. (2015). Voting technology, political responsiveness, and infant health: Evidence from Brazil. *Econometrica, 83*(2), 423–464.

Gavazza, A., Nardotto, M., & Valletti, T. (2019). Internet and politics: Evidence from UK local elections and local government policies. *The Review of Economic Studies, 86*(5), 2092–2135.

Jiang, J., Meng, T., & Zhang, Q. (2019). From Internet to social safety net: The policy consequences of online participation in China. *Governance, 32*(3), 531–546.

Khazaeli, S., & Stockemer, D. (2013). The internet: A new route to good governance. *International Political Science Review, 34*(5), 463–482.

Klapper, L., & Lusardi, A. (2020). Financial literacy and financial resilience: Evidence from around the world. *Financial Management, 49*(4), 589–614.

Lijphart, A. (1997). Unequal participation: Democracy's unresolved dilemma. *American Political Science Review, 91*(1), 1–14.

Lo Prete, A. (2018). Inequality and the finance you know: Does economic literacy matter?. *Economia Politica, 35*(1), 183–205.

Lo Prete, A. (2022). Digital and financial literacy as determinants of digital payments and personal finance. *Economics Letters, 213*, 110378.

Lo Prete, A. (2024). Political participation and financial education: Understanding personal and collective tradeoffs for a better citizenship. *Economics Letters, 244*, 111943.

Lo Prete, A., & Revelli, F. (2017). Costly voting, turnout, and candidate valence. *Economics Letters, 158*, 10–13.

Lo Prete, A., & Sacchi, A. (2023). *Civic engagement and government spending: Lessons from global warming.* EST Working Paper 202319.

Lusardi, A., & Mitchell, O. (2011). Financial literacy and retirement planning in the United States. *Journal of Pension Economics and Finance, 10*(5), 509–525.

Lusardi, A., & Mitchell, O. (2023). The importance of financial literacy: Opening a new field. *Journal of Economic Perspectives, 37*(5), 137–154.

McDonald, J. (2008). The benefits of society online: Civic engagement. In K. Mossberger, C. J. Tolbert, & R. S. McNeal (Eds.), *Digital citizenship: The internet, society, and participation* (pp. 47–66). MIT Press.

OECD. (2019). *Skills matter: Additional results from the survey of adult skills.* OECD Skills Studies. OECD Publishing.

Tomaszewicz, A. (2015). The impact of digital literacy on e-government development. *Online Journal of Applied Knowledge Management, 3*(2), 45–53.

UNESCO. (2018). *A global framework of reference on digital literacy skills for indicator 4.4.2.* UNESCO Institute of Statistics Publishing.

United Nations. (2020). *E-government surveys. E-government in support of sustainable development.* United Nations Department of Economic and Social Affairs.

United Nations. (2022). *E-government survey 2022. The future of digital government.* United Nations Department of Economic and Social Affairs.

Chapter 8

Ruling the Digital Environment at Last?

Enea Fiore, Daniela R. Piccio and Antonella Seddone
University of Turin, Italy

Abstract

Digital political advertising has been essentially unregulated for a long time. More recently, a number of notable scandals, such as the Facebook–Cambridge Analytica affair and the external meddling in Brexit and the 2016 US elections, have compelled the European Union to take regulatory action. After discussing the growing role of political advertising for political parties and candidates and the major challenges this implies in terms of electoral integrity, this chapter explores the genesis, significance as well as the limitations of the Transparency and Targeting of Political Advertising (TTPA) Regulation. Introduced in 2024, the TTPA establishes a common regulatory framework across EU Member States ensuring minimum transparency requirements that digital platforms must comply with, including disclosure about the origins, parameters and funders of political advertisements directed to European citizens. While emphasising the important step forward of this Regulation for the countering of information manipulation and foreign interference in elections and the relevant shift in the EU relationships with platform services, we point to a number of problems that remain unaddressed, including the manipulative and deceptive use of political content, hate speech, misinformation and political polarisation.

Keywords: Online political advertising; EU regulation; electoral integrity; foreign interference; micro-targeting; computational propaganda

1. Introduction

On March 20, 2024, Regulation (EU) 2024/900 regarding the Transparency and Targeting of Political Advertising (TTPA) was published in the Official Journal of the European Union (EUR-Lex, 2024).[1] This legislative intervention was the conclusion of a lengthy process. With this policy measure, European institutions took a step forward in tackling crucial aspects concerning the operation of digital platforms hitherto limited to the development of codes of conduct, reports and general guidelines (Battista & Uva, 2023; Just & Saurwein, 2024; Tereszkiewicz, 2018). The TTPA represents the first attempt by a political entity to regulate the complex system of digital ecosystems by establishing standards that private enterprises must adhere to in order to operate within the European Union area. It formalises the fundamental principles, limitations and regulatory obligations, thereby constituting a major paradigm shift. The scientific literature has previously emphasised the role of digital platforms, especially social media, as conducive environments in which phenomena like populism, misinformation, polarisation and hate speech thrive, evolve and solidify (Ben-David & Fernández, 2016; Kubin & Von Sikorski, 2021; Postill, 2018; Rossini, 2022; Szabó et al., 2021; Theocharis et al., 2020). For better or for worse, digital platforms owned by private firms have become prominent actors within contemporary democracies (Margetts, 2018). With the TTPA, European institutions acknowledge their role in, as well as their responsibility for, addressing specific dysfunctional mechanisms that may represent a threat to democratic processes (Norris, 2014).

The user numbers of various social media platforms, such as X (formerly Twitter), Facebook, Instagram, TikTok or WhatsApp, are indicative of the widespread and deep influence of digital platforms on the information consumption habits of the general public (Reuters Institute, 2023). Through social media platforms, a broad spectrum of the population can be accessed (Datareportal, 2024). However, unlike traditional television media, these platforms also allow political actors to access an unprecedented amount of personal data (Kreiss, 2016; Stier, 2015). The possibility of engaging in profiling and segmenting the population enables the customisation of content according to specific interests, values and individual predispositions (Kaid, 2006). This customisation enhances the effectiveness of mobilising, influencing and potentially manipulating citizens' opinions. The potential for compromising the integrity of electoral processes is thus significant (Garnett & James, 2020). The Cambridge Analytica scandal is one of the most extensively documented cases in the literature (see e.g. Carroll, 2021; Ramsay, 2018; Youyou et al., 2015). Likewise, the electoral campaign leading up to the Brexit referendum was susceptible to foreign intrusions leveraging digital platforms to shape the attitudes of British citizens (Conoscenti, 2018; Howard & Kollanyi, 2016; Llewellyn et al., 2019).

The evolution of technology has substantially influenced and delineated the logic of political communication (Epstein, 2018). The emergence of digital technologies has significantly increased the array of resources accessible to political actors for direct engagement with their supporters, activists and the general public (Gibson & Römmele, 2001). Specifically, digital technologies have provided communication tools that are considerably more sophisticated and effective than those used in the past (Kreiss, 2016). The accessibility of personal data from users

---

[1] The full text of the Regulation is available here: https://eur-lex.europa.eu/eli/reg/2024/900/oj

engaging on digital platforms has facilitated the design of highly advanced political advertising tools (Dommett, Barclay et al., 2024). From this standpoint, micro-targeting strategies enable the targeting of specific population segments at minimal expense (Stier, 2015). Regulatory measures designed to enhance transparency regarding the identities of content sponsors and the financial resources allocated have induced private companies to release these data, providing public repositories that have made it possible to increase knowledge and awareness of these matters (see e.g. Jost et al., 2023; Kruschinski et al., 2022; Kruschinski & Bene, 2022). However, these measures have not proven entirely effective in mitigating the risks of manipulation posed by content tailored to influencing users by leveraging their individual interests, convictions and biases (Schill & Hendricks, 2024).

The purpose of this chapter is to conduct a detailed discussion of the premises and rationale of the TTPA, and above all, it aims to clarify the objectives at stake. The chapter begins with an examination of the ambivalent role of technology in making communication tools available to political actors and, thus, in shaping their strategies. Specifically, the first section explores the opportunities and challenges presented by digital platforms for the dissemination of advertising content as well as risks concerning the integrity of electoral processes. It then examines the events that consolidated these concerns in public opinion and European political agendas, namely the Facebook–Cambridge Analytica affair and its ties with the 2016 US elections and Brexit. Finally, it delves into the legislative efforts made by the European Union to regulate and constrain the use of online political advertising. The chapter concludes with a discussion of the role of social media within democratic processes.

2. How Technology Has Reshaped Political Communication: Opportunities and Challenges of Political Advertising in the Digital Environment

The literature widely recognises that technological progress has consistently played a crucial role in shaping the interactions between political actors and their constituents, especially in terms of political communication methods and strategies (Epstein, 2018; Farrell & Webb, 2000; Gibson & Römmele, 2001; Kreiss, 2016; Norris, 2004). During the period often referred to as the 'golden age of political parties' (Blumler & Kavanagh, 1999), political parties could engage their affiliates and sympathizers through their extensive organisational structures at the grassroots level (Römmele, 2003). Communication endeavours were mainly concentrated around crucial election periods through the utilisation of rallies, canvassing and leveraging the horizontal mobilisation of activists (Norris, 2004). The advent of nationwide television in the 1960s brought about a markedly different political communication framework (Blumler & Kavanagh, 1999), enabling political parties to connect with a broader audience, and thus engage with previously hard-to-reach segments of the electorate (Röemmele & Gibson, 2020). Political parties started to rely on professional consultants to develop communication strategies for their day-to-day political activities (Negrine & Lilleker, 2002). The proliferation of television channels and the variety of products and content broadcasted in the TV environment, coupled with the rise of the internet as a novel communication system, propelled political communication into what scholars have identified as the third phase of political communication, also termed as the 'age of media abundance' (Blumler & Kavanagh, 1999). The possibility of appealing to different audience segments underscored the need for tailored communication messages (Maarek, 2011), ultimately enhancing the reliance on a business-oriented marketing approach (Röemmele & Gibson, 2020). More recently, Blumler (2015) has highlighted the shift in political communication towards a fourth phase marked by the emergence of intricate and multifaceted media systems. The growing importance of digital environments has resulted in a paradigm shift that bears a striking resemblance to the influence of TV's emergence (Epstein, 2018). The internet and the web provide a unique platform for political actors, parties and leaders to engage with their supporters directly, bypassing the traditional mediation typically offered by journalism (Coleman, 2005). Within the digital landscape, political actors have fewer constraints. As a result, they have greater capacity and autonomy in crafting their own profile and agenda (Enli & Skogerbø, 2013; Gilardi et al., 2022). Digital platforms, especially social media, help political actors engage with an audience different from the conventional mass audience of the TV era, one marked by distinct demographics and interests (Stier, 2015). This has increased the importance of consistently and precisely adjusting political communications in order to align them with the unique features of social media platforms (Hoffmann & Suphan, 2017).

Notably, through social media, political actors access a wealth of valuable data that facilitates a profound comprehension of their potential audience. Data-driven campaigns are formulated, organised and executed by extensively leveraging the data offered by digital platforms. More precisely, Dommett, Kefford et al. (2024, p. 13) define a data-driven campaign in terms of 'accessing and analyzing voter and/or campaign data to generate insights into the campaign's target audience(s) and/or to optimize campaign interventions. Data is used to inform decision making in either a formative and/or evaluative capacity, and is employed to engage in campaigning efforts around either voter communication, resource generation and/or internal organization.' In other words, data are instrumental in comprehending the electorate by pinpointing particular segments and outlining their attributes, preferences and individual values. The formulation of communication messages revolves around these specificities, adapting and customising messages according to the target audience's characteristics. Furthermore, through engagement metrics generated by tailored content, it becomes possible to assess the effectiveness of communication campaigns, thus facilitating their strategic fine-tuning.

The targeting opportunities on digital platforms have resulted in the extensive adoption of advertising practices with an increasing allocation of resources by political parties (Dommett, Kefford et al., 2024; Fowler et al., 2021; Kruschinski et al., 2022). Advertising has been a key component of political campaigns since the introduction of TV platforms, with substantial investments of resources. Nevertheless, advertising on digital environments – and social media in particular – has a distinct significance and potential compared with traditional mass media (Fowler et al., 2021). Social media, in fact, operate with a wholly different dynamic, emphasising networks and horizontal interaction according to a faster and more continuous timeline (Van Dijck & Poell, 2013), with reduced costs per impression (Bossetta, 2018; Magin et al., 2017). Indeed, on the one hand, television advertisers can target specific individuals on the basis of general sociodemographic characteristics such as age, gender and geographical location. However, on the other hand, digital advertising strategies can utilise personalised information about individuals, including self-reported interests, demographics and media consumption preferences, to devise micro-targeting strategies (Kreiss, 2016; Stier, 2015). As a result, online advertising enables a more sophisticated and precise targeting of audiences compared to television.

Given these characteristics, it is not surprising that political actors are increasingly relying on these tools. They enable more efficient outreach to potential voters and facilitate the mobilisation of volunteers and funders for campaigning at a lower cost than traditional marketing strategies (Kaid, 2006). Moreover, through digital platforms, political actors can also engage with and mobilise segments of the population that are more removed from politics.

For these reasons, the expansion of the online political sphere initially sparked expectations about the capacity of digital technologies to promote a more inclusive idea of democracy (i.e. Bode et al., 2013; Bohman, 2004; Stockemer, 2018). More recently, however, scholars have expressed concerns about online tools' unintended and unforeseen impacts on contemporary democracy (Margetts, 2018; Persily, 2017). On the one hand, digital platforms have been identified as environments conducive to various phenomena, including hate speech, negativity and incivility, which can diminish citizens' willingness to engage in political activities (i.e., Ben-David & Fernández, 2016; Kubin & Von Sikorski, 2021; Postill, 2018; Rossini, 2022; Szabó et al., 2021; Theocharis et al., 2020). On the other hand, the simplified access to personal data through digital platforms has raised further concerns related to privacy rights, as well as to the ways in which such tools undermine basic procedural democratic conditions (Mavriki & Karyda, 2020). More specifically, the growing use of big data technologies and micro-targeting tools by political parties and leaders to influence voters' perceptions, particularly in the run-up to significant electoral events, has prompted inquiries into the manipulation (van Dijck, 2014) and integrity of the electoral process (Norris, 2014).

Overall, scholars have pointed out that the risk of disrupting the functioning of basic democratic processes is significantly heightened in the realm of digital advertising. As highlighted by Zuiderveen Borgesius and colleagues (2018), the practice of micro-targeting has the effect of objectifying citizens, thereby diminishing the quality of public discourse, intensifying political polarisation and enabling the spread of misinformation. This is particularly the case now that digital platforms have become the primary space for political debate and communication in election times (Balkin, 2021; Persily et al., 2020), and individuals mostly depend on information distributed online through intermediaries such as Facebook, Twitter and Google. Consequently, they are exposed to an unprecedented and remarkably diverse range of content in terms of trustworthiness. The operational framework of social media is based on algorithms that prioritise the dissemination of the most popular content shared by acquaintances, resulting in the inundation of users with material from relatively homogenous social circles that reinforces existing viewpoints and contributes to increasing polarisation (Rhodes, 2022). In modern high-choice media environments, therefore, the flood of information presents challenges for individuals in assessing the credibility of information, rendering them vulnerable to manipulation (Helbing & Klauser, 2019).

Further challenges arise from the opaque nature of political content within digital platforms. Aral and Eckles (2019), for example, point out the challenges associated with differentiating between legitimate political messaging and manipulative tactics like disinformation and foreign interference. The task is particularly daunting in the case of paid advertisements designed to target specific segments of the population according to their attitudes and interests and which are thus conceived not only to gain their attention or interest but also, and more specifically, to mobilise and persuade them. Notably, micro-targeting techniques within the digital sphere enable political parties to present themselves as single-issue entities to each voter. This enables them to tailor their messaging in order to emphasise different concerns for each recipient, skewing perceptions of a party's priorities and creating ambiguity regarding its policy stances (Mavriki & Karyda, 2020).

Not least, digital platforms offer readily accessible data that enable online monitoring of individuals, thereby facilitating governmental targeting, surveillance and the potential silencing of dissent. Electoral procedures typically govern the roles and actions of political actors. However, within digital realms, novel and diverse actors find it easier to intervene (or interfere) in public discourse about matters related to political and public interests (e.g. Tenove et al., 2018). Established mechanisms are not specifically tailored to exert precise control on external actors, thus making the detection of misconduct or the imposition of sanctions more complicated.

Overall, the scholarly literature has been particularly attentive to the threats of digital political advertising to the free and fair conduct of elections and has advocated regulatory measures (Dommett & Bakir, 2020; Dommett, Kefford et al., 2024). As we shall see in the following section, real-world events have indeed given substance to these concerns, eventually leading to increasing legislative efforts by European Union institutions.

3. Political Advertising in the Spotlight: Cambridge Analytica, Brexit and the 2016 US Elections

Three interrelated events have contributed more than others to linking concerns about the bad practice of using online political advertising with fears about electoral integrity: the Facebook–Cambridge Analytica scandal in 2018 and its connections with Brexit, and the results of the US presidential election in 2016. These events occurred within a short time-span and received significant attention from the mass media. As a result, online political advertising became a prominent topic for decision-makers at the EU level.

In early 2018, a joint inquiry conducted by *The Guardian* and *The New York Times* revealed that the political consulting firm Cambridge Analytica had collected the personal data of 87 million Facebook accounts without their explicit consent.[2] These data were gathered in order to be exploited for political propaganda. The Facebook–Cambridge Analytica affair marked a turning point in the understanding of social media practices and the perils of private firms' online micro-targeting. Although Facebook's role in the scandal is still being debated, the social network's accessibility has made massive amounts of sensitive information available to data miners and brokers. Several private organisations, including Cambridge Analytica itself, have been established specifically to harvest these data and provide computational propaganda services. This refers to 'the assemblage of social media platforms, autonomous agents, and big data tasked with the manipulation of public opinion' (Woolley & Howard, 2016).

Cambridge Analytica was established in 2013 as a subsidiary of SCL Group, a specialised company in voter targeting and disinformation campaigns that maintained strong connections with governmental and military agencies (Carroll, 2021; Ramsay, 2018). However, while SCL was focused on foreign operations and services, especially in developing countries, Cambridge Analytica specialised in domestic affairs (Hernandez, 2023). Essentially, Cambridge Analytica illegally harvested sensitive data and allegedly used them to target voters with personalised messages. Its activities supported numerous political figures and electoral campaigns in different countries, including the United Kingdom, the United States, Mexico, Kenya, India, Malaysia and the Philippines (Hernandez, 2023). These operations were backed and directed by prominent right-wing and conservative international figures such as Robert Mercer, Alexander Nix and Steve Bannon. In particular, Steve Bannon, who was Cambridge Analytica's vice president, also served as chief strategist and senior counsellor for former US President Donald Trump. However, the concerns surrounding the convergence of ultra-conservative public figures and military-derived computational propaganda reached a tipping point when the links among Cambridge Analytica, Brexit and the 2016 US elections became public. It then became clear that cutting-edge computational propaganda tactics deployed by both foreign and domestic actors could threaten democratic processes in liberal democracies.

The 2016 EU membership referendum in the United Kingdom was, at the very least, a theatre of external interference. Contrary to general belief, the Conservative Party's win in the 2015 elections marked the first case in Europe of a massive data-driven electoral campaign (Anstead, 2017). In the UK, the amount of money

---

[2]See https://www.theguardian.com/news/series/cambridge-analytica-files and https://www.nytimes.com/2018/04/04/us/politics/cambridge-analytica-scandal-fallout.html

that political parties spend on social media and Google advertising has consistently increased with each national election since 2015, doubling between 2017 and 2019 (Dommett & Bakir, 2020). Overall, the debate in the United Kingdom and Europe about online political advertisements and micro-targeting has been affected in two ways by Brexit: First, the way in which groups affiliated with the British conservative polity ran the Leave campaign; second, the unprecedented presence of foreign actors employing disinformation tactics with the explicit purpose of influencing the democratic process in favour of the United Kingdom's withdrawal from the European Union. Regarding the first point, a House of Commons report (2019a) and various articles from *The Guardian*'s thorough investigation into Cambridge Analytica's activities reveal that different groups led by Vote Leave (the official Leave campaign recognised by British authorities) were evading electoral spending regulations (Cadwalladr, 2017; Waterson, 2019; Waterson & Hern, 2019). Specifically, they spent more than half of their 7-million-pound official campaign budget on hiring a Cambridge Analytica-related Canadian firm, AggregateQI, to target UK voters (McGaughey, 2018). During the campaign for the EU referendum, the 'Better for the Country Ltd' company, property of the right-wing UK Independence Party donor Arron Banks, was fined by the Information Commissioner's Office (ICO) for sending half a million spam text messages to support the Leave Campaign (ICO, 2016). On the second point, the deceitful tactics by domestic actors were accompanied by a sequence of computational propaganda manoeuvres performed by external agents, particularly from Russia (House of Commons, 2019b). Domestic and foreign actors used wide networks of trolls and bots (i.e. automated social network accounts) on different social media to engage in posting and spreading pro-Brexit messages. For instance, on Twitter, Eurosceptic users outnumbered and out-tweeted pro-Europeans in the referendum campaign (Hänska & Bauchowitz, 2017). In the week before the referendum vote, about 1.5 million Brexit-related tweets were documented. Out of these, almost 2/3 were pro-Brexit, and less than 1% of the accounts generated more than 1/3 of the tweets (Howard & Kollanyi, 2016). This level of engagement would be unsustainable for human users. Moreover, Bastos and Mercea (2019) geolocalised nearly half a million referendum-related Twitter accounts and only nearly 6% of the latter were based in the UK. When all of these data are considered together, they paint a very opaque image of online campaign strategies for the referendum. Furthermore, there is a significant bias towards supporting the Leave side.

The 2016 US presidential elections raised the same concerns about foreign interference in domestic political processes. Investigations by US authorities revealed that as early as 2013, the Russian state-linked Internet Research Agency (IRA) had been conducting extensive computational propaganda campaigns to misinform and polarise American voters (Mueller, 2018). The investigations determined that over 11.4 million American users on Facebook had been exposed to advertising from IRA (US House Permanent Select Committee on Intelligence, n.d.). In practical terms, the IRA is a troll farm designed to interfere in elections by several means, which include encouraging far-right voters to be more confrontational, promoting political apathy and nihilism among minorities and spreading sensationalist-conspiratorial misinformation among voters (Howard et al., 2018). The IRA established several specialised social media groups focussing on different topics such as immigration, the Black Lives Matter movement, regional issues and religion. For instance, the IRA-controlled groups 'Woke Blacks' and 'United Muslims of America' called for abstention from (or boycotting) voting for black and Muslim American communities (Mueller, 2018). However, while the Russian interferences have received considerable attention, they have not had as much impact as the propaganda generated by actors within the country (Boyd-Barrett, 2019; Eady et al., 2023). Overall, the 2016 US elections evidenced an unprecedented surge in advertising expenditure. Spending on online political ads in the 2016 presidential election increased by 800% compared to the 2012 election. Donald Trump allocated approximately $83.5 million to online media, which was four times greater than the amount allocated by his Democratic opponent and nearly twice the amount spent by President Obama four years earlier (Williams & Gulati, 2018). Trump's substantial dominance on social media ensured that his authoritarian-populist messages spread much more rapidly and effectively compared to Clinton's campaign. Specifically, his posts were three times more viral on Twitter and five times more on Facebook (Persily, 2017). According to various sources, Cambridge Analytica provided statistics and data to Trump's team in order to identify potential voters and deliver targeted content to them. In addition, it made efforts to dissuade possible Clinton voters from going to the polls, including young women, white liberals and African Americans (Bakir, 2020; Kaiser, 2019). Although the propagandistic activities of internal players and external agents may not necessarily involve a direct collaboration, it is noteworthy that both groups are actively spreading similar right-wing nationalist messages. As a result, the debate on regulating online political advertisements has gained considerable momentum.

4. Filling the Regulatory Gap?

The aforementioned events have catalysed the demand to provide the European Union with regulatory instruments to tackle risks associated with the abuse of online political advertising. To do this, the European Union has been centring its regulatory efforts on a range of specific marketing strategies. The first is the use of psychographic profiling to classify population segments according to psychological variables, starting from individual digital tracks. Data analytics companies collect online data, such as Facebook likes, favourite elements or common internet searches, to profile voters and develop predictive behavioural models. Profiling from digital records has reached a high level of accuracy. On examining a sample of just 68 Facebook likes, Kosinski and colleagues (2013) were able to infer ethnicity with 95% confidence, gender with 93%, religion with 82% and voting preferences with 88%. While profiling is not a deceptive practice per se, private stakeholders can exploit psychographic data to develop communication campaigns to target voters and influence elections. Thus, data brokers can deliver to previously profiled individuals personalised emotionally-charged political messages built upon voters' beliefs, biases and vulnerabilities (Zuiderveen Borgesius et al., 2018). In order to sway election results, these messages are crafted using predictive models and adapted in real time to mirror the ongoing political discourse on crucial matters (Risso, 2018). Although Europe may appear less vulnerable than the United States to micro-targeting (Zuiderveen Borgesius et al., 2018), threats to electoral integrity and, by extension, to democracy itself have become a recurrent topic in the public discourse. A further concern that has prompted the European Union to advocate for regulation is the systematic use of these methods for computational propaganda. As shown above, this may involve domestic actors, who use them to gain an electoral edge over political opponents, as well as foreign actors employing them to sway the vote in a direction favourable to their interest. Indeed, Brexit and the US election are just two examples of numerous reported cases of computational propaganda and political micro-targeting. For example, the literature has investigated the cases of Germany (Neudert et al., 2017), Canada (McKelvey & Dubois, 2017), Poland (Gorwa, 2017), Russia (Sanovich, 2017), China (Bolsover, 2017) and Brazil (Arnaudo, 2017).

Building on these concerns, European Union institutions have adopted various measures, including Action Plans, soft law instruments such as Guidelines and Recommendations, Special Committees, European Parliament resolutions and Codes, whose overarching stated goals are to shed light on covert foreign information manipulation and interference and prevent extra-EU agents from infringing and subverting democratic processes in the European Union and its member states, in particular by digital means. Such initiatives (summarised in Fig. 8.1) led to the adoption, on the eve of the 2024 European Parliament elections, of Regulation (EU) 2024/900 on the TTPA.[3]

Along with the protection of citizens' data privacy, the spread of disinformation, particularly by foreign actors, and the interference in the free democratic processes lie at the very core of the Regulation.

> This is a major step in protecting our elections and achieving digital sovereignty in the EU. Citizens will be able to easily spot political advertising online and who stands behind it. The new rules will make it harder for foreign actors to spread disinformation and interfere in our free and democratic processes. We also secured a favorable environment for transnational campaigning in time for the next European Parliament elections.[4] (Statement by MEP Rapporteur Sandro Gozi)

Notably, this is not the first attempt by EU institutions to establish a framework regulating online political advertising. Previous efforts were made in 2018 when a Code of Practice on Disinformation was established to ensure greater

---

[3]See Footnote 1.
[4]European Parliament Press Room: https://www.europarl.europa.eu/news/en/press-room/20230626IPR00819/political-advertising-deal-on-new-measures-to-crack-down-on-abuse

Ruling the Digital Environment at Last? 159

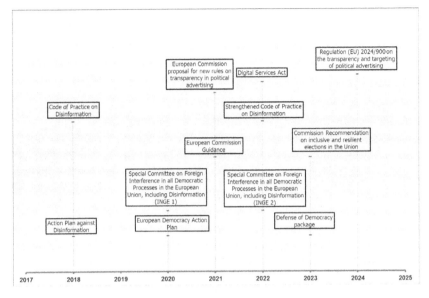

Fig. 8.1. Supranational Initiatives on Social Media Platforms.
Source: Elaboration by authors.

transparency and accountability of online platforms and monitor and improve their policies on disinformation.[5] Signatories, including Facebook, Google, X, Mozilla and other key players in the advertising sector, agreed to comply with self-regulatory standards. The Code aimed to enhance the transparency of political advertising through the introduction of new internal policies and tools. The objective was to counter inauthentic content and fake news, make paid-for communication clearly distinguishable from editorial content and enable citizens to verify the sponsors' identity and the amounts spent on political ads. The shortcomings of the Code, whose implementation was left to the online platforms themselves, have been stressed from many quarters (Wolfs & Veldhuis, 2023), including the European Commission itself. In 2021, indeed, the latter issued a Guidance on strengthening the Code, which ultimately resulted in the adoption of the Strengthened Code of Practice on Disinformation in 2022.[6]

Overall, the introduction of this new regulation followed a lengthy process and marked a new beginning for the relationship between EU institutions and platform services. Until its adoption, individual platform services had developed their own (changing) online advertising standards with a striking variety of approaches

---

[5]See https://digital-strategy.ec.europa.eu/en/library/2018-code-practice-disinformation
[6]The Strengthened Code of Practice on Disinformation is available at the European Commission website: https://digital-strategy.ec.europa.eu/en/library/2022-strengthened-code-practice-disinformation

(Helberger et al., 2021, p. 295).[7] This newly adopted regulation forces service providers to operate throughout the Union in compliance with a common set of rules. Firstly, standard transparency provisions in political advertising are established so that citizens can identify a political advertisement and be protected against disinformation, manipulation and potential interference from third countries. In particular, the Regulation requires that political advertising services must clearly and unambiguously label political advertisements on their platforms. They additionally have to disclose information about the sponsor's identity, the aggregated amounts spent by sponsors and (if relevant) the specific elections to which political advertisements are linked. Political advertisement providers, moreover, are required to keep records of their political advertising campaigns, enable notifications from natural or legal persons for non-compliant political advertisements and transmit any necessary information (if requested) to national competent authorities and/or other interested entities, including researchers, civil society organisations' members, political actors, observers and journalists. Transparency for platforms' users will also be enhanced by the establishment by the Commission (not before April 2026) of a European-wide user-friendly public repository for all online political advertisements directed at EU citizens to be made available from the moment of publication of the advertisement and for seven years after the political advertisement was last presented online. Specific rules are established on foreign interference in elections, as third-country entities are banned from sponsoring political advertising in the EU (both at the EU level and at the Member States' national, regional or local level) in the three months before an election or referendum is held.

Besides transparency measures, the TTPA Regulation regulates the use of targeting techniques in online political advertising. In line with the General Data Protection Regulation (2016) and the Digital Service Act (2022), political advertising online will be permitted only under strict conditions. In particular, targeting techniques that involve the processing of personal data are permitted only when explicit consent is provided and when such techniques do not involve profiling. Additional safeguards related to transparency and accountability include the duty for platform services to provide information on the policy and describe the use of such techniques. This enables citizens to understand the criteria for targeting individuals and constrains platforms to disclose which specific groups have been targeted.

5. Discussion and Conclusion

With the adoption of the TTPA Regulation, economic actors such as Facebook, Google and X, which traditionally relied on self-governance of online

---

[7]For example, Twitter banned all political advertising in 2019, a decision that was reversed by X in 2023; Google introduced political advertising bans in electoral periods, and since 2023 it has required sponsors to disclose any use of Artificial Intelligence; a similar policy was recently introduced by Facebook and Instagram, although it adopted a more liberal approach.

communication services, must abide by the Regulation's requirements when providing political advertising and services involving the publication, dissemination or promotion of political advertising within the European Union. This regulation represents an important change in the relationship between EU institutions and platform services, from a laissez-faire, libertarian regulatory environment approach (Beyersdorf, 2019; Mehta & Erickson, 2022) to mild forms of digital governance. Justified by growing concerns about the misuse of technology by marketing techniques in relation to voting manipulation and election interference, the presence of a common set of rules that ensure a certain degree of transparency of political advertising throughout the European Union clearly represents progress for electoral integrity. This allows citizens to be informed about the content, the origin and the funding of political ads while contributing to fighting online disinformation more efficiently. Notably, and besides the scholarly concerns mentioned above, the need for increased transparency with regard to online advertising has often emerged as one of the most frequently mentioned concerns of EU citizens with regard to online political advertising. According to recent Eurobarometer data, for example, about one-third of the respondents (32%) considered the transparency of political advertising as a crucial feature in defining an election campaign as free and fair. Likewise, 27% of the respondents emphasised the need for transparency in the use of targeting techniques for political advertising.[8] Overall, there is broad support among EU citizens for increased transparency with regard to disinformation and false or misleading content, and this Regulation is moving in the right direction to counter this phenomenon.

At the same time, the newly adopted regulation is limited in its scope. As explained in the opening sentence of the Explanatory Memorandum for the Regulation proposal, '[t]his proposal aims first and foremost to contribute to the proper functioning of the internal market for political advertising by laying down harmonised rules for a high level of transparency of political advertising and related services. These rules will apply to providers of political advertising services.'[9] Thus, and in line with the European Union's regulatory competence, the TTPA contributes to the proper functioning of the internal market, preventing distortion of competition for political advertising services across borders, and it does not interfere with the Member States' individual approaches to online political advertising regulation. As a result, many of the concerns that have been discussed in this chapter remain unaddressed. First, the transparency obligations established may prove ineffective in terms of safeguarding the democratic process against manipulation if citizens pay little attention to disclosure labels and messages – which empirical research has shown almost unanimously to be the case

---

[8] Flash EB 522 – Democracy (2023). See https://europa.eu/eurobarometer/surveys/detail/2966

[9] European Commission Proposal for a Regulation of the European Parliament and of the Council on the Transparency and Targeting of Political Advertising, Brussels, November 25, 2021 (available at: https://eur-lex.europa.eu/legal-content/EN/TXT/HTML/?uri=CELEX:52021PC0731)

(Binford et al., 2021; Dobber et al., 2023). Second, while regulating platforms and political actors' duties in relation to transparency and targeting use, many other concerns specifically pertaining to the online political sphere, such as hate speech and polarisation, will persist and so will the broader election integrity concerns about equality of opportunity for all electoral contestants and non-discriminatory media access for political parties and candidates. Regulating the offline electoral integrity cycle has taken almost a century and with partial success. Ruling the digital environment may take the same amount of time and eventually lead to similar outcomes.

References

Anstead, N. (2017). Data-driven campaigning in the 2015 United Kingdom general election. *The International Journal of Press/Politics*, 22(3), 294–313.

Aral, S., & Eckles, D. (2019). Protecting elections from social media manipulation. *Science*, 365(6456), 858–861.

Arnaudo, D. (2017). *Computational propaganda in Brazil: Social bots during elections* (pp. 1–39). Computational Propaganda Research Project.

Bakir, V. (2020). Psychological operations in digital political campaigns: Assessing Cambridge Analytica's psychographic profiling and targeting. *Frontiers in Communication*, 5(67), 1–16.

Balkin, J. M. (2021). How to regulate (and not regulate) social media. *Journal of Free Speech Law*, 1, 71–96.

Bastos, M. T., & Mercea, D. (2019). The Brexit botnet and user-generated hyperpartisan news. *Social Science Computer Review*, 37(1), 38–54.

Battista, D., & Uva, G. (2023). Exploring the legal regulation of social media in Europe: A review of dynamics and challenges—Current trends and future developments. *Sustainability*, 15(5), 4144.

Ben-David, A., & Fernández, A. M. (2016). Hate speech and covert discrimination on social media: Monitoring the Facebook pages of extreme-right political parties in Spain. *International Journal of Communication*, 10, 27.

Beyersdorf, B. (2019). Regulating the most accessible marketplace of ideas in history: Disclosure requirements in online political advertisements after the 2016 election. *California Law Review*, 107, 1061.

Binford, M. T., Wojdynski, B. W., Lee, Y. I., Sun, S., & Briscoe, A. (2021). Invisible transparency: Visual attention to disclosures and source recognition in Facebook political advertising. *Journal of Information Technology & Politics*, 18(1), 70–83.

Blumler, J. G. (2015). Core theories of political communication: Foundational and freshly minted. *Communication Theory*, 25(4), 426–438.

Blumler, J. G., & Kavanagh, D. (1999). The third age of political communication: Influences and features. *Political Communication*, 16(3), 209–230.

Bode, L., Edgerly, S., Sayre, B., Vraga, E. K., & Shah, D. V. (2013). Digital democracy: How the internet has changed politics. In *The international encyclopedia of media studies* (pp. 1–20). Blackwell Publishing.

Bohman, J. (2004). Expanding dialogue: The Internet, the public sphere and prospects for transnational democracy. *The Sociological Review*, 52(1_Suppl), 131–155.

Bolsover, G. (2017). Computational propaganda in China: An alternative model of a widespread practice. *Computational Propaganda Project*, 1–31. https://ora.ox.ac.uk/objects/uuid:b081ab3f-a54d-40ad-896d-462d1f386042

Bossetta, M. (2018). The digital architectures of social media: Comparing political campaigning on Facebook, Twitter, Instagram, and Snapchat in the 2016 US election. *Journalism & Mass Communication Quarterly*, 95(2), 471–496.

Boyd-Barrett, O. (2019). Fake news and 'RussiaGate' discourses: Propaganda in the post-truth era. *Journalism*, 20(1), 87–91.

Cadwalladr, C. (2017). The great British Brexit robbery: How our democracy was hijacked. *The Guardian*. https://www.theguardian.com/technology/2017/may/07/the-great-british-brexit-robbery-hijacked-democracy. Accessed on April 3, 2024.

Carroll, D. R. (2021). Cambridge Analytica. In G. D. Rawnsley, Y. Ma, & K. Pothong (Eds.), *Research handbook on political propaganda* (pp. 41–50). Edward Elgar Publishing.

Coleman, S. (2005). New mediation and direct representation: Reconceptualizing representation in the digital age. *New Media & Society*, 7(2), 177–198.

Conoscenti, M. (2018). Big data, small data, broken windows and fear discourse: Brexit, the EU and the majority illusion. *De Europa*, 1(2), 65–82.

Datareportal. (2024). Digital 2024: Global overview report. https://datareportal.com/reports/digital-2024-global-overview-report

Dobber, T., Kruikemeier, S., Helberger, N., & Goodman, E. (2023). Shielding citizens? Understanding the impact of political advertisement transparency information. *New Media & Society*, 26(11), 1–21.

Dommett, K., & Bakir, M. E. (2020). A transparent digital election campaign? The insights and significance of political advertising archives for debates on electoral regulation. *Parliamentary Affairs*, 73, 208–224.

Dommett, K., Barclay, A., & Gibson, R. (2024). Just what is data-driven campaigning? A systematic review. *Information, Communication & Society*, 27(1), 1–22.

Dommett, K., Kefford, G., & Kruschinski, S. (2024). *Data-driven campaigning and political parties: Five advanced democracies compared*. Oxford University Press.

Eady, G., Paskhalis, T., Zilinsky, J., Bonneau, R., Nagler, J., & Tucker, J. A. (2023). Exposure to the Russian internet research agency foreign influence campaign on Twitter in the 2016 US election and its relationship to attitudes and voting behavior. *Nature Communications*, 14(1), 62.

Enli, G. S., & Skogerbø, E. (2013). Personalized campaigns in party-centred politics: Twitter and Facebook as arenas for political communication. *Information, & Society*, 16(5), 757–774.

Epstein, B. (2018). *The only constant is change: Technology, political communication, and innovation over time*. Oxford University Press.

EUR-Lex. (2024). *Regulation (EU) 2024/900 of the European Parliament and of the Council of 13 March 2024 on the transparency and targeting of political advertising*. https://eur-lex.europa.eu/eli/reg/2024/900/oj

Farrell, D. M., & Webb, P. (2000). Political parties as campaign organizations. In R. J. Dalton (Ed.), *Parties without Partisans* (pp. 102–125). Oxford Academic.

Fowler, E. F., Franz, M. M., Martin, G. J., Peskowitz, Z., & Ridout, T. N. (2021). Political advertising online and offline. *American Political Science Review*, 115(1), 130–149.

Garnett, H. A., & James, T. S. (2020). Cyber elections in the digital age: Threats and opportunities of technology for electoral integrity. *Election Law Journal: Rules, Politics, and Policy*, *19*(2), 111–126.

Gibson, R., & Römmele, A. (2001). Changing campaign communications: A party-centered theory of professionalized campaigning. *Harvard International Journal of Press/Politics*, *6*(4), 31–43.

Gilardi, F., Gessler, T., Kubli, M., & Müller, S. (2022). Social media and political agenda setting. *Political Communication*, *39*(1), 39–60.

Gorwa, R. (2017). *Computational propaganda in Poland: False amplifiers and the digital public sphere* (pp. 1–32). Computational Propaganda Research Project.

Hänska, M., & Bauchowitz, S. (2017). Tweeting for Brexit: How social media influenced the referendum. In J. Mair, T. Clark, N. Fowler, R. Snoddy, & R. Tait (Eds.), *Brexit, Trump and the media* (pp. 31–35). Abramis Academic Publishing.

Helberger, N., Dobber, T., & de Vreese, C. (2021). Towards unfair political practices law: Learning lessons from the regulation of unfair commercial practices for online political advertising. *Journal of Intellectual Property, Information Technology and Electronic Commerce Law*, *12*(3), 273.

Helbing, D., & Klauser, S. (2019). How to make democracy work in the digital age. In D. Helbing (Ed.), *Towards digital enlightenment: Essays on the dark and light sides of the digital revolution* (pp. 157–162).

Hernandez, A. D. (2023). Cambridge Analytica. *Class, Race and Corporate Power*, *11*(2). https://www.jstor.org/stable/48749656?seq=6

Hoffmann, C. P., & Suphan, A. (2017). Stuck with 'electronic brochures'? How boundary management strategies shape politicians' social media use. *Information, Communication & Society*, *20*(4), 551–569.

House of Commons. (2019a). Aggregate IQ. *Disinformation and 'fake news'*. Final report. https://publications.parliament.uk/pa/cm201719/cmselect/cmcumeds/1791/179107.htm#_idTextAnchor034. Accessed on March 30, 2024.

House of Commons. (2019b). Foreign influence in political campaigns. *Disinformation and 'fake news'*. Final Report. https://publications.parliament.uk/pa/cm201719/cmselect/cmcumeds/1791/179109.htm#_idTextAnchor061. Accessed on March 30, 2024.

Howard, P. N., Ganesh, B., Liotsiou, D., Kelly, J., & François, C. (2018). *The IRA, social media and political polarization in the United States, 2012-2018*. Computational Propaganda Project, University of Oxford. https://demtech.oii.ox.ac.uk/wp-content/uploads/sites/12/2018/12/The-IRA-Social-Media-and-Political-Polarization.pdf

Howard, P. N., & Kollanyi, B. (2016). Bots, #StrongerIn, and #Brexit: Computational propaganda during the UK-EU referendum. *Comprop Research Note 2016*, *1*, 1–6.

ICO - Information Commissioner's Office. (2016). Better for the country ltd. https://web.archive.org/web/20171024185403/https://ico.org.uk/action-weve-taken/enforcement/better-for-the-country-ltd/. Accessed on March 31, 2024.

Jost, P., Kruschinski, S., Sülflow, M., Haßler, J., & Maurer, M. (2023). Invisible transparency: How different types of ad disclaimers on Facebook affect whether and how digital political advertising is perceived. *Policy & Internet*, *15*(2), 204–222.

Just, N., & Saurwein, F. (2024, February). Enhancing social-media regulation through transparency? Examining the new transparency regime in the EU. *TechREG™ Chronicle*, *2024*(2), 1–9.

Kaid, L. L. (2006). Political advertising in the United States. In *The Sage handbook of political advertising* (pp. 37–61). SAGE Publications.

Kaiser, B. (2019). *Targeted: My inside story of Cambridge Analytica and how Trump, Brexit and Facebook broke democracy*. HarperCollins.

Kosinski, M., Stillwell, D., & Graepel, T. (2013). Private traits and attributes are predictable from digital records of human behavior. *Proceedings of the National Academy of Sciences, 110*(15), 5802–5805.

Kreiss, D. (2016). Seizing the moment: The presidential campaigns' use of Twitter during the 2012 electoral cycle. *New Media & Society, 18*(8), 1473–1490.

Kruschinski, S., & Bene, M. (2022). In varietate concordia?! Political parties' digital political marketing in the 2019 European Parliament election campaign. *European Union Politics, 23*(1), 43–65.

Kruschinski, S., Haßler, J., Jost, P., & Sülflow, M. (2022). Posting or advertising? How political parties adapt their messaging strategies to Facebook's organic and paid media affordances. *Journal of Political Marketing*, 1–21.

Kubin, E., & Von Sikorski, C. (2021). The role of (social) media in political polarization: A systematic review. *Annals of the International Communication Association, 45*(3), 188–206.

Llewellyn, C., Cram, L., Hill, R. L., & Favero, A. (2019). For whom the bell trolls: Shifting troll behaviour in the Twitter Brexit debate. *JCMS: Journal of Common Market Studies, 57*(5), 1148–1164.

Maarek, P. J. (2011). *Campaign communication and political marketing*. John Wiley & Sons.

Magin, M., Podschuweit, N., Haßler, J., & Russmann, U. (2017). Campaigning in the fourth age of political communication. A multi-method study on the use of Facebook by German and Austrian parties in the 2013 national election campaigns. *Information, Communication & Society, 20*(11), 1698–1719.

Margetts, H. (2018). Rethinking democracy with social media. *Political Quarterly, 90*(S1), 107–123.

Mavriki, P., & Karyda, M. (2020). Big data analytics: From threatening privacy to challenging democracy. In *E-Democracy–Safeguarding Democracy and Human Rights in the Digital Age: 8th International Conference, e-Democracy 2019*, Athens, Greece, December 12-13, 2019 (pp. 3–17). Springer International Publishing.

McGaughey, E. (2018). Fraud unravels everything: Brexit is voidable and Article 50 can be revoked. *British Politics and Policy at LSE*. https://eprints.lse.ac.uk/89602/

McKelvey, F., & Dubois, E. (2017). *Computational propaganda in Canada: The use of political bots* (pp. 1–32). Computational Propaganda Project.

Mehta, S., & Erickson, K. (2022). Can online political targeting be rendered transparent? Prospects for campaign oversight using the Facebook Ad library. *Internet Policy Review, 11*(1), 1–31.

Mueller, R. (2018). United States of America v. Internet research agency llc [and 15 others]. *United States Justice Department*. https://www.govinfo.gov/app/details/GOVPUB-J-PURL-gpo89499

Negrine, R., & Lilleker, D. G. (2002). The professionalization of political communication: Continuities and change in media practices. *European Journal of Communication, 17*(3), 305–323.

Neudert, L., Kollanyi, B., & Howard, P. (2017). *Junk news and bots during the German parliamentary election: What are German voters sharing over Twitter?* (pp. 1–6). Computational Propaganda Project.

Norris, P. (2004, January). The evolution of election campaigns: Eroding political engagement. In *Conference on Political Communications in the 21st Century, St Margaret's College, University of Otago, New Zealand* (pp. 1–27).

Norris, P. (2014). *Why electoral integrity matters*. Cambridge University Press.

Persily, N. (2017). Can democracy survive the internet? *Journal of Democracy, 28*(2), 63–76.

Persily, N., & Tucker, J. A. (Eds.). (2020), *Social media and democracy: The state of the field, prospects for reform*. Cambridge University Press.

Postill, J. (2018). Populism and social media: A global perspective. *Media, Culture & Society, 40*(5), 754–765.

Ramsay, A. (2018). Cambridge Analytica is what happens when you privatise military propaganda. *Open Democracy*. https://www.opendemocracy.net/en/dark-money-investigations/cambridge-analytica-is-what-happens-when-you-privatise-military-propaganda/. Accessed on April 2, 2024.

Reuters Institute. (2023). Digital news report 2023. https://reutersinstitute.politics.ox.ac.uk/digital-news-report/2023

Rhodes, S. C. (2022). Filter bubbles, echo chambers, and fake news: How social media conditions individuals to be less critical of political misinformation. *Political Communication, 39*(1), 1–22.

Risso, L. (2018). Harvesting your soul? Cambridge Analytica and Brexit. In C. Jansohn (Ed.), *Brexit means Brexit? Akademie der Wissenschaften und der Literatur* (pp. 75–90).

Röemmele, A., & Gibson, R. (2020). Scientific and subversive: The two faces of the fourth era of political campaigning. *New Media & Society, 22*(4), 595–610.

Römmele, A. (2003). Political parties, party communication and new information and communication technologies. *Party Politics, 9*(1), 7–20.

Rossini, P. (2022). Beyond incivility: Understanding patterns of uncivil and intolerant discourse in online political talk. *Communication Research, 49*(3), 399–425.

Sanovich, S. (2017). *Computational propaganda in Russia: The origins of digital misinformation* (pp. 1–25). Computational Propaganda Project.

Schill, D., & Hendricks, J. A. (Eds.). (2024), *Social media politics: Digital discord in the 2020 presidential election*. Taylor & Francis.

Stier, S. (2015). Democracy, autocracy and the news: The impact of regime type on media freedom. *Democratization, 22*(7), 1273–1295.

Stockemer, D. (2018). The internet: An important tool to strengthening electoral integrity. *Government Information Quarterly, 35*(1), 43–49.

Szabó, G., Kmetty, Z., & Molnar, E. K. (2021). Politics and incivility in the online comments: What is beyond the norm-violation approach? *International Journal of Communication, 15*, 1659–1684.

Tenove, C., Buffie, J., McKay, S., & Moscrop, D. (2018). *Digital threats to democratic elections: How foreign actors use digital techniques to undermine democracy*. Research Report. Centre for the Study of Democratic Institutions, University of British Columbia. http://doi.org/10.2139/ssrn.3235819

Tereszkiewicz, P. (2018). Digital platforms: Regulation and liability in the EU law. *European Review of Private Law, 26*(6).

Theocharis, Y., Barberá, P., Fazekas, Z., & Popa, S. A. (2020). The dynamics of political incivility on twitter. *Sage Open, 10*(2), 1–15.

U.S. House of Representatives' Permanent Select Committee on Intelligence. (n.d.). Exposing Russia's effort to sow discord online: The Internet Research Agency and advertisements. https://democrats-intelligence.house.gov/social-media-content/

Van Dijck, J. (2014). Datafication, dataism and dataveillance: Big Data between scientific paradigm and ideology. *Surveillance and Society, 12*(2), 197–208.

Van Dijck, J., & Poell, T. (2013). Understanding social media logic. *Media and Communication, 1*(1), 2–14.

Waterson, J. (2019). Facebook Brexit ads secretly run by staff of Lynton Crosby firm. *The Guardian.* https://www.theguardian.com/politics/2019/apr/03/grassroots-facebook-brexit-ads-secretly-run-by-staff-of-lynton-crosby-firm. Accessed on April 3, 2024.

Waterson, J., & Hern, A. (2019). Obscure no-deal Brexit group is UK's biggest political spender on Facebook. *The Guardian.* https://www.theguardian.com/politics/2019/mar/09/obscure-no-deal-brexit-group-is-uks-biggest-political-spender-on-facebook. Accessed on April 3, 2024.

Williams, C. B., & Gulati, G. J. J. (2018). Digital advertising expenditures in the 2016 presidential election. *Social Science Computer Review, 36*(4), 406–421.

Wolfs, W., & Veldhuis, J. J. (2023). Regulating social media through self-regulation: A process-tracing case study of the European Commission and Facebook. *Political Research Exchange, 5*(1), 1–23.

Woolley, S. C., & Howard, P. N. (2016). Political communication, computational propaganda, and autonomous agents: Introduction. *International Journal of Communication, 10*, 4882–4890.

Youyou, W., Kosinski, M., & Stillwell, D. (2015). Computer-based personality judgments are more accurate than those made by humans. *Proceedings of the National Academy of Sciences, 112*(4), 1036–1040.

Zuiderveen Borgesius, F., Möller, J., Kruikemeier, S., Ó Fathaigh, R., Irion, K., Dobber, T., …, & de Vreese, C. H. (2018). Online political microtargeting: Promises and threats for democracy. *Utrecht Law Review, 14*(1), 82–96.

Section 5

Environment

Chapter 9

Environmental Challenges in the Platform Society: Insights From Mobilisations Against Data Centres

Cecilia Biancalana

University of Turin, Italy

Abstract

The chapter explores the environmental impacts of digital activities, which are often perceived as immaterial. Despite the notion of the 'cloud' implying weightlessness, information and communication technologies (ICTs) and the internet contribute substantially to greenhouse gas emissions. The growth of digital platforms facilitating economic and social interactions poses direct environmental risks through pollution and emissions from physical infrastructures, as well as indirect risks by fostering environmentally harmful behaviours like increased online consumerism. This chapter investigates the environmental challenges of the platform society, focusing on political responses and citizen mobilizations against data centres. These centres, essential for digital operations, have substantial geopolitical, jurisdictional and socio-environmental impacts. Conflicts over data centres bring issues of data nationalism and data colonialism to the forefront, emphasising the need for deeper politicisation of their environmental consequences. By examining various global mobilisations against data centres, the chapter highlights the intersection of environmental and digital realms. It aims to stimulate new research hypotheses on the relationship between the platform society and the environment, the materiality of digital technologies and the politicisation of environmental risks associated with digital infrastructure.

Keywords: Platform society; environment; climate change; data centre; digital infrastructure; platform capitalism; data nationalism; data colonialism; social movements; protests

1. Introduction

While we engage in everyday digital activities like surfing the internet, writing emails, storing photographs in virtual drives and conducting transactions on e-commerce platforms, we often perceive these actions as immaterial, as detached from the physical world. The term 'cloud', which denotes the online storage of data, evokes notions of weightlessness and distance.

Contrary to this perception, these seemingly weightless actions have a substantial material footprint (Kinsley, 2014) on the natural environment: indeed, information and communication technologies (ICTs), and the internet in particular, contribute significantly to the emission of greenhouse gasses (GHGs). The platform society, characterised by the flourishing of digital platforms that mediate economic transactions and social interactions, can therefore represent a concrete risk for the environment.

Not only are there direct consequences, emanating from the pollution and emissions generated by the physical infrastructures that sustain this digital ecosystem but there may also be indirect ones when the platform society fosters environmentally unfriendly behaviours exemplified by the surge in online consumerism.

In the last few years, some studies have focused on the potential of ICTs as drivers of decarbonisation (Wu et al., 2016; for the energy sector see Strüker et al., 2021). While it is true that the so-called 'platform society' can in some ways support the green transition, despite its profound socio-political implications, environmental risks remain understudied in the literature, particularly within the realm of political science. Moreover, the politicisation of this issue remains largely uncharted territory.

My aim in this chapter is to take this (so far) understudied subject into consideration. I will initially scrutinise the potential environmental risks posed by the platform society. These risks will be categorised into direct and indirect consequences, painting a comprehensive picture of its environmental impact. Subsequently, I will focus on the political responses to this emergent phenomenon and in particular on citizens' mobilisations.

In this context, the study of mobilisations against data centres – huge edifices that house the servers driving the digital realm – is of pivotal importance. Data centres bring 'with them competing jurisdictional claims, geopolitical influences and socio-environmental legacies' (Au, 2022). They affect geography and geopolitical sovereignty (Aamore, 2018) and also lead to contentious politics. According to Pickren (2018, p. 227), 'the energy and water needs of the data center industry, as well as the impact of this industry on the livelihoods of local land-users, require deeper politicization.'

The last part of the chapter provides a description and summary of some mobilisations against data centres taking place in different parts of the world. These mobilisations and conflicts at the intersection between the digital and environmental realms, and which take place in different geographical and socio-political contexts, bring out a number of key issues. Discussed in particular will be questions related to data nationalism and data colonialism.

This research is a work in progress. The aim of this chapter is not to provide a comprehensive and systematic literature review or a map of protests nor is it to establish definitive conclusions. Rather, its intention is to stimulate new hypotheses for research on the emerging interrelationship between the platform society and the environment, the materiality of digital technologies, the risks raised by digital infrastructure for the natural environment and its politicisation.

2. Environmental Impacts of the Platform Society: Direct and Indirect Consequences

To understand the environmental risks posed by the platform society, it is useful first to delineate and categorise these impacts. This can be done by drawing a distinction between direct and indirect impacts.

Direct impacts concern the repercussions stemming from the physical infrastructures that form the backbone of the platform society. In fact, for the platform society to function, it requires a physical substrate. This encompasses a spectrum of considerations: the strain on resources, including energy and water consumption and the environmental footprint of structures like data centres. These colossal hubs of digital activity have become focal points of concern due to their substantial energy demands and the associated water consumption. Moreover, one must consider the problem of e-waste – which concerns the disposal of electronic devices – and that of the extraction of rare metals (Pirina, 2022).

Extant studies point out that the ICT sector accounts for approximately 2.1%–3.9% of global GHG emissions (Freitag et al., 2021), which is more than the carbon footprint of the aviation industry. The main sources of these emissions are the production and disposal of electronic devices, as well as the energy and water consumption of data centres and communication networks. Analyses agree that both data traffic and the energy demand by ICTs is increasing and so too is the demand for data centres and network services, with the consequence these emissions are likely to increase.

Moreover, while ICTs have potential in the process of decarbonisation (Wu et al., 2016), for instance by optimising energy use for heating and lighting buildings, or through smart grids and the Internet of Things (Strüker et al., 2021), it has been demonstrated that cloud computing and AI software can also aid the discovery, extraction, distribution, refining and marketing of oil and gas (Dobbe & Whittaker, 2019), thereby posing a threat to global efforts in the fight against climate change.

Indirect impacts concern the influence of the platform society on the behaviours of citizens, which may inadvertently pose threats to the environment. An example is provided by the rise of the so-called 'sharing economy' and the 'gig economy', where digital platforms facilitate the utilisation and exchange of resources, labour and services. On the one hand, it is possible to link the sharing economy with sustainability (see Boar et al., 2020). For instance, we can think of platforms that help travelers to share their car instead of travelling alone. On the other hand, scrutinising the environmental impacts of these services reveals a complex range of harmful effects.

For instance, while sharing a car to go to work can reduce emissions, and while artificial intelligence can help drivers find optimal routes through cities and thus reduce traffic congestion, it is also true that the platform society can also foster some types of behaviour by citizens that are harmful to the environment. A study carried out by the EP in 2021 (Gawer & Srnicek, 2021) focused on ride-sharing services and stated that 'As a result of their popularity, many cities have seen significant surges in the numbers of vehicles on their streets. The end result has been significant increases in vehicle miles traveled overall and in traffic congestion in many cities. Moreover, ride-sharing services are largely *linked to reduced use of more environmentally friendly public transport options.* Unsurprisingly then, these platforms are linked with significant increases in pollution and carbon emissions' (Gawer & Srnicek, 2021, p. 55). A report by the International Energy Agency has also suggested that self-driving vehicles may encourage increased travel (IEA, 2017).

E-commerce provides another example. A prominent feature of the platform society, e-commerce has experienced a remarkable surge in popularity over the past few years, especially since the Covid-19 pandemic. It now represents one of the most widespread interactions that people have with the digital realm. However, the convenience of e-commerce comes at an environmental cost. Beyond the immediate concern of excessive packaging (Escursell et al., 2021), e-commerce undoubtedly levies a substantial toll on the environment through the carbon emissions generated by the logistics and transportation sectors, even though that toll is difficult to quantify, and different findings on e-commerce's environmental impact exist (Xie et al., 2023).

In sum, whether we take into consideration the production of devices or the infrastructure that underpin the network society, the latter's energy consumption is huge, and it contributes more and more to the production of GHG emissions. Moreover, at the societal level, the platform society can foster environmentally negative behaviours, such as choosing an Uber over public transportation, or using Amazon rather than local businesses. It is also clear that emissions will not be reduced without political efforts. It is for this reason that it is important to look at how politics is dealing with these issues.

3. What About Politics: The Role and Different Types of Social Movements

A comprehensive study of the response of politics to this emerging issue of the environmental impact of the platform society would necessarily encompass a wide range of aspects. It would require examination of political parties' positions on the matter, as well as an analysis of state regulations, policies and potential policy proposals. However, given that the issue is still in its nascent stages, a significant emphasis should be placed on the role of citizens' mobilisations and social movements.

Social movements play a pivotal role in shaping the discourse and agenda surrounding this emerging concern. They often serve as catalysts for change by mobilising public awareness and pressing for shifts of policy. By focusing on social movements, we can obtain crucial insights into the initial steps taken by civil society in response to this issue, and gain better understanding of the most important matters at stake.

Mobilisations concerned with the negative impacts – from an environmental point of view – of the platform societies stand at the intersection among environmental movements, social justice movements, movements against platform capitalism and NIMBY/LULU movements. How are these concerns linked?

Environmental movements have a long history. In addition to mainstream environmental movements, in recent decades numerous localised and issue-specific movements, such as NIMBY (Not In My Backyard) and LULU (Locally Unwanted Land Uses) campaigns, have emerged. These movements typically arise in response to specific environmental threats posed by nearby developments, such as landfills, incinerators and hazardous waste facilities. While sometimes criticised for their localised focus and perceived self-interest, NIMBY and LULU movements have played a crucial role in raising awareness about environmental justice issues and pressing for the more equitable distribution of environmental burdens.

In contrast, movements opposing the negative impacts of platform capitalism have a relatively short history. Platform capitalism, characterised by the dominance of tech giants and their control over digital infrastructures, data and economic activities, has significantly reshaped societies and economies, particularly in Western democracies. These movements have emerged in response to various issues such as data privacy violations, monopolistic practices, labour exploitation and the erosion of democratic processes. Despite their shorter history, resistance movements against platform capitalism have become increasingly visible and active. They campaign for the greater regulation of tech companies, fairer labour practices for gig economy workers and more robust protections for user data and privacy (Woodcock, 2021, p. 127).

Mobilisations that concern themselves with the negative impacts, from an environmental point of view, of the platform societies appear to follow two distinct trajectories that can be linked to the two types of environmental risk discussed earlier. The first trajectory is pursued by social movements against platforms and platform capitalism, which are incorporating environmental concerns into their advocacy efforts. Mobilisations of this kind tend to confront what have been called the *indirect* impacts of the platform society on the environment. One example of a movement against platform capitalism that also considers environmental issues is Make Amazon Pay, a global campaign and coalition that aims to hold Amazon accountable for its business practices, which critics argue negatively impact workers, communities, and the environment. In fact, on its website, one reads that Amazon, besides squeezing workers and communities, is also squeezing the planet:

While Amazon celebrated a 0.4% drop in total emissions in 2022, it would still take the company until the year 2378 to reach its stated 2040 target of net zero emissions.[1]

The second trajectory highlights the emergence of localised movements that specifically target, among the other digital infrastructures, data centres. These movements recognise the environmental footprint of these infrastructures, challenging their proliferation and demanding more sustainable alternatives. By focusing on the physicality of data centres, these local movements underscore the critical need to address the environmental implications of an increasingly digitalised world. One can say that this kind of movement deals with the *direct* environmental impacts of the platform society.

Data centres represent the socio-technical infrastructure of platform capitalism. As said above, the term 'cloud' gives the impression that data do not exist in any solid form. But in reality, they are stored in data centres. Data centres represent the materiality of the immaterial and are essential for the functioning of the internet as we know it. They are usually huge industrial buildings located in specific places; they require state regulation, and they are linked with local communities.

The movements that oppose them stand at the intersection among contentious data politics (Beraldo & Milan, 2019), NIMBY movements and environmental justice movements. Besides GHG emissions, protests against these projects often stem from concerns about their impact on local communities in terms of pollution, noise, water and energy consumption, and the visual footprint of enormous facilities. In particular, hyperscale data centres are the target of mobilisations.[2]

These movements tackle issues at the intersection between the physical and digital world. They raise new and important questions for the social and political scientists who examine the consequences of the evolution of the platform society.

4. Mapping Mobilisations Against Data Centres

According to Pickren (2018, p. 237), 'mapping out where data centers are, where and how they draw natural resources, and the economic, social, and environmental impacts on communities remains a crucial task that has important implications in terms of understanding the relationship between computing and socio-natural change.'

However, to my knowledge, there is currently no comprehensive mapping of protests against data centres.[3] Without claiming to be exhaustive, in this section I will provide a description and summary of some mobilisations against data

---

[1] https://makeamazonpay.com/
[2] Hyperscale data centers are distinguished by their vast size, high-capacity computing and storage capabilities and the extensive use of automation to manage large-scale operations.
[3] But see for instance: Lehuedé, S. (November 2, 2022). Big tech's new headache: Data centre activism flourishes across the world. *Media@LSE*. https://blogs.lse.ac.uk/medialse/2022/11/02/big-techs-new-headache-data-centre-activism-flourishes-across-the-world/. Accessed on July 1, 2024.

centres. This exercise can be useful as a first attempt to map these protests around the world. I identified mobilisations by means of a press review conducted in December 2023 on the Google News website using the keywords 'protest' and 'data center.' To be noted is that the press review was conducted in English, resulting in an over-representation of English-speaking countries or cases covered in English. Consequently, this compilation does not claim to be an exhaustive review; rather, it aims to serve as an illustrative example of diverse mobilizations occurring globally.

There emerged three distinct geographical areas in which mobilisation occurred: Europe; the United States and South America. Within Europe, cases of protests against data centres were found in the Netherlands, Ireland and the United Kingdom. In the United States, mobilisations were found in Arizona, New Mexico, North Virginia and West Virginia. In South America, I found cases of mobilisations in Chile and Uruguay. The mobilisations against data centres centred on three major concerns: energy and water consumption; impacts on agriculture and landscape and various forms of pollution, including noise and visual pollution.

In the case of the Netherlands (see also van Es et al., 2023), three mobilisations were identified in the cities of Hollands Kroon (Microsoft data centre), Zeewolde (Meta data centre) and Wieringermeer (Microsoft data centre). In the Netherlands, protests against data centres have become intertwined with farmers' protests against stringent nitrogen regulations, linking with right-wing populism mobilisations and highlighting concerns related to rural areas.

There are numerous data centres in the Netherlands because the country has invested heavily in these facilities, including hyperscale centres. Simultaneously, the country is endeavouring to reduce nitrogen emissions. A potentially harmful pollutant produced by cars, agriculture and heavy machinery used in construction, nitrogen damages ecosystems and poses health risks. Since the Netherlands produces four times more nitrogen than the EU average, the Dutch government aims to halve emissions by 2030, partly by convincing farmers to reduce livestock herds, leading to farmer protests.

Data centres themselves contribute to nitrogen production, and the construction permits granted to these large companies are viewed as problematic by farmers. For instance, the Farmer–Citizen Movement, an agrarian and right-wing populist political party, opposes data centres. In the case of Zeewolde (Meta data centre), farmers have expressed concerns about using the land for projects instead of cultivation and energy consumption, and they have successfully halted the project.

Similar concerns about land preservation are voiced in East London (Essex), where the Campaign to Protect Rural England (CPRE) has opposed the construction of a data centre. Concerns are also raised about stress on the power grid in the area.

In Ireland, movements against data centres emphasise their excessive energy consumption, which could lead to blackouts. Like the Netherlands, also Ireland hosts numerous data centres, particularly in the vicinity of Dublin. According to the 'Not Here Not Anywhere' movement website, data centres contribute to 18%

of the country's total electricity usage, which is equivalent to the consumption of 1.5 million homes. Electricity consumption by these data centres registered a significant increase of 31% in 2022, placing unprecedented strain on the electricity grid. The grid operator estimates that data centres will account for up to 27% of Ireland's electricity demand by 2028.

The consequences of potential blackouts are highlighted by the movement, with a particular emphasis on vulnerable groups. Moreover, it is pointed out that the issue of growing energy demand is closely linked to fossil fuel sources. The concern is that the inevitable growth in energy demand will likely be met, at least in part, through the use of fossil fuels, exacerbating environmental challenges. In Ireland, concerns about data centres align also with environmental mobilisations (Extinction Rebellion) and opposition to platform capitalism (Make Amazon Pay).

Partially different concerns are found in South America, specifically in Chile (cases of Cerrillos and Quilicura) and Uruguay (Canelones). In Chile, as well as in Uruguay, the major issue revolves around water consumption, which is particularly critical in those drought-prone countries.[4] The problem arises because a significant amount of water is required to cool servers as they process data. If the demand grows as expected, the world will need 10–20 times more data centres by 2035, resulting in much higher water usage. The problem is that many of these centres are likely to be built in economically and water-challenged nations that are already facing droughts intensified by climate change.

Consider that, according to the initial structural design, the cooling system of the Google data centre in Cerrillos required 169 litres per second in an area where people have been grappling with droughts for years. In a local referendum, the community voted against the data centre. More recently, Google has announced that it will implement a less water-intensive cooling system. In Quilicura, another neighbourhood in Santiago, similar actions are being taken in response to a data centre project recently announced by Microsoft.

5. Emerging Questions at the Intersection Between the Digital and Physical Worlds: Data Nationalism and Data Colonialism

I have identified various mobilisations against data centres in different parts of the world, many of which may not have been covered in the press due to a lack of media coverage in English. However, my aim is not to provide a comprehensive mapping of these mobilisations. Instead, the goal of this chapter is to understand which new and important questions for social and political scientists can be drawn from these experiences. As I have noted, mobilisations against data centres occur at the intersection between the digital and physical worlds, raising important questions about the evolution of the platform society.

---

[4]Similar concerns have been expressed in the United States, in particular in Arizona and New Mexico.

Here, I will focus especially on the cases of the Netherlands (Wieringermeer) and Chile (Cerrillos). These two experiences are useful because they help us to explore the concepts of data nationalism and data colonialism.

We have seen that in the Netherlands, mobilisations against data centres have merged with populist right-wing movements. Therefore, one may ask how the claims of the populist right intersect with concerns about the environmental impact of the platform society. In Wieringermeer, where there was a protest against a Microsoft data centre, the citizens of the 'Save the Wieringermeer' group argued on their website that 'only 25 to 35 percent of the total data centre capacity in the Netherlands is used for Dutch data.'[5]

> More data centers are not necessary. There is already an excess capacity compared to data usage in the Netherlands. In fact, only "25 to 35% of the total data center capacity in the Netherlands is used for Dutch data," according to a study by Buck IC to the Minister of Economic Affairs on June 26, 2021. The remaining capacity is used for data from other countries. For example, according to information from Microsoft itself, all the data space of the existing Microsoft facility at Agriport is only used for data from other EU countries, the Middle East, and Africa.

This can be considered a form of 'data nationalism' and raises crucial questions about territorial national sovereignty in the digital age (Goode, 2021). Data nationalism has been defined as the effort by nation-states to ensure control over data for a range of normative and security-based purposes (Daskal & Sherman, 2020). In this case, it is not so much an effort by a nation-state as it is a campaign by groups advocating for the local use of resources that supply a global network. It is an effort to territorialise the internet and give it a national connotation linked to sovereignty over a territory: that national sovereignty which right-wing populists say they want to protect (Basile & Mazzoleni, 2020). As Daskal and Sherman state, this contradicts the idea of an open and global internet and prefigures a new way of imagining the Web:

> The once heralded vision of a free, open, and globally interconnected internet has been replaced by an increasingly strong push to demand data be stored locally, erect virtual borders, and keep foreign influence out – motivated by an array of economic, normative, and security-related costs. (Daskal & Sherman, 2020, p. 13)

On the other hand, there is a case which, in a different way, also highlights issues related to territorial sovereignty and the local and physical effects of the platform society. The Chilean experience, where data centres used to power the

---

[5] https://reddewieringermeer.nl/

internet in first-world countries consume water that the inhabitants desperately need for drinking and agriculture, can be linked to a concept that differently mobilises territorial sovereignty: the concept of data colonialism. Why should economically disadvantaged nations allocate their scarce resources, such as water, to facilitate internet usage probably in wealthier countries? Activists denounce what seems to them an injustice:

> It is outrageous that, in this context, Google's data center project in Cerrillos declared that the cooling system for its servers would use 169 liters per second of water. The average water consumption per inhabitant in Cerrillos is 15 cubic meters, and we are around eighty-five thousand inhabitants in the commune. The data center intended to use twice as much water as the citizens! (INC, 2023, p. 58)

In reality, like the concept of data nationalism, the concept of data colonialism has also been used differently in the literature. 'Data colonialism', as defined by Couldry and Mejias (2019), is the process by which governments, non-governmental organisations and corporations claim ownership of and privatise the data produced by their users and citizens. It is the capture and control of human life itself through the appropriation of data for profit.

However, in this case, I believe that the word 'colonialism' in 'data colonialism' could be understood in its old sense as the practice of acquiring and maintaining political, economic and cultural control over another country, often through settlement and exploitation of its resources: it has indeed been demonstrated that data colonialism can be manifested in the direct link between the expansion of data infrastructure (Lehuedé, 2022) because digital infrastructures constitute yet another sphere of life where coloniality and imperialism still persist (Au, 2022). Mobilisations against data centres in the Global South illustrate this point.

6. Conclusion: The Cloud Is Material in Its Nature, and We Can Learn From It

This concluding chapter has examined a dimension of the platform society's evolution that remains partly unexplored: the environmental risks that it poses. While we are accustomed to thinking of the platform society and the internet in general, as an immaterial phenomenon detached from our physical lives, this chapter has described serious environmental risks.

My examination of the environmental risks posed by the platform society has shown both direct and indirect risks. The former are those that stem directly from the production, operation and disposal of the various physical infrastructures that make the Web function. The latter are those that arise from changes in citizens' behaviours facilitated by the dynamics of the platform society, such as e-commerce or car sharing.

In this chapter, I have focused on the political responses to these challenges and particularly on social movements and grassroots mobilisations. My research focused on data centres as physical representations of the cloud. In my view, mobilisations against these data centres furnish insights into emerging issues and contradictions of the digital age, demonstrating how the physical and the digital worlds are interconnected and raising issues related to territorial sovereignty and the use of natural resources.

The aim of the chapter has not been to provide a comprehensive mapping of the protests against data centres. Instead, it has been to consider those protests in order to identify shared features and emerging issues for the evolution of the platform society. In particular, examination of environmental protests against data centres in the Netherlands and Chile, despite their contextual distinctions, revealed significant issues relevant to the platform society: data nationalism and data colonialism, both of which are linked to territorial sovereignty. These two cases, though distinct, represent two sides of the same coin and prompt reflection on issues at the intersection between the digital realm and the environment.

Just as Dutch farmers claim that their data centres should store only Dutch data, Chilean activists emphasise that the water used for cooling the data centres is taken away from local people suffering from drought. What unites the two cases is the awareness of a digital infrastructure that exploits local environmental resources 'to the benefit of actors and institutions residing elsewhere' (Pickren, 2018, p. 237). The goal of this chapter has been to highlight emerging issues and themes and to suggest hypotheses for analysis. Future research could study in more detail how these diverse and distant mobilisations ultimately raise the same issue regarding the environmental impact on the places where people live by something as immaterial as the 'Cloud.'

References

Amoore, L. (2018). Cloud geographies: Computing, data, sovereignty. *Progress in Human Geography*, *42*(1), 4–24.

Au, Y. (2022). Data centres on the moon and other tales: A volumetric and elemental analysis of the coloniality of digital infrastructures. *Territory, Politics, Governance*, *12*, 1–19.

Basile, L., & Mazzoleni, O. (2020). Sovereignist wine in populist bottles? An introduction. *European Politics and Society*, *21*(2), 151–162.

Beraldo, D., & Milan, S. (2019). From data politics to the contentious politics of data. *Big Data & Society*, *6*(2). https://doi.org/10.1177/2053951719885967

Boar, A., Bastida, R., & Marimon, F. (2020). A systematic literature review. Relationships between the sharing economy, sustainability and sustainable development goals. *Sustainability*, *12*(17), 6744.

Couldry, N., & Mejias, U. A. (2019). Data colonialism: Rethinking big data's relation to the contemporary subject. *Television & New Media*, *20*(4), 336–349.

Daskal, J., & Sherman, J. (2020). Data nationalism on the rise. *Data Analyst*. https://datacatalyst.org/reports/border-control-the-rise-of-data-nationalism/

Dobbe, R., & Whittaker, M. (2019). AI and climate change: How they're connected, and what we can do about it. *AI Now Institute, Medium, 17*. https://ainowinstitute.org/publication/ai-and-climate-change-how-theyre-connected-and-what-we-can-do-about-it

Escursell, S., Llorach-Massana, P., & Roncero, M. B. (2021). Sustainability in e-commerce packaging: A review. *Journal of Cleaner Production, 280*, 124314.

Freitag, C., Berners-Lee, M., Widdicks, K., Knowles, B., Blair, G. S., & Friday, A. (2021). The real climate and transformative impact of ICT: A critique of estimates, trends, and regulations. *Patterns, 2*(9), 100340.

Gawer, A. R., & Srnicek, N. (2021). Online platforms: Economic and societal effects. *Panel for the Future of Science and Technology (STOA) European Parliament*. https://www.europarl.europa.eu/stoa/en/document/EPRS_STU(2021)656336

Goode, J. P. (2021). Artificial intelligence and the future of nationalism. *Nations and Nationalism, 27*(2), 363–376.

IEA (International Energy Agency). (2017). Digitalisation & energy. *Impact of digitalisation on energy, demand in transport, buildings and industry*. https://www.iea.org/reports/digitalisation-and-energy#downloads

INC (Institute of Network Cultures). (2023). *Theory on demand #50. Resisting data colonialism – A practical intervention*. Institute of Network Cultures.

Kinsley, S. (2014). The matter of 'virtual' geographies. *Progress in Human Geography, 38*(3), 364–384.

Lehuedé, S. (2022). Territories of data: Ontological divergences in the growth of data infrastructure. *Tapuya: Latin American Science, Technology and Society, 5*(1), 2035936.

Pickren, G. (2018). 'The global assemblage of digital flow' Critical data studies and the infrastructures of computing. *Progress in Human Geography, 42*(2), 225–243.

Pirina, G. (2022). I costi umani e ambientali del digitale. *il Mulino, 71*(3), 57–64.

Strüker, J., Weibelzahl, M., Körner, M. F., Kießling, A., Franke-Sluijk, A., & Herrmann, M. (2021). Decarbonisation through digitalisation: Proposals for transforming the energy sector (No. 69). *Bayreuther Arbeitspapiere zur Wirtschaftsinformatik*.

van Es, K., van der Weijden, D., & Bakker, J. (2023). The multifaceted and situated data center imaginary of Dutch Twitter. *Big Data & Society, 10*(1). https://doi.org/10.1177/20539517231155064

Woodcock, J. (2021). *The fight against platform capitalism: An inquiry into the global struggles of the gig economy* (p. 127). University of Westminster Press.

Wu, J., Guo, S., Li, J., & Zeng, D. (2016). Big data meet green challenges: Big data toward green applications. *IEEE Systems Journal, 10*(3), 888–900.

Xie, H., Chang, S., Wang, Y., & Afzal, A. (2023). The impact of e-commerce on environmental sustainability targets in selected European countries. *Economic research-Ekonomska istraživanja, 36*(1), 230–242.

www.ingramcontent.com/pod-product-compliance
Lightning Source LLC
Jackson TN
JSHW011837090425
82326JS00004B/107